A
VILLAGE IN A VALLEY

Beverley Nichols's Thatch Cottage and a neighboring house at Glatton.
Courtesy of the Bryan Connon Collection.

A VILLAGE
IN A VALLEY

by
BEVERLEY NICHOLS

With a Foreword by
BRYAN CONNON

TIMBER PRESS

Jacket and interior photographs
are the property of Bryan Connon,
reproduced with permission.

Drawings by Rex Whistler

Copyright © 1934 by the Estate of Beverley Nichols.
All rights reserved.

First published in 1934 by Jonathan Cape
Foreword and Index copyright © 2005 by Timber Press, Inc.

Published in 2005 by

Timber Press, Inc.
The Haseltine Building
133 S.W. Second Avenue, Suite 450
Portland, Oregon 97204-3527, U.S.A.

www.timberpress.com

For contact information regarding editorial, marketing, sales, and
distribution in the United Kingdom, see www.timberpress.co.uk.

Reprinted in 2007

ISBN-13: 978-0-88192-729-0

Printed in the United States of America

Catalog records for this book are available from the Library
of Congress and the British Library.

CONTENTS

A village store in Glatton in 1933. This was the model for Miss Hazlitt's shop, the subject of chapter 11. Courtesy of the Bryan Connon Collection.

FOREWORD

BEVERLEY NICHOLS TOLD ME THAT the huge success of *Down the Garden Path* came as a complete surprise, and he had to work at speed to pen the sequel *A Thatched Roof*. "Pen" is the operative word, for he wrote in longhand which was then typed up by his secretary Barbara Dormer: not for him new-fangled machines which, he said, stopped his inspiration and gave him a headache! When his publishers demanded yet another sequel, he despaired of finding a theme until his friend Cyril Butcher suggested he write about Allways itself. The result was *A Village in a Valley*. As before, it was mixture of fact and fiction laced with Beverley's sense of humour. I defy anyone not to be amused by chapter one which like much of his work is in the great comic tradition of English writers such as Jane Austin and P. G. Wodehouse.

By the time it was published in 1934, most people knew that Allways was the pseudonymous name for Glatton, the ancient village where Beverley had his sixteenth-century cottage. But, they asked, were his vividly drawn characters real or fictional? Today we know that some in the earlier books were based on folk he knew, such as Mrs. M., partly a portrait of his mother, but in the new book there were several fresh recruits. Among them was the millionaire Lady Osprey (whom he named after the sea hawk with its vicious claws), whose dominating interest in life was herself. She shocked the village by proposing to sell off some of her land for building new houses, which would ruin the unspoiled appearance of All-ways. She justified this sacrilege by claiming her wealth was in imminent peril and her income might be reduced to a mere pittance of £10,000 a year! (In 1934 a High Court Judge earned an annual income of £5,000, and a bank clerk £300.) Her astonishment that anyone dared oppose her plan typified her selfish attitude to life. Beverley eventually admitted that his villainess was a thinly disguised Lady Astor. Some readers guessed this from his description of Lady Osprey's sumptuous country mansion, which bore an uncanny resemblance to Lady Astor's home "Cliveden" (now a luxury hotel). Instead of taking legal proceedings for libel, she laughed off Beverley's slur on her character and tried to absorb him into her social circle. She did not succeed.

He was not so lucky with another lady, a prominent local figure, whom he light-heartedly portrayed by mocking the extravagant phrases of the local newspaper which reported her activities. Although he changed her name and that of the newspaper, it was obvious who he meant, and very unwisely he described the photograph which had appeared in the paper as bearing a very horsy face, strangely like a male impersonator. The lady was not amused and called her lawyer. The upshot was a paragraph in *The Times* of January 3, 1935, apologizing for Beverley's derogatory and offensive comments and agreeing to pay £100 to a local charity. In the second edition of the book there were judicious cuts, with the spaces filled by asterisks.

Beverley introduced a serious element with his new character, the lonely but feisty spinster Miss Bott. She was typical of the many thousands of women who were affected by the slaughter of the 1914 war and the resultant shortage of marriageable men. The public had every sympathy for the Miss Botts of this world but some felt that Beverley's book was not the right setting to portray the misery of enforced spinsterhood. Beverley, however, was never afraid of offending those who chose to avoid life's harsh realities. Needless to say, all readers were happy with the story of Victor, Miss Bott's nephew. He was a sensitive, middle aged bachelor, whom she tried to bully into leaving his comfortable London apartment for a ramshackle old manse, which as Beverley put it, only an insane millionaire would consider purchasing. Victor was a wickedly funny portrayal of one of Beverley's more fastidious friends, to whom the country was terrifying enemy territory. There were several possible candidates, but when I suggested John Gielgud, Beverley just gave me an enigmatic smile and said nothing.

We had met Miss Hazlitt, based upon Beverley's governess Meig Herridge, in earlier books, but she became a leading character in this one. The story woven around her was pure fiction but sadly prophetic. It was many years later that Miss Herridge wrote to Beverley from the hospital, where she had just had a major operation for cancer. "All my affairs are in

God's hands and it is not for me to be anxious at all." She believed her suffering was God's way of testing her faith, and she only accepted morphine when the pain was too extreme to endure. Beverley said "I may have invented some of her adventures but I could never have invented her nature or her spirit. She was the nearest to being a saint that I have ever met in this world."

The ending of the *A Village in a Valley* has puzzled many readers. As if in a dream, Beverley foretells how he will return to Allways as a ghost in the distant future. It is significant that when he wrote it he was mentally and physically exhausted by his frantic schedule and, not surprisingly, became ill. Following a brief rest, his work began again, and over the next few years he published *The Fool Hath Said*, a defence of Christianity, a travel book entitled *No Place Like Home*, and *How Does Your Garden Grow?*, taken from radio talks with, among others, Vita Sackville-West. He also reported the 1936 Olympic Games from Berlin and produced a weekly column for a Sunday newspaper. As if this were not enough, he provided the impresario C. B. Cochran with a new play and wrote and composed a lavish musical show which opened in London in 1937. For years he had worked at this hectic pace and his friends assumed that he must be a wealthy young man well able to afford his lifestyle and the cost of his London home and his country cottage, both with resident staff. Only a few people knew that he was responsible for his parents, whose income had dwindled to almost nothing because of the war, and that he supported his invalid brother Alan and his wife and children. (It was a well-kept family secret that Alan suffered constantly from epileptic fits; at the time epilepsy was regarded by an ignorant public as being synonymous with insanity.) Under any circumstances, all this was a heavy financial burden, but it became particularly onerous following heavy losses on the stock market. Beverley had to face the fact that his expenditure exceeded his income. With great reluctance he agreed to sell Thatch Cottage. It went on the market in September 1937, but he kept back the land on which he had planted the wood because he hoped to see the trees mature, but this too had to be sold after a few years.

On his last day in Glatton he gave his beloved dog Whoops (a gift from Lady Cunard) to his old friend Geoffrey Harmsworth, who had a family home in the country. (Whoops lived happily for many years, but Beverley rarely saw him again.) After he had taken a last look at the garden, he locked the door of the cottage and went across to the church, carrying a spray of honeysuckle. There he placed the spray on a grave whose tombstone read "John Borie An American who loved England." And he recalled the night in Chicago in 1918 when he met the Borie family and the Allways story began.

He went back to Glatton only once, some twenty years later. To his horror he found the countryside ruined by motorways and urban sprawl. The spirit of Lady Osprey had triumphed! Two houses had been built on sections of the once-famous garden but, surprisingly, the statue of Antinous which once featured in so many photographs, was still there. Beverley was shocked by the depredations of time and got into his car and drove away. "The glory had departed and the magic had flown. I was deeply upset."

If he had visited the cottage, he would have found it little changed. The section of wall on which special guests signed their names had been carefully preserved; among the famous were Cecil Beaton, Rex Whistler, Winston Churchill, and Vivian Ellis, the British composer to whom he dedicated *A Village In A Valley*.

Beverley never completely recovered from the loss of his home at Glatton but he went on to design more gardens and to give us all immense pleasure reading about them. He also continued to write books and plays of great diversity, but it was his gardening books which generated a lasting affection for him. Many others tried to emulate his style but none could write with such humour, passion, and simplicity.

BRYAN CONNON
Eastbourne, Sussex

A
VILLAGE IN A VALLEY

by
BEVERLEY NICHOLS

illustrated by
REX WHISTLER

Facsimile of the original edition of 1934

A VILLAGE IN A VALLEY

Beverley Nichols

Jonathan Cape
LONDON

CONTENTS

For
VIVIAN

CHAPTER I

CHURCH PARADE

THE accents of Allways are many and various, and nowhere are they heard to better advantage than in church. Especially during the singing of the *Benedicite*. For each verse of this great canticle, as you may remember, begins with the interjection O. And as the chant progresses, it is difficult not to be struck by the extraordinary number of different sounds which different people make, on being confronted by the same vowel.

The vicar, for example, says '*Oooh!*' He says it with a bright smile, like a child who has climbed a fence and suddenly sees an orchard whose trees are fiery with fruit.

'*Oooh, ye Ice and Snow, bless ye the Lord!*' cries the vicar, with such boyish exultation that one feels he would like to run out and make a snowball, here and now, and throw it up with a shout of glee, to the grey sky . . . up and up till a white hand fluttered out, far above, and caught it, and turned it into a star.

Miss Wilkins, on the other hand, says 'U'. She pronounces it, not like 'you', but like the French 'U'. And there is something terribly sad about her eyes and her mouth when she says it, because Miss Wilkins is extremely aesthetic, and she thinks that all beauty is so sad, isn't it? This does not, however, deter her from singing the *Benedicite* with the greatest relish, especially when there are any r's to be rolled.

'*U, all ye Gr-r-reen things upon the Ear-r-rth, bless ye the Lor-r-rd.*'

There is nothing in the least Scottish about Miss Wilkins, but she once had singing lessons, and never since has she been able to sing a word with 'r' in it without worrying it to death. Sometimes, indeed, she will put in an 'r' where no 'r' exists. I swear, though you may not believe it, that I have heard her sing 'Rose in the-rr bud'. But we must not here consider such secular things. The reason I mentioned Miss Wilkins's passion for r's was because it is inclined to set the rest of us awry. If you have a very tiny congregation, and only two in the choir, and an organ like a sparrow chirping, it is a little confusing when a tall and elaborately dressed young woman takes so long about her r's. When she sings 'ye Gr-r-reen things upon the Ear-r-rth' I have visions of long fronds unfolding, of long green ferns and trailers sprouting out from between her teeth, and it is all very distracting.

Mrs. M., the efficient, capable Mrs. M., who is always right about everything, sings a pure 'Oh!' She would. But she sings it somewhat perfunctorily, because she is so very anxious to get on to the verse, and do her 'seconds'. Mrs. M.'s 'seconds' are entirely her own. When the tune goes up, she goes down, and when the tune goes down, she goes up. If she is not quite sure what the tune is going to do, she chants with great determination on one note. But I am sure she feels that this is a waste of time – she would rather be striking out a line of her own.

'*Oh! ye Wells, bless ye the Lord!*' cries Mrs. M. She goes down deep on the word 'wells', thereby showing her sense of the dramatic.

And as I stand there, with the sunlight splintering through the stained glass, and making little pools of blue and orange on the flimsy paper of my Prayer Book, I think that Mrs. M. may indeed call upon the wells to bless the Lord, for hers is the only well in the village which did not run bone-dry last summer. And it is difficult to forget the very ungodly look of exultation which always appeared on her face as she looked over the hedge to watch the water-cart passing down the dusty road, to fetch a few buckets of muddy fluid for the rest of us.

'*Ho! ye Beasts and Cattle, bless ye the Lord.*' The 'ho!' comes from Miss Bott, stocky, jovial, utterly unself-conscious, and so excessively untidy that one realizes she must either be a great lady or a great saint. And when one knows her better one is inclined to think she is a little of both. That is why I hesitate to mention that as Miss Bott enjoins the beasts and cattle to bless the Lord, she turns round to me and winks broadly. You see, I don't feel at all like asking the beasts and cattle to bless the Lord, for two reasons. Firstly because whenever they pass my little front lawn, which is blazing with crocuses at the moment, one particularly beastly beast goes out of its way to plant its foot right in the middle of a clump of blossom. Secondly because, in the farm opposite, one cow has been singing mournful contralto solos all day and night. I asked the cowman if somebody had taken away its calf, but he said that nobody had done anything of the sort, as it was not that sort of cow. It had no reason at all to go on like that.

Unless, perhaps, it was blessing the Lord?

'*Ow! Ye Whiles, and all that move in the Waters, bless ye the Lord.*'

And when you hear that Ow! you blink, and start, and look nervously across to the choir to see if anybody has been hurt. But all you see is a mild little man with glasses and a moustache, and that fascinating form of *coiffure* which consists in three or four long strands of hair carefully plastered across a bald head, horizontally, from the left ear to the right.

'*Ow! ye Whiles . . .*'

It is Mr. Joy who gives us the *OW!* Mr. Joy is the keeper of the village shop. And though he has lived in Allways for fifteen years he is still an unrepentant Cockney. He still smiles in a kindly but pitying way at the simple manners of the villagers. He loves Allways, and he is a fierce defender of its rights and customs, but he will have his little joke. 'This way to the bargain basement, sir,' he always says, when he opens the trap door that leads to his cellar. 'Early doors, seven-thirty,' he chuckles, when there is a village concert. I am devoted to Mr. Joy, but I do wish he would modify that 'ow!' when he is singing the *Benedicite*.

'*Ow! ye Whiles . . .*'

I also wish that I had a mind which would occasionally stop still, and not go racing down every avenue which opens before it. Because, when I hear that superbly arrogant command to the whales, telling them to bless the Lord, I see the whole thing literally. I see a waste of sunlit waters, dotted with vast, if somewhat vague, amphibians. I see two very large whales — the parents of course —

14

spurting hugely and piously into the air, blessing the Lord. Obviously a whale, in such circumstances, would be compelled to spurt. I also see a tiny and somewhat sickly whale — the good little boy of the family — giving a much feebler spurt, which goes up into the air with a rather ridiculous dribble. And finally I see an excessively small, pink, and bright-eyed whale — the truant daughter — doing very high and irreverent spurtings in a cloud of spume and foam. And the sad, lowering mournful eye of God glares down, like the mystic Eye in the drawings of Blake, and threatens dreadful things to this little whale which mocks him in the waters.

Oooh!

U!

Oh!

Ho!

Ow!

The voices boom out, the little organ manfully accompanies them, and thus the chant continues. It is a sunny morning in spring, and through the windows one sees a blowing tapestry of sky and branches and cloud, threaded with many a fleeting pattern as the birds fly to and fro. A sunny morning, indeed! The whole church is dancing with lights, the gayest possible lights, for the church of Allways has a fine glass window, and when the sun is shining through it the most charming fantasies are evoked. The crimson rose, in the angel's hand, gives birth to a miraculous progeny, and spreads ghostly flowers over a row of old oak pews from which the sap has long departed. The blue glazed sky behind the seraphim is freshly radiated, and the blue pours down lavishly upon the ancient brick, flooding the floor with colour, till you would say that the very pavements were washed with the waters of God. And the robes of green and gold which the glaziers fitted, centuries ago, round the shoulders of the prophets, high above us — they seem to be spread over us all, by the sun, like a blessed garment. The purple mantle of Abraham floats out, out, it trembles in a beam of light, it is linked with the golden tassels of the seraphim and gently it enfolds us, blesses us.

Oh! ye Servants of the Lord, bless ye the Lord, praise Him and magnify Him for ever. . . .

Oh . . . ye Servants of the Lord. . . .

You look up, quickly. Why did you hear that 'Oh' so clearly? It was very soft, very gentle, but somehow, it rang out above all the other warring interjections, it had a shining clarity that compelled attention. There it is again!

Oh! Ye holy and humble men of heart, bless ye the Lord. . . .

You peer across the church, striving to find the singer of this bird-like note. Over the square shoulders of Mrs. M. and the drooping shoulders of Miss Wilkins, and the hunched shoulders of Miss Bott, and the draped shoulders of the vicar, and the little Cockney shoulders of Mr. Joy. And there, in the shadows, you see the plain, bespectacled face of a woman of about fifty. Her mouth is wide open, ridiculously wide open, and the hands that clutch her shabby Prayer Book are worn and gnarled. Her throat is swelling with the effort of her song, and there is a strand of mouse-like hair drifting into her eyes.

But you say to yourself 'That woman is beautiful. Terribly, austerely beautiful. Her cheeks are painted with a colour that is not of this world, and a wild bird is singing in her throat . . . a bird that has strayed from some divine thicket.'

And you will be right. For you are looking at Miss Hazlitt, plain, grey Miss Hazlitt, singing her heart out, in the shadows.

CHAPTER II

SAINTS AND SINNERS

WHEN Miss Hazlitt came to Allways the *Huntingdonshire Courier* did not make very much of this event. For the *Huntingdonshire Courier* is a very thick, large, and rustly newspaper, whose word is law over a radius of at least ten miles, and whose journalistic thunderbolts have been known to explode as far as Peterborough to the north and Biggleswade to the south. So naturally it had not much space to chronicle the advent of Miss Hazlitt.

But it *did* chronicle it, just to show us, I suppose, that its eye was omniscient and that not even the least important of us could escape its vigilance. It said, in a corner of the page which was headed 'News from the Five Counties':

A welcome addition to the society of Allways has arrived in the person of Miss Lilian Hazlitt, L.R.A.M., who is now in residence at Cobble Cottage.

I do not know why this harmless sentence should make me think of a gaunt, knobby spinster, with chilblains, pushing an upright piano through her front door, but it does. It is far from the truth. For Miss Hazlitt was not gaunt, nor knobby, and she was far too poor to have a piano, however cracked or tinny.

'Is she a professional?' asked Mrs. M., whose eagle eye had detected the mystic letters in the *Huntingdonshire Courier.*

'Oh no, Mrs. M. But when I was six, and she was my governess, she played very prettily.'

And even as I said it, there seemed to come, from somewhere in the distance, the ghostly tinkle of an old piano. It was as though the wind were sighing in the simple cadences of Stephen Heller, and the brook, as it dropped over the ledge of grey stone, expressed its surprise in a constantly repeated cadenza by Czerny.

'Yes, she played very prettily,' I said again.

§ 11

We were walking away from Cobble Cottage, late one afternoon. We had been helping Miss Hazlitt to move in. I had rather dreaded the effect that the overpowering Mrs. M. might have on poor Miss Hazlitt. I feared that her grim sense of realism might triumph over her efforts to be tactful, and that she might not be able to conceal her disapproval of Cobble Cottage which, it must be admitted, was little better than a ruin.

But it was Miss Hazlitt who, with her indomitable optimism, triumphed over Mrs. M. I remember the following dialogue:

'The cottage seems a little damp.'

Miss Hazlitt beamed. 'Then I shall have every excuse for making fires, even after May! Won't that be splendid? My mother would never have a fire, not after the first of May. But if the cottage is *damp* . . .'

Mrs. M., baffled by her radiant smile, tried another tack.

'I'm afraid your sitting-room faces north.'

'So it does,' exclaimed Miss Hazlitt, happily. 'And oh! there's a weathercock on the shed, and I shall be able to see which way the wind is blowing!'

'And the garden's over-run with weeds.'

'So it is!' And Miss Hazlitt sighed with pleasure. 'Covered with wild flowers! I shall have to make a list of them.' And she turned to me. 'Do you remember when we went for walks in the Devonshire lanes, and I taught you all the names of the wild flowers? Have you forgotten them? Look!' And she bent down to the damp brick floor (we were in the little washhouse) and picked a weed that had thrust itself through the brick. 'Do you remember what this is?'

'Shepherd's Purse.'

'Oh yes . . . *yes!*' she cried, and there was a delight in her voice, a ringing, silver peal of delight, that gave one a new hope in life.

'I'm so thankful,' she said, turning round and looking at the damp, decayed room. 'For everything!'

I looked at her. Thankful. She was holding an old weed in her hand. She had picked it off the floor of her broken-down cottage. The hand which held it was covered with a glove that had been neatly but obviously darned. The hand itself, as I well knew, gave endless pain to its owner, for she was crippled with neuritis. She was alone in the world. Alone, on exactly seventy-five pounds a year. And she was thankful.

One would have thought that, on purely utilitarian grounds, the opponents of religion would have been a little shaken when confronted by Miss Hazlitt. Even if religion is a drug, it seems to be a rather more effective drug than the average atheist can purchase from the average apothecary.

§ III

I would like to give one little example of this perpetual theme of Miss Hazlitt's thanksgiving. Allways is only a tiny village and much of its happiness, I believe, has been due to her. In the disasters which later befell her, she always found cause for praise. Things which we should describe as the blows of Fate, she regarded as proofs of the loving-kindness of God.

It was an evening in March, a few days after Miss Hazlitt's arrival.

I had reached my cottage just as the light was fading. Glancing hurriedly at my watch I saw that there would be a bare ten or fifteen minutes to make the tour of the garden. This would mean that I should have to run at top speed to the bottom of the field to see if the double daffodils were out, tear back again to peer at the japonicas, rush round the wood like a wild animal, speed back to the greenhouse and almost bury my nose in a quantity of seed-boxes which any sane person could see were completely barren. However, good gardeners are not quite sane. And all good gardeners will understand me when I refer to this mad urgency to see the garden before it is dark. I think that a large proportion of the road accidents, during the shorter months of the year, must be due to ardent gardeners who are terrified lest they should arrive home too late to 'make the tour'.

You may therefore imagine my disgust when, exactly as I was opening the French windows and preparing to dash out, I was summoned back by the voice of Mrs. M. She had opened my front door of her own accord, which is one of her most maddening habits.

'You've heard?' she said, breathlessly.

Oh Lord . . . Mrs. M. always began with 'you've heard?' And she knew very well that you hadn't, and didn't want to.

'I'm terribly sorry,' I said, giving an agonized glance at

the sky. 'But I've been away for a week, and I *must* see the garden before it's dark, and . . . .'

She interrupted me. For the first few sentences I did not hear her. All I knew was that the veils of night were drifting down thick and fast . . . drifting over the daffodils, turning their gold to grey, weaving their spell round the branches of my wood, dulling the first shrill green of the may trees, clouding the pools of anemones. Thick and fast drifted the veils of night, robbing my garden of its colour and its sparkle. Soon, in a few minutes, the garden would be a maddening mystery, in which I should stumble groping, lighting matches, and finding only blades of grass, running my fingers over branches, and finding nothing but cold bare wood.

And then, for the third time Mrs. M. said:

'I tell you, it's a wonder she wasn't killed. And after all, she *was* your governess!'

I turned round, forgetting the encroaching darkness.

'What has happened?'

What had happened was this. The daily woman whom Miss Hazlitt had engaged, to help her in the rough work of cleaning up, had been taken suddenly 'queer'. Miss Hazlitt had ministered to her with the bottle of brandy which, for years, had been in her possession for emergencies. (In five years, the brandy had only sunk one inch.) She then went to bed.

Not so the daily woman. She had always been a little weak in the head, and the brandy revived a strong suspicion, which she had entertained all her life, that she was Queen Elizabeth. After she had drunk half the bottle, this suspicion was so strong that she began to take off her clothes, in order to don the royal robes. By the time the bottle was finished, she *knew* that she was Queen Elizabeth, and removed the small amount of apparel which remained. However she could not find any royal robes, so she put a saucepan on her head, went to the front door, and stood in the bright moonlight, waiting for courtiers.

It was very late, and it is doubtful whether, in the ordinary way, any courtiers would have been forthcoming. However it happened that Mr. Joy's son, on holiday from London, had been complaining bitterly to his father that nothing ever happened in the country, and that he was so fed up, that he would go for a stroll before turning in.

'Not that there'll be anybody to see,' he said. 'At least, nobody that a chap would look twice at in London.'

And in a sense, he was speaking the truth. For when he was suddenly confronted, in the lonely lane, by a very large and completely naked woman, with a saucepan on her head, assuring him that she was Queen Elizabeth, he did not look twice at her. He uttered a wild shriek and took to his heels.

How Miss Hazlitt took charge of the situation, how she got the woman to bed, calmed down the would-be helpers, and, indeed, sent everybody home with the impression that something very sweet and natural had happened — all that is Allways history. This story has gone on for too long, for all I really want to do is to give you her reaction to the affair.

I went round to see her that night. She was sitting in a room that was almost bare. It was cold and musty, in spite of the glow of the lamp.

'It must have been horrible,' I said, when at last I brought the conversation round to the subject of the woman who had gone. 'Drunkards have the same effect on me as madmen, a sort of sick terror. And she was drunk *and* mad.'

Her face clouded, and her kind eyes looked pained. 'But you must not look at it like that,' she said. 'It might have been so very much worse. But I was protected.'

'Well . . .' There was nothing much that one could say to *that!*

Miss Hazlitt stared into the fire, and shook her head. 'I prayed for her, last night. I prayed that she might be better and that she would go away quietly in the morning. And she did.'

The firelight flicked.

'You see, God *does* answer prayer.'

I dared not look at her. So utterly unreal was this situation. If you told that story in the Ritz bar in Paris, Lord, what a laugh you'd get! Monsieur Charles, the barman, would double up, as his agile fingers slipped the extra bit of ice into the *champagne nature.* A funny old woman, thanking God because her maid-of-all-work, who had been mad drunk the night before, had gone off, without kicking up a hell of a row! Gee . . . that's great! Tell us another!

But it was not funny, as Miss Hazlitt told it, in the feeble light of her pale fire, over which the plumes of smoke hovered so petulantly.

Backgrounds make a difference. A mood can make or mar a story. I wonder if our moods are the same? Yours, and mine?

§ I V

This is the chronicle of Allways. Of a very tiny village in the quietest county in England. It is the story of doors opening and shutting on to empty lanes, of smoke ascending into tranquil skies, of whispers, about nothing, borne on the

wind, over wide fields and broad brooks. A story? Hardly
even that. For a story has form. It has a beginning, a
middle and an end. But our story has no beginning, no
middle, and no end. Neither have the bushes of wild
roses that cluster over the grass track that leads up the
hill, off the village green. They begin somewhere, one
supposes, but one doesn't worry where. I didn't worry
where, when I began this book. I saw a figure in Allways
who was very like a wild rose, in her simplicity and her
sweetness. That was about all.

But we must get some form into all this, or we shall be
drooling all over the place, before we know where we are.
And so I think, we had better begin our little exploration
by glancing at the pages of the *Huntingdonshire Courier*.

One fine day in July, some weeks after Miss Hazlitt
arrived at Allways, a copy of the *Huntingdonshire Courier*
was delivered at the kitchen door, bearing tidings which
were of the utmost importance to our little village. I will
not tell you what those tidings were, just yet, partly
because it was a long time before I happened upon the
paragraph myself, but principally because it will be fun
to show you this fascinating newspaper in a little more
detail. It is so infinitely more exhilarating than most of
the great London newspapers. After you have read it you
never feel bored nor disgusted, nor do you ask yourself
what England is coming to. No — you feel as though you
had had a country holiday. And as long as there are
people like the people who are reflected in these pages,
there is not much need to worry about England.

And though I may smile at some of its little foibles, let
me tell you that in its leaders you will find as sound sense,
and as good clean, ringing English, as in any of the great
Metropolitan dailies.

24

I bore the *Huntingdonshire Courier* into the garden, and
settled down in the deck chair for an enjoyable two hours
reading. You need at least two hours to do justice to the
Huntingdonshire Courier. (And in future I shall call it the
H.C., in order that those who read this book aloud may not
run the danger of contracting lockjaw.)

I smoothed it out, lit a cigarette, and studied the advertisement column on the front page. These advertisements
are delightful with their country flavour. In them, you
hear the whistle of the ploughboy, the homely noises of the
farmyard. Many of the advertisements, I admit, are still
somewhat mysterious to me. Thus, the first advertisement
I read was as follows:

> Good General Farm Labourer Wanted. Small, or no
> Family.

Did this mean that the required gentleman must either
be small or childless? In other words, did the adjective
'small' apply to the gentleman or to the family? If it
applied to the gentleman, a very singular picture was
evoked — the picture of a small gentleman, with a quantity
of children, competing for the required position with a
very large gentleman, who, for reasons best known to
himself, was without issue. It was very puzzling.

The next advertisement I saw was at the top of the
Poultry Section, but I hastily averted my eyes from it,
because it was headed *Sex-Linked Pullets.* And that sounded
too painfully like the modern girl.

Page Two proved to be dominated by an enormous
photograph of a walrus defending its young. But no — it
was none other than Sir Percy X —— the well-known
M.F.H., surrounded by a group of apparently terrified
keepers. Sir Percy, whose main wealth is derived from

the rents of tenements in Glasgow, is an ardent sportsman, and I read the report of his speech with interest.

'These are funny times,' said Sir Percy. 'Some people might call them very funny indeed.' (Hear hear). 'A lot of pacifists' (laughter) 'and vegetarians' (loud laughter) 'were moving heaven and earth to prevent sport.' (Cries of 'shame' and 'Good old Sir Percy'.) 'But he asked them, where would we all be without sport? We should all be on the dole. All of us. What would the keepers do? And the ghillies in Scotland? These nincompoops (laughter), said that sport was cruel. . . .'

At this point, I put down the paper and made several loud scraping noises with my heels on the gravel. I also said several obscure adjectives which are usually applied to the more depraved type of goat. And for once in a way, I wished I had a gun, and I wished that Sir Percy were a rabbit, physically as well as mentally. It would have been the greatest pleasure to show him what 'sport' really was, with a touch of the trigger.

But the evening was too beautiful to worry about such pests as Sir Percy for long.

You may skip the next few paragraphs, if you hate lolling back in a chair, and letting life drift by. For that is all I did, for a moment or two.

§ v

How quiet it was in the garden! How utterly tranquil the world!

So, at least, it seemed. For how could I know that in the newspaper which I now laid, for a moment, on my knees, there was a paragraph of such sinister import? How could I know, or even care, in the face of beauty such as this?

For this was the first summer of the Great All White Experiment, in the garden, and it was proving triumphantly successful. When, last year, I announced 'Next summer I'm going to have no flowers in my front garden which aren't pure white,' everybody said 'You're mad. It'll be horrible.'

And then they added: 'And anyway there aren't enough white flowers, in summer.'

'Aren't there? Come and see.'

And I took them a tour of the garden to show them some of the white flowers which one could use. I showed them a drift of white snap-dragons, which had seeded themselves on a bank near the toolshed. And great clusters of sweet rocket, from which I should take cuttings. And Michaelmas daisies, obviously, and candytuft, and tobacco flowers, and that creamy feathery spiraea whose name I always forget.

But when I came to plan out the garden there were endless white flowers which I had forgotten. Of these the phloxes were the most valuable, and of all the white phloxes none has a more saintly quality than that which is called Jeanne d'Arc. And then there were the Canterbury bells, and white petunias, which were all the more attractive because they so often had a faint spot of purple, staining the edge of a petal, like a secret sin. And the great white peonies, beloved of the moon.

I didn't have all these things. But I had a good many of them. And as I sat there, a year later, pretending to read the *H.C.*, this is the picture I saw.

In the centre, a heaped drift of white snapdragons, planted so closely that you could not see an inch of earth. Only the sparkling white of a thousand blossoms, rising clean above the leaves, like snow on green grass.

As a frame, a formal border of the silver Centaurea — that strange plant whose leaves seem ice cold even in the heat of July, and are always stiff and shimmering, flaunting their frosty beauty in the heat of the most ardent suns.

And all round, grave and cool against the hedges, the white bells of the foxgloves and the phloxes. And at the feet of the foxgloves, a snowdrift of those cottage carnations, which are perversely named pinks.

This is really terrible. I said I was going to get form into this book, and here we are, wandering round and round the garden, and finding it impossible to leave it.

I feel in that sort of mood when, on some perfect morning, one says to a gardening friend:

'We really *must* go and call on Mrs. Z. this afternoon.

'I know. We must.'

'She's asked us fifty times. And we've never been.'

'I know. It's awful.'

'It's only eight miles. And it'll be a nice drive.'

'Yes. It will.'

'And if we never go out of this garden, we shall moulder away, and our minds will get covered with lichen, and general decay will set it.'

Pause, in which each wonders who will be the first to say that we don't care in the least if we moulder away, and become lichen-minded, provided that we are not dragged out of the garden. For it will be an intolerable agony to call on Mrs. Z., and put on a clean collar, and get the earth out of one's nails and be polite. It is an unbearable and loathsome project.

Lunch arrives, and is eaten. Shady glances are cast from one to the other as we have our coffee in the garden. There is an exquisite laziness in the air. The smell of the earth, and the hot wallflowers and the lilac — it's like mulled claret. And there are a thousand things to do, the flowers to arrange, and all those absurd little seedling laburnums to transplant. And the heads of the dead polyanthus ought to be nipped off. And there is that new spraying stuff to use on the roses.

So suddenly, one of us says:

'Let's damn well —— Mrs. Z.'

To which one replies 'I should think it's a long time since anything like that happened to her. But let's.'

Worse and worse. These pages are becoming not only pointless but coarse. I don't care. I shall sit here, looking at the white flowers, till night falls, if necessary.

And that reminds me. That phrase — 'till night falls' — has evoked a memory which I can't keep to myself. For if any gardener has read the foregoing paragraphs without being convinced that a white garden may be a lovesome thing (God wot), he cannot have thought of it as it is at night.

For it can be even more exciting by night than by day.

Your heart beats high as you step out. The moon is still hiding, and there is little to be seen. But there is everything to be touched, and smelt, and guessed. Here, as one stumbles down the path, a honeysweet drift of perfume proclaims the presence of the mock-orange. Lightly run your fingers over its branches — its leaves seem to whisper to you in the dark. Further on, beyond the arch, there is another scent, even more poignant, from the border of the night-scented stock. How glad you are that you came out to greet this delicious little blossom at its crowning hour! It was so pathetic during the day — it dropped at high noon, and was too weary to offer you its sweets.

As you walk across the lawn you can feel your way, in the thick darkness, merely by the sense of smell. You

29

realize something of the exhilaration of the animals, who *see* with their noses! You stand still for a moment. What is that lovely, luring perfume that drifts from the shadows? You close your eyes, savouring it. Of course — the tobacco flowers!

Quite still, you stay, breathing in these airs which are so heavily laden with beauty. Deeper and deeper you breathe and you are filled with an exhilaration that is keener than any sense that wine can give a man, cooler, and more lasting.

And then, when you open your eyes, you find that the moon has drifted from behind the clouds. And these dim shapes, which had been present in the darkness only as disembodied scents, proclaim themselves with ivory clarity. The tobacco flowers are like a flight of white moths, trembling on the curtains of the darkness. The white petunias are poised as delicately as any Sylphides — one feels that the first strains of a Chopin prelude would set them dancing. And whatever may be the time of the year, the flowers, if they are white, will be perfected, transfigured by the light of the moon. The snowdrops will be luminous — a twist of your imagination and you can persuade yourselves that they are white elves, met on secret business, and you can set them marching round the trunk of the damson tree.

§ v i

And, now, at last, for the light is beginning to fade, we can return to the *H.C.*

The fatal paragraph is still a little way ahead, but we are nearing it.

After reading the sporting utterances of Sir Percy X,

I turned the page, and found another large photograph
confronting me. The photograph of a woman with a very
horsy face, strangely like that of a male impersonator.
'What *can* be the reason for publishing the photograph of
a woman like that?' I asked myself, burying my nose in the
H.C., and forgetting all about the white beauty in front of
me. The *H.C.* told me that the horse-like lady was Mrs.
Grafham, and that she had just been appointed a new
magistrate for Huntingdonshire. And it said:

> 'ONE CAN TRUTHFULLY SAY that Mrs. Grafham, wife of
> Town Councillor E. W. Grafham, is a "live wire", in
> many ways, whether it be politics, social service, golf,
> hockey, or even the mundane things of ordinary
> life.'

This startling paragraph, as I read it, gave me the
impression that Mrs. Grafham was about to explode by
spontaneous combustion. It gave me a picture of a large
woman, letting out rather rude sparks in all directions,
with a golf club in one hand and a hockey stick in the
other. But ah! one must not forget that she sparked 'even
in the mundane things of life.' An obscure and somewhat
frightening sentence. Did she spit fire at provincial cock-
tail parties? Did she pass through her kitchen in a whirl of
tulle, throwing her lipstick contemptuously into the
stock-pot? What did she do?
I glued my eyes to the paper.

> 'Of Scotch extraction she revels in the fact that she
> played for Wales at hockey.'

At which, I started back, as though somebody had dealt
me a staggering blow between the eyes.
'No, no,' I muttered in delight, 'this is not true. It just

can't be true.' But another glance at the paper told me that I had read aright.

> 'Of Scotch extraction she revels in the fact that she played for Wales at hockey.'

'*Of Scotch extraction*' (I adore the word 'extraction', it always makes me think of a baby being painfully dragged from a cave with a pair of tongs) . . . she revelled, yes, she *revelled* . . . in the fact that she played for Wales at hockey. When she thought of this, she simply bounced about the house! She rushed upstairs (revelling), and turned on all the taps at once, and whistled *Traviata*, out of tune.

More, more!

> 'In the County Library, she has proved herself a tower of strength, and she . . .'

But no. *Ça, c'est trop.* A Scotch-extracted revelling tower, which is also a live wire, is a phenomenon which one does not often encounter even in the pages of the *H.C.* I stared in a sort of drugged delight at Mrs. Grafham. And then, for fear that the spell would break, I turned the page.

§ VII

The fatal paragraph is now coming very near indeed. But before we reach it, one peculiarity of the *H.C.* must be noted. And that is, its extremely morbid preoccupation with Death. As I turned the remaining pages, I discovered that at least two-thirds of the news was all about local people 'passing away', and being buried, and covered with wreaths. Indeed, so many and so varied were its accounts of funerals, and so gloating its descriptions of them, that a stranger, unacquainted with the qualities of our local journalism, would have imagined that a fierce and virulent plague had swept the county, and that he was reading a special number issued to commemorate the disaster.

'Sorrowful Assembly at Funeral Service,' I read.

And underneath, there was the heading 'To be Cremated at Nottingham'. This heading, unfortunately, had been placed just over a peculiarly winsome picture of Miss Marlene Dietrich, whose charms were enumerated in the next column. The typesetters of the *H.C.*, you see, have a lot on their minds, and they cannot always be too particular. I was very glad they can't. Because the singular idea of Miss Marlene Dietrich being cremated at Nottingham gave me a new and poignant interest in that lady.

Underneath the picture of Miss Dietrich there were three columns of the gloomiest prose, beginning with a description of the church, whose rostrum, we learned, was 'relieved by the greenery of palms and ferns'. Then there was an account of the sermon, which ended with a great peroration:

'I think that our friend sailed gladly down the River of Time, and when he came to face Eternity, out went all his sails.' A metaphor which, I felt, was a little rollicking for such an occasion, and would be more suitable for the description of a regatta at Cowes.

After this, there was an astonishingly long list of the names of mourners and those who had sent 'floral tributes'. Try as he may, the reader is unable to study the list of these floral tributes without noting how the typesetter carefully arranges the inscriptions so that they shall mount to a crescendo of regret.

The first wreath in the list is just inscribed, 'With sympathy'.

After that we get:
With deep sympathy.
With deepest sympathy.
With deepest sympathy and regret.
With very deepest sympathy and regret.
With very deepest sympathy and heartfelt regret.
With very deepest sympathy, heartfelt regret and remembrance.
With very deepest sympathy, heartfelt regret and fondest remembrance.
And so on.

There must be some very rigid etiquette about the things one writes on wreaths. For I noted that as the relationship became nearer, the sympathy, regret, remembrance etc. became more and more profound.

But the only tribute which touched me, a stranger to these grim facts, was the one at the very end, squeezed in, just above the name of the undertaker.

'With love to a good master. Annie.'

I don't know why those simple words should be so moving, but they are.

The reader of these remarks may mutter 'Bad taste'.

Perhaps. But Death, I have often thought, is in rather bad taste itself.

§ VIII

And now, at last, we come to the long-promised paragraph.

It was contained under the Allways Notes on the page which was headed 'News From the Five Counties'. The Allways correspondent of the *H.C.* is Mr. Joy, the keeper of the village shop, and of all his duties this is the one which he takes most seriously. Fluent with his tongue, he is even more fluent with his pen, and he has a journalistic cliché for every possible occasion.

Never once — not even when a violent thunderstorm gave all the children colds — has he failed to observe that 'an enjoyable time was had by all', when reporting the annual outing to Skegness. Never once, in describing a funeral, has he neglected to note the presence of a 'sorrowful assembly', and 'a large number of floral tributes'. Never once, in describing a village concert, has he omitted to record that the piano solos were 'tasteful', the comic songs 'mirthful', and the recitations 'much appreciated'.

I turned to see what he had written this week. Nothing very much, apparently. There had been a 'pound day' for the local hospital, and there was a long list of the people who had sent pounds of tea, sugar, jam, etc. There had also been a whist drive, with 'refreshment carried out by Mesdames Watts and Jackson' — a phrase which made me think of two French ladies, highly *maquillées*, rushing out into the garden with a quantity of meringues. (If you knew Mesdames Watts and Jackson you would realize that my mental picture was definitely inaccurate.)

And then, at the end of the notes, there were the following paragraphs.

I read them casually.

A most successful garden fête was held at Allways on Tuesday, in the delightful floral gardens of the Rectory. The fête had the honour of being opened by the Dowager Lady Osprey.

Lady Osprey, who was warmly received, said that England's ship of state had passed through stormy waters, and was not not yet 'out of the wood'. However, if we all put our shoulders to the helm, she had no doubt that we could scale the highest peaks. One thing, she said, was ruining the life of the agri-

35

cultural labourer, and that was super-tax. She herself would be forced to sell some of her property unless the Chancellor of the Exchequer could be made to see reason. She had much pleasure in declaring the fête open.

I put down the paper, and yawned. Another garden fête — another outburst by that sour old millionairess — how could that have any effect on Allways?

I was soon to learn.

CHAPTER III

A GREAT LADY

THE name of Lady Osprey loomed large over Allways, and indeed over all Huntingdonshire. Although she lived some thirty miles away, at the vast castle of Farthingdale, it seemed as though the shadows from her fantastic turrets and battlements drifted across the county in order to remind us of her presence.

Lady Osprey was immensely rich and immensely social. Hardly a week passed by when the English illustrated magazines omitted to show her thin and raddled face peering from the centre of distinguished groups of Farthingdale house-parties. What attraction the British public found in regarding these recurring dozens of singularly plain men and women, disposed in angular attitudes on a flight of steps, it would be difficult to explain. Did the British public know these persons? Certainly not. Did it obtain any erotic excitement from them? Well, if it obtained erotic excitement from the representation of six perfect English ladies, with hook-noses, balancing themselves on shooting sticks, and looking with angry expressions at their feet, it was lucky.

Under Lady Osprey's skilful guidance, Farthingdale loomed large in the social life of England. I had been there to luncheon, once or twice, on Sundays, but I did not much relish the experience. My car always looked so tiny as I swept into the immense drive. This would not have mattered if the gravel had not been so new and sharp that the tyres made a noise like a minor bombardment, so that

37

you felt that dozens of distinguished people would glare out of the windows to see what was happening. For the very valleys echoed to the crunching of that gravel, and when one suddenly stopped, by the front door, it sounded as though an avalanche were falling.

Moreover, the butler always took a malicious delight in asking me to move the car farther on. 'Would you mind, sir . . . His Royal Highness has not yet arrived.' So one had to get in the car again, panic-stricken, and make another crunching noise over the gravel, wondering, meanwhile, which Royal Highness it was, and if there would be female Royal Highnesses too, and how on earth one was to know which was which, and would it be better to call everybody 'ma'am' and 'sir', or would that make them think that one had come to tune the piano?

Besides, the flowers made me grind my teeth with envy. As one walked through the overheated corridors, which were so thickly carpeted that one could hear faint pre-prandial rumblings in one's inside, one saw banks of gloxinias, forests of azaleas, and buckets of orchids. A single one of those gloxinias would be an event in All-ways. I should walk round and round it, and take it into the house for one day, and back to the greenhouse for another. I should give parties for it, and it would have an awful effect on Mrs. M. I should know each velvet petal by heart, and study all its blood relations, and even try to paint it. And when it died — however, we must not be morbid.

But at Farthingdale, the gloxinias were lost. I longed to take one away, and show it what life could be, if it were really appreciated and not treated as if . . . well, as if it were only a gloxinia. However, I never took anything away from Farthingdale, except a headache.

A GREAT LADY

§11

You may wonder why we have suddenly left the quiet and homely lanes of Allways for these uncomfortably exalted circles. It is not really so irrelevant as it sounds. It was on a Friday that I read the sinister paragraph about Lady Osprey's speech in the *H.C.* On the following day I had forgotten all about it. But it was recalled to me, for a fleeting moment, by my neighbour Undine Wilkins, who paid me a brief and mysterious visit after lunch.

Undine, you may remember, is the willowy young lady who always sings the *Benedicite* so aesthetically in church. Her clothes, which are very expensive, look as if they were lengths of material pinned on to one of those wax figures that make one jump when one sees them, lit up in attitudes of shameless abandon, late at night in the Brompton Road.

She said she would *adore* some coffee. She also said how exquisite the 'snapdwagons' were . . . and how *excruciating* it must be for the poor bees to have to *plunge* through the entrance to the snapdwagons in order to obtain the pollen, and then, with heavy carelessness, she said 'Oh — by the way, Angela Osprey is lunching with me to-morrow. Do come too! If you haven't anything better to do?'

I stared at Undine. *Angela* Osprey. So they were on those terms?

I wondered what was in the air.

'I'd love to,' I said. And then I added hastily, 'Provided she doesn't make a speech.'

'A speech? Why should she?' Undine gazed at me with an astonishment that was quite unassumed.

'Didn't you read the report of her speech in the *H.C.* yesterday?'

'No! What did she say?'

'She said that England was passing through rough water, and was not yet out of the wood. It sounded rather amphibian.'

Undine, whose spirit is not exactly drenched in humour, gave me a vague smile, and murmured 'terribly'. Then she rose to go, adding 'Nobody else. Except Mrs. M. And the Professor, for coffee.'

And she did one of her celebrated glides through the narrow front door.

When she had gone, one problem began to intrigue me. No . . . it had nothing to do with Lady Osprey's speech, whose significance had not yet dawned upon me, nor upon anyone else in Allways. The problem was this. What would she do about her Visitors' Book? For this was a very important thing in Undine's life.

The idea of Undine's Visitors' Book was one of those ideas which might, without prejudice, be described as 'arch'. For instead of having an ordinary Visitors' Book, she had ruled off a square of the white wall of her 'den', and people wrote their names on the wall.

Only a few people were chosen for the honour of writing their names. In fact the village at large knew nothing about it, because on all normal occasions the list, which was quaintly headed, in Tudor script — VISITORS' BOOKE — was covered by a large picture, which was only taken down when somebody of a certain distinction hove into view. I had just scraped into the 'booke', by the skin of my teeth, and I don't think that I should have been asked, had I not seen it one day by accident, during a spring cleaning.

'Whatever is all that written on the wall?'

'Oh!' Undine had said, regarding me doubtfully, as though pondering my eligibility. Then, a little more brightly, having decided that I had some claim, under the arts . . . 'Oh — you *must* sign your name. All my *real* friends do.' And she tripped to the desk, and brought me a large quill pen, dyed violet.

I glanced hastily at the list, and the first name I saw was that of Charlie Chaplin, who passed through Allways about five years ago, when he was touring England. If I remember rightly he spent about forty minutes here, and a bare three minutes in Undine's cottage, so that her friendship with him must have blossomed with remarkable speed.

I also saw the names of two cabinet ministers, who had once come down in the depths of winter and made very cross little speeches in the village hall, because there had been a rumour that the local Tory candidate was not 'safe'. Also, a number of stars of stage and screen, who had never been within a hundred miles of Allways. But there was nobody from the village. Of that I made quite sure.

Therefore what would happen at lunch? One thing was quite certain, and that was that Lady Osprey would not be allowed to depart from Tudor Cottage without signing her name — no, not even if Undine had to take her by the scruff of the neck and rub her nose on the wall. Another thing that was quite certain was that nothing would induce her to ask Mrs. M. to sign.

The lunch promised to be interesting.

§ III

'No really . . . my chauffeur would *much* rather lunch at the inn . . . he's so particular . . . and I'm sure your little cook would be put out.'

Thus, in the first minute of her arrival, did Lady Osprey,

before she had even entered the house, show her charming consideration. But she was wrong to refer to Undine's cook as 'little', because that lady weighed thirteen stone and looked as if she were permanently inflated. However Lady Osprey invariably belittled other people's possessions.

'Charming . . . charming!' she murmured, as we went inside. 'Were the ceilings always like this, or did you have the floor raised? Oh yes, *quite* genuine, I'm sure, one can see that!' (Thank heavens, she was early, and Mrs. M. had not yet arrived, so there was a hope that Undine would be able to get her to sign her name before lunch). 'Oh — I nearly bumped my head! No really, it doesn't worry me at all . . . I'm used to it . . . you see, I often visit my tenants in their little cottages, and I feel quite at home. And this room is the . . . ?'

'This is the Garden Room,' simpered Undine. We were all feeling a little overpowered, and I fear our remarks sounded flat.

'Ah yes! And there . . .' she peered through the window, '*there* is the garden! I see you have antirrhinums!' She made the word 'antirrhinums' sound like stomach trouble — the sort of thing you cure with bicarbonate of soda.

'Yes,' said Undine faintly. In spite of her new mauve tulle, she looked very insignificant, for Lady Osprey was wearing one of those incredibly elegant costumes which are invidiously described by the French as 'le sporting'. She had no jewels at all except a brooch of immense rubies, which, on any other woman, would instantly have suggested Woolworth's.

At last, the moment came.

It was still only twenty minutes past one. We had a good five minutes before Mrs. M. would arrive.

'You *must* come and see my den,' said Undine.

'Your . . .?'

'My den.'

'Your den?'

The word 'den', if repeated often, sounds like a bark, or a cough — it loses reality, and becomes like a word in a German grammar —

Der die das

Den die das . . .

That was what echoed through my head. But Lady Osprey was equal to the occasion.

'Oh your den!' she said. 'But of course. Let us all go!'

We went in. Ah — there it was. My fondest hopes were realized. The picture had been taken down! The Visitors' List was exposed in its full glory. Lady Osprey's eagle eye detected it at once.

'Oh!' she said, advancing towards it.

'Oh yes,' murmured Undine, with so much nonchalance that I feared she would suffocate, 'you must sign your name'.

Lady Osprey looked at her sharply. 'On the wall?'

'Let me see,' said Undine, ignoring her. 'Where can we find a pen?'

The question was hardly necessary, because a large quill pen, newly sharpened, was already poised in her hand, with ink dropping on it.

Lady Osprey took it vaguely 'Oh sign . . . sign!' I murmured. 'Mrs. M. may be announced at any moment, and then there will be hell to pay.' I willed Lady Osprey to sign. But she stood there, glaring at the names on the wall, the pen wobbling in her hand.

'But my dear, what a distinguished list!' The tone in which this remark was delivered was glacial. 'Quite a

43

galaxy! Charlie Chaplin! Quite an educated hand, he
writes, doesn't he? Though I never *quite* forgave his very
odd behaviour to the Prime Minister when he was over
here. Ah . . . and Lady Julia . . . she's been staying
with you! Poor Lady Julia! She's often proposed herself
to me, too . . . but of course . . . how nice it must be to
be able to ask *anybody*.

'Oh, sign, sign!' I willed her.

But she burbled on.

'Not that I really mind . . .' she continued, 'my dear
old father always used to say that if one was sure of one's
own position one could ask the cook to dinner . . . but then,
it's the *other* people one has staying with one, isn't it? They
mightn't be so broadminded. Although I must say I think
she *looks* worse than she is . . . so smothered in cosmetics
. . . I once stayed in a house where she had been asked,
to fill up, you know, and when I was passing her bedroom,
the door happened to blow open, and I have never *seen*
so many cosmetics in my life. "But what do you do with all
of them, darling?" I asked her . . . after all, I *had* to go in
. . . and she explained what each of them did. Of course
I was so sorry for her that I didn't like to point out that the
whole lot of them hadn't been able to get her a husband.
Poor darling Lady Julia. So maligned!'

Another flourish of the pen.

'Oh sign . . . sign!' I breathed. This was as bad as one
of those early wild west films where the villain is chasing
Pearl White . . . (was it?) . . . round the scullery, with the
worst possible intentions, and the hero is careering over the
mountains to her rescue. Heavens, the girl has tripped up!
And now he *will* do something most unpleasant . . . but
no, for we are shot back to the hero who is just sliding
down a completely perpendicular precipice. Oh dear,

she has escaped, and is trying to get out of the window . . . but no . . . he is dragging her back by the ankle . . . ah! the hero has slid down the precipice, and is now charging through a river . . . oh, oh, *oh!* she has sat in the sink! But ah! she is out again, but no . . . he is pushing her back over the kitchen table, what *can* the poor girl do . . . hooray . . . the hero is over the river, and the little boys in the threepenny seats have begun to cheer, so perhaps there is hope that nothing really fundamental will happen to Miss White after all.

That was how I felt as Lady Osprey stood pen in hand. And Undine was also feeling the strain. Glancing nervously towards the door, she forced a fierce smile to her face, pointed to the wall and said, 'There would be a nice little place. Just above dear Sally!'

Sally, I may say, was a Duchess who had once opened a garden fête, with considerable reluctance, at Allways.

'Oh really . . . not *above* dear Sally,' crooned Lady Osprey. 'Sally mightn't like my signing above her, because Sally is just, well *just* a tiny bit of a snob! Poor Sally! Of course . . . .'

'I will dip the pen in the ink again,' quavered Undine. 'Thank you.'

Undine darted to the ink-pot, but before she could return to the wall, Lady Osprey was off again. 'Of course,' she said, 'snobbery is the one thing I do *not* understand. My dear old father . . . you remember the Sargent picture of him? The Queen always thought it was the *image,* though personally I don't think he quite got the chin . . . still, a genius . . . and I don't grudge it to the National Gallery at all . . . I often go there and pay my sixpence . . . just to be alone with him . . . not that one ever can be, even on the days which aren't free . . . however . . . my dear old father always said that he couldn't understand snobs at all. Neither can I. But I'm a snob for *one* thing.'

She paused dramatically.

'Yes?' Undine was holding the pen so close to her that I feared it would go into her eye. Lady Osprey gently took it and laid it down on the table.

'Brains!' she said. 'Yes . . . I'm a snob for brains. That's the only thing that really interests me in the least. I remember once . . .'

'I think it may drip on the carpet,' I murmured in desperation.

Lady Osprey moved the pen an inch. 'I remember once giving a dinner before the war where there were seven Garters.'

This was such a vision of grandeur that for the moment I almost forgot Mrs. M.

There is very little that the normal person can say, after such an announcement. Seven garters takes a lot of beating. I suppose one might say that once one had to have the plumbers in because seven Maharajah's had all been in the bathroom together, but such a statement would not have the true ring of reality, besides sounding not quite nice.

'Seven, I think it was,' said Lady Osprey with a slight frown. 'Let me see, who were they? There was Lord Curzon, of course. And Lord . . .'

She began to say the names, one by one. And oh, rapture! at last she was taking up the pen . . . she was lifting it to the wall to sign. Then she paused.

'But that only makes six!' she said. 'Who *was* the seventh?'

I felt like saying 'Crippen,' and making her sign by force. But at that precise moment the bell rang. It was Mrs. M.!

The next few moments passed like a horrible dream.

46

'Who *was* the seventh?' repeated Lady Osprey.

I heard the front door open, and Mrs. M.'s voice. I nearly yelled at Lady Osprey 'The seventh Garter was Mahomet and he wore it suspended from his left nostril, and Lord Curzon said he would report him to the Lord Chamberlain . . .' when the miracle happened. . . .

A bright smile suddenly came over Lady Osprey's face. 'Why, of *course* . . . how foolish of me . . . it was King Edward!'

Saying which she sprawled her name quickly across the wall, just above Sally's. And the second after Undine had seized it from her, and was hanging the picture on the wall, Mrs. M. was announced.

I have never so much admired Undine as at that moment. For she gave a final pat to the picture, and turned, and cooed . . . 'Ah Mrs. M. We were just looking at my little treasures.' Then she put down the pen with great deliberation on the table, and said, 'I don't believe you have met?'

After which, there was the usual polite conversation. But Mrs. M.'s eye strayed constantly towards the picture. What had been going on? What did it all mean? And why had nobody told her about this before?

CHAPTER IV

WARNING SHADOWS

THE lunch 'went off' very well indeed. Austin waited beautifully, the mutton was very hot, and Lady Osprey said it was wonderful to think that so many vegetables grew in Undine's little garden.

But it was not till the end of lunch that she revealed the sinister purpose of her visit. Till then we indulged in literary conversation.

'Mr. Nichols is writing a book,' said Undine, during one of those awkward pauses which often happen in houses where there is only one to wait at table. That is the moment when the principal guest is regarding her mutton, but cannot begin to eat it because it is not yet surrounded by vegetables, and will not be so surrounded till the least important guest (who is usually me) has humbly and hastily grabbed a piece of mutton for himself.

'Really?' said Lady Osprey, kindly, 'You must tell me all about it. . . .'

I was about to decline to do so, when she assisted me, by adding, in quite final tones 'some day'.

'I see,' she continued, 'that poor Lady Julia, whose name I saw in the other room. . . .'

Mrs. M.'s eyes opened wide. Lady Julia's name? In the other room? Her curiosity was agonizing. . . .

'I see that she has got her book published at last. Have you read it?'

No. We had not read it. We had only heard it 'very highly spoken of', which meant that we had seen one or two advertisements of it in the Sunday papers, where we had been informed that it was 'Piquant . . . the memoirs of the charming chatelaine of Longacre . . . Contains many lively stories . . . Lady Julia has a ready pen . . . should command attention'.

'I thought it so wise of her to have the book illustrated by sketches instead of photographs,' purred Lady Osprey. 'I don't think that *photographs* of Longacre would be very appealing, not to the general public, but the sketches really made it look almost impressive. It was very clever how the artist got those nice cloud effects . . . did you notice? Very natural, and the clouds completely hid all those ugly little villas by which Longacre is surrounded, now that she'd had to sell so much of her property, poor darling. If she'd had it photographed, the clouds mightn't have been placed so conveniently . . . although I must say that whenever I've been to Longacre the weather has been appalling . . . I suppose its because it lies in such an unhealthy district.'

All this with hardly a pause for breath. I was about to say something in favour of poor little Longacre, which was really a charming place, when Lady Osprey continued, in saccharine tones:

'Such a lot of trouble, too, she's been to about her ancestors. Poor darling, I'm afraid it must have cost her a great deal in research. The College of Heralds, they tell me, is very expensive, especially when they have to look up such a lot of very sordid people. Who was it that she made such a fuss about? Sir Robert or Sir James? Or both? Baronets weren't they, in Charles I's reign? Yes? And both married the same milkmaid, or something like that. Personally I should have thought that was the sort of thing one would prefer to hush up, if it really happened, but of course, it may all be fiction. So much of the book *is* . . . not that I've really read it, only dipped into it, still I couldn't help wondering.'

At this point Austin, who had been poised behind Lady Osprey for a very long time, with a salad, gave her a perceptible nudge. She stared distantly at Austin, observed the salad as if it were a peculiarly repellent form of weed, and then she turned to me, and beamingly continued:

'Of course, my dear, the whole thing's copied from *you*. But completely. Your lovely books, "The Garden Gate" and what was the other one? It's always by my bed, to send me to sleep. You really ought to sue her for something, yes, you really ought . . . not that you will, of course, because the poor darling couldn't pay, and you're far too kind-hearted. She's got *all* your characters in it, only she's given them all titles, and taken away their sense of humour. And that bit about religion . . . you know . . . you treated it so lightly, I laughed *so* much . . . but with her it's quite impossible, really embarrassing, like being talked at by the vicar. However I see she's gone into a second edition, not that that means anything does it, because you can have an edition of only half a dozen copies, can't you? Still, I do hope it succeeds, because she's such a sweet woman, really, and always seems to find *good* in things, however bad they may be. Look at the way she managed to get quite nice advertisements out of her reviews, by taking a sentence here, and a sentence there, and leaving out the whole of the rest of it, and putting in a few dots. I *do* call that looking on the bright side of things, and I hope she makes a great deal of money out of it, because I shall have to lunch there some time next summer, and last time I lunched I couldn't eat anything at all.'

'But you're not eating anything now,' breathed Undine,

in a voice that was meant to be arch, but was very troubled about something.

'Darling, I'm *gorging* myself,' said Lady Osprey, without enthusiasm, pushing her mutton a little farther away from her, and balancing a brussels sprout on the end of her fork. She disliked being interrupted, when she had 'got going'. She turned to me again, and purred:

'Of course, there were bits in the book which the Prime Minister couldn't *endure*, but I told him that was just because he was so old fashioned. Those references to her "secretary", for instance. You remember, the Argentine boy who fell down the well. Such a very odd thing to do . . . and we all know *why* . . . some people have even gone so far as to say . . . but she couldn't . . . I *never* believed that . . . I've seen the well-head myself, and no woman could possibly lift it, besides he was an extremely powerful young man. Of course, some people say he was drunk, and . . . but really, why should she? Naturally, I wouldn't breathe a word of this, normally, but then she does say *such* a lot about him in the book, doesn't she? And those poems of his, which she translated . . . did you like them? I suppose they may have sounded very nice in Argentine, but in English they made me shudder. Still, one can't have everything perfect in a book, and really I think she's done it amazingly well, considering what a drab life she's led, with that frightful father, who lies on his back all day, although his spine's as good as mine, and considering that she's really never met anybody, except in my house. But still, poor darling, I do hope her book is the *greatest* success — I'm sure it deserves to be — don't you?'

We felt, after this, that it certainly did.

§ 11

At last Lady Osprey began to come to the point. Her method of doing so was somewhat indirect. She began with a long lamentation about her poverty.

'One really doesn't know what one will do to make both ends meet, does one?' she said. 'I mean, when one's overdraft reaches *six* figures, it *is* time to think a little. Don't you agree?'

Personally I should think it was time to take the first train to Greece, or some other country where the extradition laws are kind to foreigners. But then I had not several million pounds worth of gilt edged security. So I politely agreed that, in such circumstances, a little thought should be taken.

'Of course,' she went on, 'if I were *absolutely* ruined, I mean if they took almost everything from me, and just left me, well, I never was much good at figures, but let's say one was reduced to ten thousand pounds a year . . .' (all our eyes met, at that moment, as if by a signal, and were then hastily redirected to Lady Osprey) . . . 'I think I should leave England altogether. One couldn't bear to live in it, could one? Not on those terms. And I think I should take a flat in Paris. I couldn't afford a car, of course, nor a chauffeur, but I think I could just manage a maid. She adores me, you know . . . such a character. Yes, I think she'd come. And though naturally, one couldn't entertain, I might occasionally have a few friends in to tea, and I hope . . .' she sighed, 'I *hope* that some of the people whom I had entertained in the past might sometimes remember me . . . and ask me to dine.'

Her voice was so sad that I felt she might at any moment

begin to weep, gently, so vividly was she visualizing the horrors of life on ten thousand a year. However she pulled herself together.

'And that reminds me,' she said, as though it were an afterthought, 'of what I really wanted to talk to you all about.'

§ III

There was a deathly silence. Mrs. M. paused, her coffee-cup in the air, with her little finger sticking straight up. Lady Osprey sighed, and looked down.

'I'm afraid, I'm very much afraid, I shall have to put all my land round here up for sale.'

'Ah!'

We all said the same thing, in different ways. Undine politely, Mrs. M. very sharply, as though she were a detective who had just found a blood-stain on the bath-mat. And I said it fairly sharply too, for I wondered where all this was leading.

'After all, it only pays me a bare two per cent . . two and two-thirds to be exact, but the charges on it bring it down to *just* over two.' (Poor Lady Osprey never had any head for figures!)

'That's very sad,' I said. 'But I suppose it won't make much difference? I mean, you'll give first choice to the present holders? The farmers and people?' (Fortunately, we ourselves were all freeholders.)

'Well, as a matter of fact . . .' she hesitated a little . . . 'there was some talk of a building scheme. And I hardly thought it was my place to stand in the way of it. In fact, my agent tells me that he has sold one piece this morning. I was quite astonished at the price it fetched, far more than I anticipated.'

'Where was it?' I asked sharply.

'Well, of course, it *was* a good site. That little piece opposite the church.' She rose to her feet and peered out of the window. 'Let me see . . . no, you can't quite see it from here.'

Undine, for once in her life, spoke with a ring of genuine emotion.

'You don't mean to say you've sold the little field at the end of my garden?'

Lady Osprey raised her eyebrows. 'Certainly. Have you any objection?'

'I have a very strong objection indeed.'

'Really?' Lady Osprey glared at her.

'May I ask to whom you sold it?'

'A Mr. Galloway. That was the name, I believe.'

Galloway! A nice enough little man, and a widower. But he had six of the loudest-voiced children in Allways.

The seriousness of Lady Osprey's decision began to dawn on me. For it meant that all the land from the Great North Road to Allways, and beyond, right up to the 'folly' where the bluebells grew, would now be on the market as 'desirable building sites'. These quiet fields, which had been handed down from generation to generation of farmers, would now be thrown open to the rag, tag and bobtail.

Mrs. M. broke in sharply.

'And does this mean that all your plots will be sold? The field at the end of my garden for instance?'

'I haven't the pleasure of knowing your garden,' began Lady Osprey, 'but . . .'

'I'm afraid,' said Mrs. M., 'that nobody *will* have much pleasure in knowing it, if this sort of thing is going to happen all over Allways'.

She too was genuinely moved.

'Really . . .' Lady Osprey took a step back. 'I think that you are all behaving very strangely. I come to lunch with Miss Wilkins, at great inconvenience to myself . . .'

'And even greater to me,' snapped Undine.

Lady Osprey's eyes blazed. 'I come to lunch,' she continued, 'in order to tell you about certain plans which I have been compelled to make in order to put my affairs in order. Those plans may possibly affect your little village. Therefore, as a neighbourly act, I come out of my way to inform you of them.' She paused, and made a noise like a snort. 'I think the whole thing is . . . is most regrettable.' She turned to me. 'I *think*,' she said, 'that you will agree with me.'

I was very angry indeed. I hope I managed to control my voice.

'I do,' I said. 'It must be terrible to be so hard up that one's got to ruin England in order to save oneself. It must be quite terrible. I'm so sorry for you, Lady Osprey.' I gulped. This was one of those awful moments when one knows that one will think of the most acidly brilliant things to say in ten minutes, when it's too late.

Fate came to my rescue. I saw something glimmering on the floor. It was one of the fabulous rubies which had fallen from her pendant. I picked it up and handed it to her. She was rigid with anger and did not put out her hand to take it. I dropped it on to the table. 'I hope that the price you got for Undine's little field will go some way to paying for the insurance on this.'

That finished it. Lady Osprey went through the movements of what is known as 'sweeping out'. There was a frightful silent pause in the hall while the chauffeur was hurriedly summoned from the inn. There were icy farewells. There were tears on the part of Undine, and fulminations on the part of Mrs. M.

Three things emerged from that lunch.

Firstly, I was never asked to Farthingdale again.

Secondly, there was a blank patch on the wall of the den, where Lady Osprey's name was angrily erased by Undine, after Mrs. M. had left.

Thirdly — but that will have to wait for the next chapter.

CHAPTER V

PRESERVING THE AMENITIES

AND now it was that panic seized the members of the little community of Allways.

Even the Professor, normally so cool-headed, was observed to leave his desk on more than one occasion, and to stand blinking at the small coppice at the end of his garden. And he had been heard to say that he 'supposed he ought to buy it, before it was too late'.

The others showed their distress in far more emphatic terms.

Mrs. M. called on me, the day after Lady Osprey's visit. Her ostensible reason for calling was to ask if I would lend her Perkins, the 'odd man', that evening, as she could not get through all the watering that had to be done, and she thought that Perkins was 'quite a good waterer'.

However, I too had observed the admirable watering capacities of Perkins, and I had no intention of parting with him. He was the world's champion waterer. He really loved it. There was a strain of poetry in him, I think. For often, on sultry summer evenings, I have watched him, a tiny little man with a drooping moustache, holding out a can over the thirsty flowers, with another can dripping on the old brick pavement. And he has turned to me with a sort of ecstasy and whispered, 'saving 'em, sir, saving 'em!' It is almost as though he were an evangelist, saving souls instead of flowers — as though the sweet brown pond-water, that poured from the can, were a holy water

which he had taken from some secret well of the spirit.
Of all the happy memories which my garden has given
me one of the happiest is the silhouette of Mr. Perkins,
standing there in the dusk, with the cool water hissing on
to the parched earth, turning to me and whispering:
'saving 'em, sir, saving 'em!'

When I told Mrs. M. that Mr. Perkins was my Waterer
in Chief, and that nothing would induce me to part with
him, she surprised me by refraining, for once in a way,
from argument. She merely shrugged her shoulders and
said, 'Oh well — it doesn't matter. I suppose it's hardly
worth bothering about one's garden any more. We shall
probably all be surrounded by factories in a few months'.

'Factories?' I stared at her. 'Is anybody going to build
a factory here? Have you heard anything?'

'Not directly.'

I heaved a sigh of relief. When Mrs. M. tells you that
she has not heard anything 'directly', it means that she
has heard nothing at all, directly or indirectly, and that
her fertile imagination is at work.

How fertile her imagination was, may be guessed from
the following dialogue:

'But Mrs. M., what *sort* of factories?'

'Does it matter?'

'Perhaps not. But you can't just say "factories" as though
you were talking of mushrooms. What *could* make anybody
want to build a factory in Allways?'

'They always seem to choose the prettiest places.
Haven't you ever noticed that, when you are travelling
by train?'

'I know. But they choose them for some particular
reason.'

'As far as I can see, they choose them to be unpleasant.'

She shot her rabbit's teeth at me, and proclaimed:

'He only does it to annoy
Because he knows it teases.'

We argued for some time and then parted.

I was not greatly alarmed by Mrs. M.'s prophecies. Why should anybody build a factory at Allways? We were four miles from the nearest town of any importance. We had no natural advantages of any sort. Above all, we had no water. There was only the little stream at the end of my field, and even that had dwindled to a feeble trickle, protesting in a plaintive treble as it shivered its way beneath the long and hungry grasses. And water was, one understood, a vital factor in industry.

I shrugged my shoulders, and thought no more of it. I had to go to London for a month, and I felt sure that by the time I returned, the whole thing would be forgotten.

Just before I went, I called on Miss Hazlitt, to see how she was getting on. If anybody was likely to suffer from the sale of Lady Osprey's land, it was Miss Hazlitt. For her tiny little plot was quite unprotected, and surrounded on all sides by acres of bare fields.

When I told her, jokingly, that Mrs. M. had prophesied a rash of factories all over Allways, and that probably she would have a warehouse for potted meats overlooking her shrubbery, her face lit up.

'Yes?' she said. Then she smiled happily. 'We never know, do we?'

'Know what?'

'What is in store for us. That is one of the things which makes life so exciting. We never know what has been planned. All we know is that it is all for the best.'

Unconquerable Miss Hazlitt! Even if they *had* built a

factory at the end of her shrubbery, she would have seen it, with the eyes of her spirit, as a thing of beauty.

But of course, they never would. I went away, smiling to myself, at the foolishness of Allways.

§ 11

And then the smile faded, very suddenly.

It was a month later.

I was driving back to Allways. Up the Great North Road. Here is the turning. The car winds leisurely through the curving lanes. The rabbits sit up, stare, and scurry away. The hedges are very lush and sparkling, for there have been heavy rains. Oh — it is good to be back!

I turned the corner. I always accelerated a little at that corner, because Undine Wilkins' cottage was just round the bend, and if she was in her garden I would have to get out and talk, and look at *her* herbaceous border, when all the time I was itching to look at mine.

But on this occasion, as soon as I had turned the corner, I stopped, with a grinding of brakes. The new bungalow had leapt into view.

God almighty!

Forgive me. But if ever there were an occasion for blasphemy, this was one. For the thing itself was blasphemous. It was a little to the side of Undine's cottage, so that at least she would not have to look at it from her windows. But it completely spoiled one's view of the church. Its squat, glaring silhouette was plastered flat against the church's grey and nebulous outlines. It stared at one arrogantly, through its hard little brazen windows. It was redder than you would have thought possible —

with the red of apoplexy. And its head, I mean its roof, glistened with bald new tiles.

It was an absurd thought, but somehow, as I saw it planted there, with the church behind, I thought of a nasty little Bolshevik sentry standing at the entrance to some sacred building which had been violated by a revolution.

As ill luck would have it, Mr. Galloway, its owner, came out of the door, just as I was about to start the car again. His pleasant, rosy face, whose hue matched the bricks of his loathsome dwelling, was beaming with the pride of ownership.

'Well sir,' he said, touching his cap, 'it's finished!'

I gave a sickly smile. What could one say? He was such a nice little man. So thrifty, and clean, and anxious to please.

'So I see.' And then: 'I expect you're glad to be in.'

At this point, a sound like a screech-owl announced the presence of Ivy, the youngest and most repellant of his daughters. Poison Ivy, she ought to have been called, for she was one of those children who dribble for dribbling's sake. I always looked at her face through half-closed eyes, and then sharply averted my eyes, and stared over her head, having seen quite enough to give me a hatred of the human race. If I ever had to wash Ivy's face I would do it with a very large sponge at the end of a very long pole, and should wear smoked glasses during the process.

Ivy clung to her father, and they stood there, blinking in the sunlight. One rapid glance at Ivy's nose and chin informed me that her face bore unmistakable traces of a peculiarly abandoned bout of dribbling, so I threw my eyes at the hard wall of the cottage. It sounds painful, and slightly inaccurate, but that was how it felt.

'Of course, it's a bit bright now,' said Mr. Galloway.

'Yes,' I gulped from the car. I *must* say something to conceal my loathing. 'But perhaps it'll tone down,' I said, weakly.

'That's what *I* say,' said Mr. Galloway, rubbing his hands with approval. 'It's bound to tone down.'

At this point Poison Ivy skipped a little nearer. I would rather have looked at the Gorgon's head than at Ivy's dribbling face at that moment. And so, I waved my hand at her, looking hard in the opposite direction, made a few more brilliant epigrams connected with the subject of toning down, and drove on.

Toning down! It would need an earthquake to tone *that* down. And it would need more than an earthquake to tone down Poison Ivy's face.

§ III

When I got home, I found an urgent note from Mrs. M., summoning me to take coffee after luncheon.

After luncheon, I was in a somewhat calmer mood. For I had made a mental survey of Allways, and had come to the happy conclusion that there was absolutely no other building site available — at least, no site near the road. The main farm covered all the frontage opposite me, and they weren't likely to sell. The Professor had an option on the field opposite the church. Mr. Joy, the shopkeeper, had no intention of selling his frontage, which adjoined that of Miss Bott, who had no intention of selling hers. The only other danger spots were covered by the inn, the post office, Mrs. M., and myself.

And so, I thought, Mrs. M. could not really have very

much to complain about. The only real danger seemed to be that one would always be running the risk of meeting Poison Ivy in the lane. But then, one could always bend down, and lace up one's shoes, over and over again till the menace passed. Or one could pretend to be calling one's dog, and skip along backwards, with airy gestures, demanding its company in ringing tones. And if the worst came to the worst, and one was forced to meet the Queen of the Dribblers face to face, the only thing to do would be to think very hard of somebody else. Of Miss Dietrich, for example, or some other exquisitely *maquillée* woman, who never dribbled. Miss Dietrich, one can be fairly certain, never dribbles. Or if she does, all the dribbly bits are cut out before the film is released.

Therefore, I imagined that Mrs. M. could not have much up her sleeve.

I was gravely mistaken. For this was the beginning of the great Allways Land Drama, of which I was the chief victim, and of which you are about to witness the first act.

§ I V

'You've seen it?' cried Mrs. M., when I arrived.

It would have been difficult to deny that one had seen it.

'Of course,' she added, in the same breath, 'that woman ought to be shot.'

'That woman,' I gathered, meant Lady Osprey.

'Poor Undine,' she went on, 'is absolutely prostrated.'

I pricked up my ears. 'Is she taking it badly?'

'She can't look at it, she told me. *Can't.* And this time I don't think it's affectation. When she turns the corner she walks backwards.'

63

The idea of Undine walking backwards into her cottage seemed rich in promise. I made a resolution to be a witness to this procedure as soon as possible.

'And before we know where we are, we shall have these things all over Allways,' continued Mrs. M. 'Now, I think we ought to do something about it.'

'We,' I feared, meant *me*. And I was right. For within five minutes, I was being taken out into the garden, made to peer through the hedge at a singularly drab field, and being informed how vitally important it was that I should buy it.

Mrs. M. spoke with such glibness that I felt certain she had been rehearsing.

'Land is going up,' she said. 'Only the other day, I had my stockbroker down and he said land was going up, and would go on going up. A very shrewd man. He said in these days it was the sort of investment a wise man would make, and stick to.'

'That land *would* stick to you,' I thought irreverently. 'It's the muddiest patch in Huntingdonshire.' Aloud I said:

'But Mrs. M., if I *did* buy any more land, and I really don't want to, I'd much rather buy a little more round my own cottage.'

'You have more than you want already.'

'I haven't got as much as you.'

'Not as much acreage, perhaps,' she countered quickly, 'but yours is more *spread* out.'

While I was trying to interpret this mysterious distinction in the spreading-out of Mrs. M.'s land and mine, she continued:

'Besides,' she said, 'this would be such a retreat. Nobody would know you were here. You could come and think things out.'

What sort of things a man could 'think out', standing in the middle of that field, in the pouring rain, it would be difficult to imagine. Besides Mrs. M. would always be popping over the hedge. I could see her, just as I decided to make the hero go to plant coffee in Kenya. 'Stuck?' she would cry amiably, as she often did, when she saw me looking pensive in my own wood.

Oh, no . . . no! That would never do. And at last Mrs. M. was convinced that I did not want the field.

Personally I thought it highly improbable that anybody else would want it, but she differed. Looking very ill-treated, because I would not fall in with her plans, she stepped back and surveyed her boundaries.

'Of course, I *could* throw up a bank here and plant it with evergreens. That would block them out.'

'Block *who* out, Mrs. M.?'

'Anybody who chose to build there.'

'But why *should* they build in that field. I still don't understand why they should.'

'And *I* don't understand why they shouldn't.'

'It's almost impossible to get at. They'd have to build a road all round your property. There's no water. No drains.'

'Those sort of people don't want water. Nor drains. They like living like pigs. And they would probably shout insulting things at the maids, over the hedge.'

I blinked. Mrs. M.'s mind was evidently already teeming with a mysterious people whose one object in life was to build houses in utterly impossible situations merely to spite her.

CHAPTER VI

ANCIENT LIGHTS

THE drama was only just beginning.

It was a drama that could have been played only in England. For only in England does there exist this white-hot passion for keeping oneself to oneself.

Only in England, do women stand at windows, and stare with frightened eyes at a distant hill, on which they can just see the outlines of a building, rising up to mar their hitherto inviolate horizon. 'The enemy is here,' they seem to mutter, 'he is at our gates!' They clutch the curtains, and stare into the distance. So, one feels, their ancestors must have stared out on to the hills, for the sight of alien lances piercing the skyline. The civil wars are over now, and neighbours are at peace, provided they speak the same language. But the war of property continues. And it is as fierce in the gardens of the suburbs as in the wide-spread acres of the great estates.

'Ancient lights!'

That is a strange archaic phrase, that one sees on dusty plaques against many little English walls. I never see that phrase without a quickening of the heart. It might well be taken as the ringing motto of the liberties of England. 'This light we had, this light we will keep. This window was ours, for dreaming, for receiving the blessing of the sun, for opening wide to the winds of the world, that they might blow in upon us, freely. This window we will guard, as we guard the freedom of our own hearts.'

'Ancient Lights!' That might also be the title of this

66

chapter. And with marked approval on glancing at the top of the page, I observe that it is.

§ 11

I called this a drama. But it is a drama of the spirit, rather than a drama of the body. And therefore, thank heavens, we are not compelled to rush out and witness a lot of harrowing sights, nor make things go off with a bang. We can sit back and give ourselves up to the exquisite luxury of intelligent reflection.

'Ancient lights.'

In America, that phrase would be meaningless.

Nothing surprised me so much, in the United States, as the endless rows of gardens, open to the road, which one passed in the suburbs of all the great cities. There was not even a hedge to protect them. It was, in fact, difficult to know where one garden began and the other ended. They might as well have been public property.

'But . . . why . . . why?' I used to ask, for the hundredth time, gazing round in distressed astonishment when I saw these parodies of gardens.

'We don't like shutting ourselves in,' was the usual burden of the answer. 'We don't think it would be neighbourly.'

'But do you like people only a few yards away, with nothing but a brick path to separate you, seeing everything you *do*?'

'We've nothing to be ashamed of,' they observed brightly.

It was all a deep, deep mystery to me. I would rather have ten square yards of sour soil, surrounded by a hedge so high that it blocked the sun out, than a hundred acres of land without a hedge. No — perhaps that is an exaggera-

67

tion, but it is not a really very gross exaggeration, and most English gardeners will share it with me.

Oh, how we hate being 'overlooked'! The eagerness with which we watch the vine creeping up the trellis! 'That will prevent Mrs. Smith from seeing us,' we mutter, with dark glee. From the way we go on we might be about to set up a coining establishment — we might be attempting to bury a large and important body in the seakale bed. We might be going to take off all our clothes and wave scarves round our heads, like the young ladies in Nature camps, whose photographs always surprise me. For they look as if they were shooing away birds from the newly-sown grass lawn. But why, with such protuberant figures, do they want the scarves? Any modern bird would take one look, bury its head under its wings, and fly off to the village pump for a drink.

However, we continue to shut ourselves in. Oh, the horror when there is a gap in the laurel hedge that separates us from the kitchen garden.

'We can see the gardener walking through to the green-house!' we gasp.

'See him?' the puzzled foreigner demands, wondering what monstrous things he can be up to.

'See him!' we repeat. Surely that is enough explanation? The expression on the foreigner's face tells us that it isn't, so we add, to clinch it, 'And he can see us!'

'See you?' repeats the foreigner blankly.

We give it up. We cannot explain to foreigners that we have a horror of being seen when we do not wish to be seen. It is not because we want to take off all our clothes. It is not because we wish to talk to ourselves, nor make faces like idiots, nor scratch our heads, nor blow out our cheeks, all by ourselves. It is just . . .

ANCIENT LIGHTS

Well, I suppose it is just because we are English. I can think of no explanation.

It is a pity that some other nations cannot catch a little of our curious psychology.

§ III

I called this a drama of the spirit. But it very soon became a drama of the body.

After Mrs. M.'s vain endeavour to persuade me to buy her field, I hoped that I might be left in peace. But no.

It happened like this. I was going for a walk with Whoops, who had not been for a walk for two days, and had been driving me to distraction with his dramatic yawns and highly affected stretchings. It is impossible to deny Whoops on these occasions. The power of canine suggestion is too great. He meets you at every corner of the garden, and stares fixedly at the gate. He stands over you, while you are watering, with an expression of martyrdom and casts his eyes longingly to the hedges. And if you definitely tell him that a walk is impossible, the measured tragedy of his slow return to the house, and the weary droop of his limbs as he sags beneath the dining-room table, are such that for your own peace of mind you have to take him.

So we set out for a walk together.

As we were passing Undine's cottage, a faint voice breathed over the hedge.

'Can I see you?'

I looked up and saw Undine. She was drooping, in an attitude of picturesque despair, over her garden gate. So startling was her appearance, that I stopped dead, to the intense disgust of Whoops, who stayed about fifty yards

69

up the lane, with his body facing towards a walk, and his head sharply turned, in interrogation.

Undine was in pitch black. She looked like those French widows who are blacker than anything known in nature. Her dress was of crepe, and with it she wore a heavy black necklace and jet ear-rings. Her powder (which was usually of the shade known as Naturel, and which is about as *naturel* as a dyed peacock), had been changed to dead white, which looked a little strange on her sunburnt face. Small drifts of powder remained at the sides of her nostrils, and under her ears, like snow which had refused to melt.

'You startled me,' I said.

'I am sorry.' Her voice seemed to come from a great distance.

'I'm just going a walk. But I'd love to come in for a moment.'

She achieved a smile and opened the gate. And then, very slowly and gracefully, she proceeded to walk up the path, backwards, in order to avoid seeing the Galloways' bungalow.

'Of course,' she murmured, 'it's all too terrible. I simply can't see it . . . I daren't.'

At this point she tripped slightly over the root of a clematis, and nearly fell, so that her smooth glide of grief was slightly interrupted.

'But you can't see the bungalow from here at all,' I said.

'It is *there*,' she replied vaguely, continuing her promenade.

'But you can't *see* it,' I repeated.

'*I* can see it,' she said.

How Undine could see the Galloway's bungalow through

a thick hedge of may and privet, to say nothing of a ten-foot mound of earth, heavily planted with Portuguese laurel, I did not inquire. I gathered that I was intended to understand that she could see it with the eyes of the spirit.

This strange progress continued all round the house, till we found ourselves in the kitchen garden, Undine walking backwards all the way. As soon as her feet touched the gravel path opposite the raspberry bed she turned round, sighed heavily, and said . . . 'There! Safe!'

I commiserated with her. What was she going to do? What *could* she do? she wailed. She could not leave Allways. It was an impossible situation, didn't I think? And certainly, I did, if her hatred of the Galloways was going to force her to walk backwards all her life. It would be an admirable training for anybody who wanted to obtain a post as lady-in-waiting to the Queen of Roumania, but as she had no such ambitions, it was just a bore.

§ I V

Meanwhile I wondered why Undine had taken me into the kitchen garden. And why she was delivering such a fierce tirade against kitchen gardens in general. There must be *some* significance in this, I felt. One does not rush people out into kitchen gardens merely to deliver lamentations against the vegetable kingdom.

'I really think,' said Undine, 'that I shall give the kitchen garden *up*.'

'But what will you do about vegetables?'

'I shall buy them. In the ordinary way.' (Which made me think, how would one buy vegetables in an extra-ordinary way? Would one put on a bathing suit and go down to the market and pick up beans with one's toes?)

'That's what I shall do,' continued Undine. 'I've gone into it very carefully, and I've come to the conclusion that for practical purposes a vegetable garden is a *little* over-rated.'

I had long come to the same conclusion myself, but had not dared to say so in public.

'I've reckoned it all out,' she sighed, 'and I find that with labour, and fertilizers, and everything, each lettuce costs me exactly five shillings. It really is a little *much*, isn't it? I mean, I simply *can't* eat them, not at that price. They'd choke me. Don't you think?'

I did. It was frightful to think of Undine being choked by a lettuce, however expensive.

'And these gooseberries,' she said, 'I *cannot* eat goose-berries. There are enough gooseberries to feed an army, but personally I hate them. To me there's something very *definitely* hateful about them. That frightful *hair* that they grow . . . and those *uncompromising* pips . . . it's sheer agony.'

'Won't you miss the asparagus bed?'

'I suppose I may. But don't you think it's rather a bore if one has a whole bed entirely to oneself, for a whole *month*?'

My unpolished mind detected a sinister significance in Undine's innocent remark. And apparently, she detected it too, for she suddenly blushed violently, and burbled on at great speed:

'I mean, one *can* get bored, even with asparagus, don't you think? And beans? It's having everything at *once*. And then when one really wants anything, it's never there. And the gardener *insists* on growing *acres* of potatoes, and I never *touch* a potato, they're rank poison to me.'

While Undine was talking, I thought how right she was!

I love a kitchen garden. I love going out and seeing cabbages, wild and untamed, and naked brussels sprouts, furiously sprouting. Nothing is more agreeable than picking a pod of peas that has been warmed by the sun, splitting it open, and running one's finger down the glistening row, gathering the peas into one's palm, and crunching them up. Broad beans too, are quite delightful. The beans, when you open the pod, look so startled and innocent, that it seems almost a sin to devour them. I love taking off the lids of rhubarb pots and seeing the pale shoots groping upwards in the dark. And pulling young spring onions out of the earth, wiping the dirt off on one's sleeve, and having an orgy of onion-eating before dinner. And persuading the week-end guest to eat onions too, in self-defence. And carving my initials on a very small vegetable marrow, and seeing the letters swell out as the sweltering weeks go by, till an enormous B.N. proudly proclaims itself under the cool shade of the leaves.

I love tomatoes, hot from the sun, and the crisp feel of lettuces with the dew on them, and the little patch of herb garden, when mint and sage and camomile and taragon and thyme send their alluring fragrance far and wide, so that one is constantly being summoned, by their scents, from the flower garden, merely to kneel down, and sniff and sniff.

All the same, from a practical point of view, it is cheaper to buy. Infinitely cheaper, safer and less troublesome. For unless you have dozens of under-gardeners, scurrying about all over the place with determined expressions, your vegetable garden will destroy you, in the end.

'And so,' said Undine, interrupting these meditations, 'I really think I shall sell it. And of course, the *one* person I should like to sell it to would be *you*!'

§ v

How I persuaded Undine that I did not require her vegetable garden, either for vegetables or for meditation, and that even if she offered it to me as a gift, I should still refuse it, and that I was already a landowner on a scale which made me feel a little guilty (seven acres is far too much for any self-respecting person) — all this must be told at some other time.

The whole idea was grotesque. Undine had much more money than I had. If she didn't want vegetables, why not turn it into a lawn? Why persuade herself that she ought to sell, and then terrify herself with the idea that if she sold, somebody would build another nasty little bungalow on top of her?

But by now the ladies of Allways were beyond reason. In their dreams they saw bungalows springing up everywhere. And they all seemed to imagine that it was my duty to prevent it.

Even Miss Bott joined in.

We were leaning over the little gate at the end of my wood, one day, looking out on to the broad field beyond. There is something very exciting about looking at an open field, naked to the sunshine, and glittering with buttercups, from the quiet shade of a wood. The wood is like a window —it protects you, —it offers a little frame for your tiny human personality. And while your body is in the shelter of the wood your spirit can rove out over the great meadows, free as the wind, and as swift.

'You're mad,' she said, 'not to buy that field.'

I sighed. Oh dear . . . she was beginning it now.

'Why?' I asked wearily.

ANCIENT LIGHTS

'Supposing somebody built on it?'

I looked at her. Yes . . . she appeared to be quite sane. 'Nobody,' I said, with infinite patience, 'is going to build on that field except . . .'

'Except?'

'Well . . . the reincarnation of Walt Whitman, or the ghost of Thoreau, or some other charming lunatic, who doesn't mind about there being no water, no road, no shelter, and no anything. And if anybody like that wanted to build, I should be only too happy.'

She tried another tack. 'It would be a marvellous investment.'

'But it's forty acres,' I said. 'And do you know how much I had to pay for a single acre, last year, to round off the wood?'

'Fifteen?'

'On the contrary, seventy.'

'Then you were robbed.'

'Perhaps I was,' I said, in grating tones. 'But then I always *am* robbed, and always shall be. I'm not proud of the fact. It just happens. It's a law of nature. I am made to be robbed, just as certain spiders are made to be destroyed when they make love.' I was quite hot by the time I got to the bit about the spiders.

'Forty times seventy is only . . .'

'Two thousand eight hundred pounds. Thank you very much.'

'It would be a marvellous investment,' she repeated. 'Now that flying's coming in. Think what a landing-ground it would make.'

I thought, regarding Miss Bott with what is called *haughteur* while I did so.

I thought of that quiet field, which was so spangled with

75

cowslips in spring that it looked like a sequin cloth, and so buttoned with mushrooms in September that it looked like a coster's jacket . . . that field which was tunnelled with mysterious rabbity caverns, down which my dog had thrust his nose a thousand times . . . that field over which I had wandered so often, with the grasses brushing my ankles, while the slow and languid brush of twilight lazily traced a purple rim on the distant hills.

I thought of that field. If you stood in the middle of it, towards November, when the evenings were drawing in, there would pass, constantly, over your head, a swift and lofty flight of starlings, from elm to scattered elm. That is one of the loveliest sounds that echoes over the winter world, the high flight of starlings, in their urgent troops, at dusk. And see, over there, that great elm looks as though there were leaves upon it. A puff of wind and the tree is bare, the leaves are gone, for they are not leaves, but wings, and they are above you now, clouding the dusky sky. And as they pass, hundreds of them, you hear a long-drawn fluttering sigh . . . like the swish of a silken garment in a high corridor of heaven. It has gone. You look up. The corridor is empty, its gathering shadows lit only by a white and lonely star. But over there, in the next elm, the branches have suddenly blossomed once again into a thousand leaves . . . the leaves that are wings . . . warm wings, that trembled there for a moment on the naked boughs, before the wind blows them once more to destinies unknown.

I thought of that field.

'Forty acres,' I thought. 'Enough for a nice little, smart, dinky snorting puss-moth with revolting smells coming out of its perky tail to lay a smear of grease all over the bank where the white violets grow. Lovely. And young men

76

with snub noses and bright Empire-building eyes will tramp over the fence where the clematis is trained and will demand a spot of water. Why do young men like that always want spots of things? Spots of whisky? Spots of sleep? Spots, spots, spots.'

I turned to Miss Bott.

'You are making me see spots before my eyes,' I said, with restrained passion.

And she nodded. I think she must have been thinking of the field too. 'I know,' she said, gruffly. 'It *would* rather put a damper on our mushrooming, wouldn't it?'

§ VI

However, nothing could stop Miss Bott, in her determination that Allways should be rendered safe from the intruder. If I wouldn't buy that field somebody equally 'desirable' must be obtained. And if *they* wouldn't buy the field, they would be made to buy something else. Allways was full of her machinations, and we expected to hear, at any moment, that she had arranged that the National Society for Preserving Ancient Monuments should buy the entire village.

'If she does,' said Mrs. M. acidly, 'I suppose we shall have to ring up the Prime Minister before we can put in a new pantry sink.'

However, Miss Bott was not aiming at anything so nebulous as a National Society. She was aiming at a very real person . . . a distant cousin, by name Victor Shelley. And she eventually hooked him.

She came round to see me one morning to tell me all about it. It was a glorious morning, when the whole earth seems to smell like a chrysanthemum, and the rose-

77

buds are very sturdy and glossy, and will open up into miracles of beauty in water, even though the outer petals are a little puckered by the frost.

'You remember Victor?'

'Of course.'

I had seen him several times in London. He was a very thin, ascetic man of about fifty — dainty in his ways, but not exactly effeminate — a man with silvery hair, who loved cats, collected miniatures, treated his few books with reverence, always lived on the right side of his income, and took three days to pack for a week-end in Paris.

'Well, he's coming up here for the week-end. And I've decided to get him to buy the Manse.'

'You've . . . *what?*'

'To buy the Manse,' she repeated airily.

'But it's the most hideous house ever built.'

'Victor can alter all that. He's got exquisite taste.'

'And it's enormous.'

'Well — he can shut some of it off.'

'But does he want to live in the country?'

'Not very much. But he will.'

Miss Bott's optimism baffled me. Only an insane millionaire, who wished to be constantly reminded of the asylum from which he had just escaped, would think of purchasing the Manse. It was a long low building that glared at you like an angry and dangerous animal. Its cavernous door gaped wide as though it were snarling. The date of the main building was about 1845, and as if that were not bad enough, dreadful wings and turrets had sprouted out, in the 'sixties and the 'eighties, making it look more like a dragon *couchant* than ever.

Moreover, it was in an impossible situation. It lay next to an unsavoury farm, which always passed rapidly from owner to owner, at a decreasing price. This farm at the moment was inhabited by three brothers who looked as if they had stepped straight out of the pages of *Wuthering Heights* — so thundery were their faces, so immense their capacity for liquor, and so staggering were their oaths.

And these were to be Mr. Shelley's neighbours — Mr. Shelley who was so set in his ways that he pined for a whole week when the elevator man, at his block of service flats, changed his uniform from blue to brown!

It was with misgiving that I accepted Miss Bott's invitation to lunch, to help persuade her cousin to become one of us. I am not a good liar, and even if I had been, Ananias himself could not have lied away the Manse.

But Miss Bott was more than a match for Ananias.

§ VII

'Oh — we are driving?' said Mr. Shelley, when he saw the car. 'I thought it was in the village?'

'No — about a mile out.'

'Isn't that a little . . . thank you, the rug *would* be more comfortable like that . . . isn't that a little . . . if we *might* have the window, just a fraction? So kind . . . a little remote?

'Just what you want, after London,' said Miss Bott cheerfully.

Mr. Shelley seemed about to reply, but closed his thin lips, and sighed through his nose.

As we drove on, I marvelled at the miracle which Miss Bott had wrought in inducing him to consider this fantastic project at all, for he was perfectly happy where he was, in London. However, perhaps he was a little touched — I think he was — by the thought that any of his relations should so eagerly desire his presence. For he was a lonely man.

Just as we were turning the last corner before you arrive at the gates of the Manse, a strange person staggered out of the hedge, carrying a very bloody rabbit in his hand. He was so drunk that I had to jam on the brakes, so that we skidded round the corner. As we passed him I had a vision of blood-shot eyes, and a hairy fist uplifted against us, while the air was thick with curses.

It was one of the brothers of the farm, Mr. Shelley's future neighbours.

'What a *frightful* looking creature!' said Mr. Shelley, in a trembling voice, as we got out. 'Did you see?'

Nobody answered. It was an embarrassing moment.

'But didn't you see?' quavered Mr. Shelley. 'The most monstrous man. Covered in blood!'

'Local colour!' observed Miss Bott, brightly. And marched us in, through the creaking gate, whistling hymns.

§ V I I I

In some ways I was glad that we had met the drunken gentleman, because Mr. Shelley was so shattered that he did not fully appreciate the uncanny hideousness of the Manse as it first burst upon our view. True, he took one look at it, and shuddered, but then he glanced over his shoulder again, to make sure that he was not being followed.

It was not till we had passed through the front door, that he had begun to take notice. He took one glance at that door, and one glance was quite enough, for it was decorated by an arch of sea-shells in concrete.

Mr. Shelley stared round him into the shadows. That

was all the impression you got of the house at first —
shadows. Only when your eyes had become accustomed to
the gloom did you see the monstrous things that lurked in
them.

'Well, plenty of room, what?'

Mr. Shelley gave a sickly smile.

'It's a little larger than I thought,' he said, weakly.

'Good! More value for money, what?'

Mr. Shelley looked at me with despair in his eye, as
though to ask what arguments he could possibly employ
against such logic. He said:

'I was thinking of servants.'

So was I. And a lot of other things besides. But it was
not my place to say so. Therefore, I averted my eye, and
stared with assumed interest at a stained glass window,
about 1890, which showed a young man rising from the
grave, with an angel hovering over him with a forbidding
expression, as though it were saying: 'If you come out of
there, young man, I'll give you what for!'

'*What* about servants?' said Miss Bott, beginning to
climb the staircase.

'I only have *one* maid. Maud, you know. She's been with
me thirty years.'

'Well — what of it?' Miss Bott paused, half-way up the
gaunt staircase.

Mr. Shelley blinked and peered around him. On all
sides one had vistas of rooms, rooms which could easily
have been used as hospital wards to accommodate thirty
beds.

'Isn't it . . . just a *little* much — for one maid?'

'Much? Rubbish!' Miss Bott waved away the suggestion.

'Her feet . . . are not what they were.'

'Well, I don't know what Maud's feet were, so I can't

say whether that's a tragedy or not. But she'll be doing step-dancing before she's been here long. Exercise, that's all she wants, exercise. Come on.'

Mr. Shelley still paused. 'But my furniture,' he quavered. 'I really didn't want to buy very much.'

Miss Bott drummed on the banisters. 'Why should you? You've got tons.'

Mr. Shelley gaped at Miss Bott, wondering, presumably, how any woman could tell so frantic a lie. And as I saw his thin ascetic face, with the kindly lips, parted and puzzled, I felt pity for him, but I also felt a very urgent desire to burst into hoots of ribald laughter. For I had seen Mr. Shelley's tiny flat. A pocket drawing-room, a pocket dining-room, two bedrooms, a maid's room, and a minute hall. And even this modest apartment was furnished with an old-maidenish sparcity — a single period piece against an almost blank wall — that was the general idea.

I tried to visualize what would happen when he came to arrange his little pieces here. He would have to put the spider-legged Queen Anne bureau in the archway between the vast double drawing-room, to give a faint illusion of furniture to that room. The little Marie Antoinette sofa could be placed in the middle of the other double drawing-room. If one sat on it one would look like a symbol of Man's Futility in a setting of *The Dynasts* designed by Gordon Craig. The little Empire clock, resting on a gilt swan, could go in the hall, with as much effect as a sparrow in the Albert Hall. As for the small Bokhara rugs — he had only rugs because the flat had parquet flooring — they could be stuck about the place like postage stamps, over the worst holes in the floor.

'Furniture!' Miss Bott repeated scornfully. 'Your things'll look all the better for having a little space round 'em. Now come on, and don't make difficulties.' She put her foot on the next step, and then suddenly shouted:

'Hell!'

There was a sound of cracking wood and falling plaster. I ran forward, fearing that the whole staircase was about to collapse. But a cheerful laugh reassured me. 'Only my clumsy old feet,' she observed brightly. 'But you'd better tread carefully there. One or two steps are loose.'

'D'you think it's safe?' pleaded Mr. Shelley.

Miss Bott was already nearly at the top of the stairs. 'Come on!' she cried out. 'I'm the heaviest of you all, and I've got up, so why can't you?'

A pale and acutely depressed Mr. Shelley tiptoed up the stairs, hugging the wall. I brought up the rear.

We went into the first room on the right. It was as large as a concert hall, and it smelt like a fungus.

'Isn't it a little musty?' asked Mr. Shelley.

'Musty?' echoed Miss Bott. 'Musty? Of course it's musty. You'd be musty if you hadn't had any fresh air inside you for donkey's years. Come on . . . let's open a window.'

This simple suggestion was not, however, easy to carry out. The window was warped with damp and only after a violent struggle, which Miss Bott tried to disguise by singing out 'Heave ho! Heave ho!' in a breathless voice, did we succeed in opening it a few inches.

However, those few inches were enough to let in a sharp and acrid perfume. I sniffed. Sniffed again. I glanced at Mr. Shelley. He too was sniffing.

'Pretty, isn't it?' said Miss Bott heartily, gazing on to a mouldering slate roof, under which a few starved laurestinus were sheltering. 'You could sleep here.'

'Could I?' breathed Mr. Shelley.

'Of course, it could make a very nice spare room.'

Mr. Shelley sniffed again.

'Got a cold?' boomed Miss Bott.

'No . . . oh no . . . it was merely . . .' he sniffed, . . .' is that *pigs?*'

'Is what pigs?' Miss Bott's voice was very sharp.

Mr. Shelley turned to me. 'Can't *you* smell something?'

I could. I could smell the most aggressively perfumed pigs that I had ever smelt. It was a smell that hit you between the eyebrows. But how could I say so? Fortunately Miss Bott snapped:

'Nonsense! I can't smell anything at all.' (I noticed however that she was surreptitiously shutting the window, by sitting on it. It went down with a bang which made us all jump.) 'I can smell nothing, and I haven't got a cold. You must have a cold or you wouldn't be sniffing so much.'

Mr. Shelley had no reply to this assertion. And when Miss Bott snorted, 'It's all imagination', and led us through the door, he assented that perhaps it was. For the odour of pigs, though still intense, was so mixed up with the odour of damp and decay, that it was a little difficult to tell which was which.

And so the tour continued. On and on we went, through room after room, each more depressing than the last. Miss Bott's spirits never flagged. I marvelled at her genius for salesmanship. As each horror presented itself, she deftly turned it into a thing of beauty — or, at least, a thing of convenience.

She was such a wonderful saleswoman that I believe she would have sold the Albert Memorial to a collector of Louis Seize miniatures.

But she did not sell the Manse to Mr. Shelley. There was something unexpectedly determined in the spirit which lurked beneath his frail body.

As we came out, wearily, and paused in the front door, breathing the odour of pigs, he summed up the whole situation by glancing at the horrific pile behind him, smiling timidly, and saying to Miss Bott:

'For *me*, I think it would be a little . . .' he paused.

'Well?'

'A little *much*.'

Miss Bott shrugged her shoulders. She was a sensible woman, and she knew when she was beaten.

'Perhaps you're right,' she said, cheerfully.

§ I x

The tour of the Manse very definitely unsettled me.

Up till then, I had regarded the Great Land Panic as a joke. But now, I began to be affected by the prevailing unrest.

I began to prowl round my few little acres, glaring over hedges to see who might come to molest me.

I took to tiptoeing round the house, staring through every window, to spy out the land, to search for distant fields where buildings might arise, and gaps in the trees through which I might one day catch sight of unwelcome roofs.

But, I must admit, that as soon as I entered the room and went to the window, I forgot why I had come up. The whole process of opening a window in a country cottage, is so exciting, especially if it is a lattice window and has a little perforated bar to fasten it, a bar which you have to move gently for fear of tearing one of the tender shoots of the vine.

You lift the latch, and push the window out. The cool air blows in, and there floats with it the eternal sigh of restless, blowing branches — a sigh of happiness, that is ever about you, in the country, though you do not notice it, till you open a window. You lean your elbows on the sill, pushing aside the curtains, and you notice that the pattern on the curtain is very faded at the edges. The painted roses are pale and wan, where the sun has caught them, and the green leaves drift like ghosts across the fabric. But on the other side, where they are in shadow, against the big black beam, the roses are still a gay crimson, and the leaves are as bright as on the day you bought them. You ought to change the curtains you suppose, and buy new ones. But you won't. You like them as they are, and you do not grudge the hues that the sun has stolen back to himself, for the sun has given you plenty of colour, in your time.

You look out again. What are you here for? Oh yes . . . to see whether anybody can spoil the view. For a moment or two you try to be methodical, to make a note of that field over there, where the cattle are grazing, to map out, in your mind, the gaps in the coppice, and to remember the parts of the road they overlook, so that you can take some sort of action about it. But even as you form these fine, business-like ideals you begin to smile. Because you can't help noticing that the chestnuts, over the way, are just spreading their fans, and that reminds you of the time when you were walking in the wood this morning and discovered a chestnut breaking bud, and were unable to resist the temptation to take one of the sticky, silky things between your fingers and open it out, spreading its fan for it. And then you were seized with remorse, in case the night should be cold or the wind unduly harsh, and you tried to stick the baby leaves together again.

Land — acreage — frontage — desirable sites — options.

You frown. You *must* try to decide something about all this. But even as you make this firm resolution, old Miss Grant passes in the road below, on her bicycle. She has one of those bicycles which go so slowly that any normal pedestrian has to slow down in order not to pass her too quickly. And she always seems to be bicycling against the wind. Her big black hat, of immense age, unmistakably Queen Anne, is blown up behind her head until it stands like a sort of arrogant crest. Her very thin and faintly disgusting dog slinks behind her.

What a long time she takes to pass! Pedal, pedal, pedal, pedal . . . against the wind, her hat standing more and more erect, and her dog assuming Russian Ballet attitudes every few yards. At last she is gone. She has gone to her field for which she pays three pounds a year, for grazing her cows. And that brings you back to finance. For three pounds a year represents a capital of a hundred pounds. And they could probably get at least two hundred for Miss Grant's field. And if they invested that two hundred in some new pill which made women thinner, or fatter, or kept them the same, or did something radical to their insides, they would probably make a fortune.

You shake your head. It is all most perplexing. Why can't people leave things as they are? Why can't they let beauty sleep?

Why?

You look out of the window. The light is fading. The drama of the day is almost done. Slowly, slowly the dusky curtain falls. The giant elms are lit with a last gleam, a theatrical flare from the dying sun, and then, they are but shadows in the wings. Only faintly now can the stage be seen, in lingering fragments — a few panes still glimmer in the church windows, there is a ripple of gold on the quiet pond, and the lawn beneath you still glows with a radiant green. But it is a green of the night rather than a green of the day, silvered over by a rising moon, whose pale face, high-lifted, casts a polite scorn on the last efforts of the honest sun. The curtain falls, falls — it has almost reached the earth now — the church windows are dimmed, the great stage manager has given his signal. As though it were an anthem, the birds sing their final song, and cease. And the world is in dust sheets, till the morning, with only the white owl as caretaker, hooting mournfully round empty corridors, and the scornful moon, like an artificial lamp, illuminating the deserted arena.

That is what happens when one goes up to a room at twilight in order to be severely practical about protecting one's estate.

§ x

I think that the other inhabitants of Allways must have been opening their windows, too, and forgetting their troubles.

For gradually, quiet descended once more upon Allways. Nobody bought any more land. Nobody built any more bungalows. And as far as one can see, there is no reason why anybody ever should.

Even the Galloway bungalow has lost something of its original repulsiveness. The ivy, and the Gloire de Dijon roses, and the wistaria and honeysuckle, have seen to that.

At any rate, Undine no longer finds it necessary to walk backwards into her cottage. Unless, of course, somebody happens to be watching.

CHAPTER VII

A SYMPHONY OF SILENCE

You will, by now, have realized that this is going to be a very quiet book. So quiet, that, I fear, a lot of people will go raving mad if they attempt to continue to read it.

'Oh dear — how can you *stand* it — this silence?'

Quite charming people have asked me that, often enough, after a few hours at the cottage.

'But it *isn't* silent,' I tell them.

'Well — I can hear that awful cuckoo, doing its stuff over and over again. And a little boy passed in the lane, about an hour ago, whistling. But that's all.'

When people like that arrive, the only thing to do is to put them in the garden, as far away as possible, with a gramophone and a packet of loud needles, and let them drug themselves with the sounds of 'civilization'.

'Civilization' is the death of the finer senses of man. If a cigarette is always between your lips, you can't ever smell the sweetness of the bean fields, on a summer evening. If you begin to drink cocktails at twelve, you forget, for ever, the keen, silvery taste of cold water in a clear goblet. Which sounds like one of the most embarrassing moralizations of *Eric or Little by Little*, but it happens to be true.

It is particularly true in the matter of sound. For the people who go crazy because there isn't a gramophone playing, or a telephone ringing, or a bus roaring by — these people are, quite literally, deaf. Otherwise they could not possibly talk such nonsense about Allways being 'silent'.

A cuckoo . . . a whistling boy . . . that was all they

heard! While even as they were speaking, I heard the following sounds:

1. A high wind in the elms. They were a long way from us, it is true, but all the morning there had been a song in their branches — a song of the sea. As the wind surged through them there was a sound akin to the sweep of surf over shingle — the wide, thundering advance, the sighing mournful retreat, as the truant surf is drawn back by the long arms of the sea.

2. A clock ticking. It was not a loud clock, but it had a cheerful, busy tick, that made you think the passage of Time was a grand joke, and that every minute you were dancing on to better things.

3. Birds innumerable. Starlings under the eaves, thrushes in the may, sparrows on the path — and not only the song of birds, but the many other sounds that birds make — the scurries in the bushes, the flutter of wings from branch to branch — even the *tread* of birds — for many birds make distinct sounds as they hop down a brick path.

4. The bleat of lambs, carried down from the hill by the vagrant wind.

5. But why bother about 5? Or 500? Either you know what I mean, or you don't. And if you are one of the few who do, I think it will be fun if we listen to the sounds of Allways together, and leave the rest of the people to play their gramophones.

§ 11

I called this chapter a symphony of silence, for that is what it really is. The symphony is always the same, and always different. For our conductor is the Weather, and he has as many moods as there are hours. Sometimes he stresses the wood wind, till you would say that there was no sound about you but the high clamour of the elms — sometimes he can bear nothing but strings, and when you go to bed at night you can remember only the way the wind hissed through the rushes on the bank of the stream.

Sometimes, when the sky is a brazen gong, vast and still, he taps very gently on it, so that there is a roll of distant thunder. You start, and wonder if he is working up to a wild finale, an *allegro tempestuoso*. But no — not yet! He puts his fingers to his lips, waves his hand, and the long grass in the meadow sways in time, at the hint of a freshening breeze. Tap, tap . . . tap, tap, tap, tap . . . What is that staccato sound? Only a big thrush, knocking a snail on the stones outside your window. It has been dry for so long, the earth is parched, the insects are in hiding — happy thrush to have discovered so rare a morsel at this season!

But the conductor has signalled to the drummer once more, and he taps again, a little louder this time, for the thunder is coming closer. And with the sound of the drums comes another sound which is exactly like pizzicato strings, the sound of the first drops of rain falling on the glass of the greenhouse. You hurry indoors, for you must not be late for the Symphony, the weather would punish you severely for that. Even as you run you note that the orchestration is getting fuller and fuller, the wind higher and higher, till it has the echo of shrill clarinets, and deep in the wood, over yonder, there is a sound of stormy 'cello music, as the boughs of the big ash trees grate together.

You are just in time. Breathless you take your seat by the window, and listen.

And now, the drums have it! Roll upon roll, till you

91

would say the straining surface of the skies would split —
louder, louder! This is intolerable, you mutter. No
composer can possibly keep it up, even with so amazing
a subtlety of rhythm. Suddenly, the conductor makes a
lightning gesture, from bronze roof to green floor. There
is a second's pause, and then the whole vast orchestra of
Nature bursts out in a throbbing melody of rain and wind,
of blowing branch and straining leaf. The thunderstorm
has begun.

§ III

I cannot think why I began with a thunderstorm, because
anything less typical of Allways cannot be imagined. I
intended to begin with a sound which must be common to
all dwellers in old cottages, though I like to think that it
is peculiar to Allways. The sound of beams cracking at
night.

It is a queer, brittle noise, as though somebody were
tapping on the door. I suppose the beams crack by day,
too, but you do not hear them then, because the birds are
singing, or the fire is burning, or some other sound is
distracting your attention. But in the stillness of the
night, as you lie in bed, with a candle by your side, as you
play games with the shadows cast by your hands on the
ceiling . . . fluttering those long, grey, ghostly fingers,
bringing to birth phantom ducks and grotesque rabbits —
as you lie there, then the beams begin their strange jerky
conversation. You start. Your hands drop on to the sheets.
Crack again! The house, you see, is sinking, sinking, little
by little, through the centuries. These are its tiny sighs of
protest, the proof that its limbs, though strong, are growing
weary.

'Well, it will last my time,' you say to yourself. And as you fall asleep, the beams crack again, as though in reproach. 'It was not very kind of you to say that.' No, you agree, it was not very kind.

Although this slow sinking of all our houses is picturesque although it gives an amusing twist to a gable, and cocks a window to one side, as though it were winking at you, it has its disadvantages. For example, every year we all begin to find that our doors are sticking, because the ceiling is pressing upon them. And we have to send for Mr. Beard, the village carpenter, to shave off a fraction of the lower part of the door for us. While he is performing this office, we hover round him, and the following dialogue takes place:

Tenant: I suppose it's the damp?

Mr. Beard: No sir, it's not the damp, it's the subsidence. (He pronounces this with an air of authority. The tenant heaves a sigh of relief. Mr. Beard has said it's the subsidence, once more. One knew it already, but it's good to hear it again.)

Tenant: Do you think it's . . . subsiding . . . more quickly than it ought to?

Mr. Beard: No sir.

Tenant: That cupboard in the spare room, though. You really can't stand in it any more. The floor's so sloping . . . you just slide down.

Mr. Beard: You always did, sir.

Tenant: How much do you think it sinks every year?

Mr. Beard: Well sir, I reckon the left wing of this house has sunk two feet since it was built. That's pretty well 400 years. That's one foot in 200 years. That's one inch in roughly seventeen years. So that makes about a seventeenth of an inch every year. Which is quite enough, sir, to account for the way this door is sticking.

But the main disadvantage of our cracking beams is experienced by those who have new and timorous maids from London. These poor creatures are scared stiff.

'But mum, I swear, there was somebody tappin' on the stairs.'

'Nonsense, it's only the beams.'

'I'm sorry mum.' A pause. 'But even if it were the beams, supposin' they cracked in 'alf, and come down on my 'ead?'

'There's no possible chance of that.'

'A big piece of plaster fell in the 'all only yesterday.'

And so on. I dare not think how often that dialogue has echoed, at Allways, between mistress and maid. Nor how often the village Ford has borne a tremulous maiden back to the railway station, back to the sounds of 'Civilization', where there are no barbaric beams to mar her rest, only the sounds of creaking radiators, of angry lifts, of passionate trams, and other comforts.

§ IV

Some of these sounds I have mentioned are shared by the whole village. Others are my own — heard only by me — and these I guard most jealously.

I would not willingly share, with anybody, the strange excitement which I gain from the dripping of water into the well. But you, who are reading this, aren't 'anybody', because, for the moment, we are living together. So I will share it with you. This is what happens.

You walk out on to the little brick pavement in front of the kitchen. You look round, like a conspirator. There is no one about. In the distance, through an open window, you hear snatches of the 119th Psalm, punctuated by dull thuds, proving that your bed is being made, the pillows beaten. (Why do so many servants always sing the 119th Psalm when they are making beds?)

Nobody about! You get down on your knees. You seize the cool iron ring of the well-cover. You heave, and heave again . . . the moss has grown thickly round it. Now, once more . . . it pulls open. You lay it back, you fall on your stomach, a cold air blows up, and you stare into the depths of the wall.

You wait.

Drip!

The dark mirror of the water is troubled — its dreams shattered. A moment ago, life was reflected placidly on its surface, such life as the well may see — the vagrant bough of the cherry tree, a darting bird, a smiling sky. But the ceaseless march of the little underground river disturbed all that. True, it has shrunk to a mere drip — it is only a ghost of its wintry, turbulent self, but it still has a spirit of its own.

Drip . . . drip . . . drip!

No instrument ever made by man has a sweetness akin to this. It is a high, fluting sound — never quite on the same note. If you wrote it musically it would be something like this. . . .

Drip! C

Drip! C♯

Drip! E

And then, after a pause, a very heavy, pompous. . . .

Drip. A♭

And all the time the mirror of the well is being shattered, its dark depths disturbed, its pattern marred. But it does not care, for in this shattering of the mirror many strange and lovely patterns are formed, as though a kaleidoscope

95

were shifting before us. The reflected branch of laburnum blossom which, a moment ago, made a single gesture, a delicate, arrogant sweep of gold, is suddenly shattered into a thousand stars, which spin to the edge of the well for a moment, quiver, and then hurry back again till they are hung once more on the mirrored stem. The cloud that hovered, as though frozen, is suddenly puffed to atoms by the water-drop — it looks as though a shell were bursting — and for a time the ripples seem to be painted with puffs of white, in violent agitation, till the storm passes, and the mirror is clear again, and the cloud, once more, has gained its repose.

'What's all this?' mutters the avenging imp, who is always peering over the shoulders of conscientious writers. 'Hundreds of words about a drip of water into a well?'

'Hundreds of words,' I reply, 'have been written about subjects that have left no deeper trace on the world.'

'Yes, but by fools.'

'Did I ever claim to be anything else, in the face of Beauty?'

And for once in a way, the avenging imp has no adequate retort.

§ v

Have you ever heard a mole? It is one of the sounds of Allways that you must certainly hear, during your stay.

It was the mole-catcher who first made me hear it. The mole-catcher looks as if he had stepped straight out of some novel by D. H. Lawrence, some novel which had been very heavily banned, barred and bolted, in case the British public might suddenly develop a morbid passion for mole-catchers. For he is very virile, and has a look in his eyes

The Church

which makes young maidens catch their breath when they meet him at the corner of a lane, when the may is in blossom. And he wears corduroy trousers and has an enormous Adam's apple and a voice like old sherry and is twenty-one and unmarried. All of which interests me less than the fact that he catches moles exceedingly well.

'How much shall I pay you?' I asked him, one evening in December, when he looked so D. H. Lawrence that he really ought to have been taken at once to the Café Royal.

'Eh?'

'How much?' I repeated, adding, diffidently . . . 'per mole?'

As soon as I had said 'per mole' I felt strangely uneasy. It sounded as though one were a beauty specialist, holding a nickel-plated mole-catcher in one hand, confronting a spotty-faced dowager, and coming to terms. 'The fee is twenty guineas per mole, moddom, although the mole in the chin is *reely* a thirty guinea proposition — that is to say — should you wish it to be permanently eradicated.'

I wished my moles to be permanently eradicated. They were doing unholy things to the roots of my new silver birches, which were far more important to me than anybody's chin. So I muttered 'per mole' again, feeling peculiarly idiotic.

'Tuppence.'

'Right.'

'I'll bring 'em to you every morning.'

'Oh!' I blinked, and looked at the mole-catcher. If D. H. Lawrence had observed him at that moment he would have burst into a Lawrence prose poem about the dark earth and the loins of the moles panting through the dark earth and the dark earth being very cool and soothing and bee-autiful to the loins of the moles. And all that sort of thing. And I thought that breakfast would really be rather an ordeal if one had to go out every morning, in a dressing-gown, and inspect battalions of mole-corpses, just before eating eggs and bacon. So I said:

'I don't think you need bring them to me. Just tell me how many you have caught. At twopence. . .' I gulped 'per mole.'

'You'll trust me?'

Trust him? Lord . . . what a question. I hate trusting people. It's a coward's game. I like people I can't trust. People with knives up their sleeves . . . people with a life of which I know nothing . . . people who have dark alleys in their souls, down which they skulk when they think I'm not looking. That's the fun of friendship, the double personality of those we love.

The avenging imp is at it again.

'You were talking, I believe, of a mole-catcher?'

'So I was.'

'Or rather of a mole?'

'Good Lord . . . I'd forgotten.'

'And the noise that a mole makes?'

'Of course.'

'Perhaps, if it is not troubling you too much, you would make a noise like a mole?'

§ VI

A noise like a mole.

I must write very softly. I must smooth out the paper. The ink must be very clear, and flowing freely. We must all put our fingers to our lip, hold our breath.

'Crunch . . . crunch . . . crunch. . . .'

No. That is not it. That is not the sound that the mole

makes, at dusk, when the blackbirds have gone to bed, and
the air is dizzy with the scents of the earth. It is subtler
than that. For the mole's snout is very tiny and delicate.
It is sensitive to a degree. It is, in fact, incapable of making
a sound so vulgar that it could be described by any man's
pen.

For it is not a 'crunch', nor a 'munch' nor even a 'swish'.
It is the sort of sound that a goblin gravedigger would
make. Not that the mole is digging a grave . . . far from it
. . . he is digging what is, to him, 'a desirable residence'.
And so we may as well leave him at peace.

There are many of these tiny sounds, made by animals
and insects, which play important parts in the Symphony of
Silence at Allways. Some of them are so commonplace
that I blush to mention them. There is the sound of the
moth as it taps impatiently against the lampshade at night,
and the quite different sound of the daddy-long-legs doing
the same thing, but doing it far more clumsily, and making
much more fuss about it. I have a sneaking fondness for
daddy-long-legs. They look as if they had been designed
by Mr. Walt Disney and might at any moment do a gavotte
across the ceiling and sit down at the piano and bang the
keys with those absurdly comic limbs.

I have also a great affection for a bluebottle, especially
on a summer afternoon, when it is being more than usually
idiotic about getting out of the open window. I go over
and watch it, and become almost as distracted as it is
itself. 'You fool . . . you damned fool . . . there is the
open window . . . and the wide air and the flowers waiting
for you. You have been up and down that piece of glass
at least seven hundred times. Why don't you go outside?
Here. . . .' And I gave it a gentle prod. But this only
arouses the violent indignation, and the bluebottle booms

away at the glass with redoubled energy, until at last I catch him in a handkerchief and put him outside. And as I watch him fly away I think how like bluebottles we are ourselves, wearily beating against the glass, when the window is open all the time.

I am writing far from Allways, and the traffic roars by in the street outside, so fiercely that you would say that the street was full of wild animals, bellowing and screaming after their prey. But above the din I hear, clear and sweet, the tiny sounds of Allways, which are so far clearer to me because I hear them with my heart, and not only with my ears . . . the soft patter of petals on to the parched earth when a rose in summer passes, the hard knock of a chestnut in the road when the November winds are full, the hiss of apple logs when the fitful rain spits down the chimney. These sounds I hear, high above the clamour of the city. Maybe I walk with dreams. But the dream is clearer than the reality.

§ V I I

Dreams!

At Allways . . . even when the human voice is heard, it has a dreamlike quality . . . the phrases that drift to you when you meet the labourers in the lane seem, somehow, as though they came from a land of make-belief.

'Fine day!'

'Ay — but a drop of rain'd be welcome.'

The greeting has been given. You pass on. The heavy boots crunch away into the distance. Did you say those words, or hear them? You do not know. They have gone. They were part of the Symphony of Silence.

It is the same with the sounds of 'civilization'. There is

a lane outside my cottage, and venturesome vehicles, occasionally charge down it, on their way to villages even more remote than Allways. But as soon as they have turned off the Great North Road they are caught in the same magic, their wheels are captured in the same silken web. All right — tell me I am romancing, and laugh at me to your heart's content. You will not alter the facts. For I swear that even Miss Grant's bicycle bell, as she ploughs slowly along, with her disgusting dog behind her, has a silvery tinkle that is not quite of this world. I should never be surprised if I saw a Poltergeist, with a peaked cap, sitting on her handle bars, ringing away, just for fun. Which makes me think that Miss Grant must ring for fun, too, for there is never any obstacle in her path, except the wind. Perhaps she *is* ringing her bell at the wind? I hope she is. It is a nice idea, which the wind . . . (the only element who has a sense of humour) . . . would appreciate.

As this chapter has to stop, some time, I suppose I must draw a line. I have not told you a thousandth of the sounds of Allways. I have not told you of the 'plop' the goldfish make, when you step on to the path by the pond, and a hundred glistening bodies dive down into the depths. Nor of the church bells, that play C D E F *G* F E D C and so on, ad infinitum. The G always gets the biggest bang, and I always wonder, on Sundays, if it objects, or if it is pleased by this attention? Anyway, it is a very sweet note, and seems somehow truer and more vibrant than the others.

I climbed the church tower once, to see if the G bell was any different from the others. I stood among the bells, with the wind lashing the tower, and the great bells hanging still and silent before me.

'Which is the G bell?' I asked the sexton.

'Eh?'

'The G bell . . . the highest?'

'The highest?'

'Yes.'

'Eh? They be all the same height. And a pretty job it wor, gitting of 'em up.'

Which was another way of looking at it.

Oh — this music — this eternal music of the English country! It is too quiet to be echoed by any human hands, too subtle to be set between staves or disciplined to the rhythms of art, too delicately coloured to be mirrored in any orchestral score. Eternally it sighs, through field and lane, and every hour a new masterpiece is born — a master-piece in which each echo has its appointed place, and even the pauses — the hushes when the birds are still and the wind has dropped — seem deliberate, ordained and commanded by the baton of the Conductor of All Things.

CHAPTER VIII

INTRUSION

AND now the silence was rudely disturbed.

And now things at last begin to happen.

And I wish, very sincerely, that they didn't. Because if they hadn't . . . but enough of these negative conditionals.

It happened like this.

One day, towards the end of September, I was sitting in the garden, making plans for next year. These plans, as each year passes by, become more elaborate, and incidentally, more futile, because I always forget to look at them when the time comes.

The idea is to draw large squares in the garden note-book, and label each square to represent a flower-bed. Then one writes angry remarks in the squares.

At the moment in question I had written:

For the ninetieth time will you realize that you want masses and NOT clusters? The three clumps of red hot pokers are just silly. They look extremely mean and slightly indecent. YOU WANT AN ARMY OF RED HOT POKERS.

I then licked my pencil, turned to the end of the book, and put down 'order army of red hot pokers'. There was a certain doubt at to how one did this, but that was a detail.

I also wrote:

For the nine hundredth and ninetieth time when will you realize that you want a BLAZE of asters? They are astonishingly amiable flowers. They want less water than the camel and they are far more decorative. What

is this odd complex you have that asters are 'common'?
If you think asters are 'common', you are 'common'
yourself.

I shook my head in self-approval. I then wrote:

'It is no use whatever keeping this note-book if you
do not do what it tells you. Last June you put down,
in great letters

INSPIRATION FOR WOOD

Underneath you wrote . . . I have just had an inspiration for the wood. In the new field I shall plant at
least twenty silver poplars, as tall as I can get them, and
in front of them a row of copper beech. The dark
leaves will show up magnificently against the pale
background. And in front of the copper beech I shall
plant a mass of syringa. Well, you put in quantities of
bamboo sticks to show where all these things were to
go, and now you have torn out all the bamboo sticks
and decided to have a shrubbery of spindle instead.
This is bad. It is extremely immoral. You are losing
control. You MUST realize that the year consists of
TWELVE months and not just the month you are
living in.

N.B. To-morrow, remove bamboo sticks and put it
all back again.

It is a very good thing to keep a gardening note-book
like this. One may only carry out a twentieth part of its
commands, but even that twentieth part has its effect. If
it were not for my gardening note-book I should never have
planted those daffodils in the further meadow, in a bold,
brave line, like a golden sword slashing through the fields
of spring. I should never have beribboned the banks of
the brook with bluebells . . . and if you think that

'beribboned' is an affected verb you are wrong, for that is just how the bluebells look, when you stand away from them with the west wind blowing . . . flying streamers of colour, fluttering in the long grass.

If it had not been for my gardening note-book I should have forgotten the scarlet oaks, which blaze so fiercely in October that a man may warm his hands at them. And at the end of May, in the front-garden, when the wall-flowers have come up, and the baby snapdragons have gone in, there would have been no colour in the garden at all had my note-book not reminded me that down the centre walk I could have a mist of cat-mint, and against the hedges a carnival of giant poppies, pale pink, rose, and scarlet . . . those superbly intoxicated flowers that are like Southern girls . . . those abandoned things, with their petals loose, and their sultry lips for ever pouting.

The gentlemen of the press who parody me may now draw an elegant picture of me shrinking in horror from the thought of being alone in a room with a rampant poppy. The idea is, as they say, 'a gift'.

Seven books could be written about my gardening note-book. But I am not writing seven books, but one book . . . (why does that sound so Biblical?) And we have now arrived at a point where delay is no longer possible.

For just as I had drawn a line in my note-book, I looked up. And over the asters I saw the face of Mrs. M.

§ 11

'Personally', she said, after she had made several vain attempts to see what I was writing, 'I should say that it was a good thing.'

It was five minutes later. The usual acid remarks had

passed, the remarks which always pass, from one gardener to another. And then she had come to business. She had produced from her bag an important looking document which was headed 'Montevideo Tin Holdings Limited.'

'But what makes you think so?'

'Well — read the prospectus. The preference shares, it seems, will be covered ten times.'

'Covered with what?'

'Covered,' she snapped. 'Paid for.'

'Why? Are the owners feeling very charitable?'

She gave me a withering smile. 'They merely happen to be BUSINESS MEN.'

I have put Business Men in capitals, because that is how Mrs. M. made it sound.

'In that case I can't see why they allow the public to have any shares. Why don't they keep them all themselves?'

'Because they have to raise capital.'

'Oh!'

'Are you being *deliberately* obtuse?'

No, I told Mrs. M., I was not. But this just happened to be one of the many things in the world of finance which I did not understand. If these shares were such an astonishing investment why, oh why take so much trouble to pass them on to the public?

It reminded me of those gentlemen who spend their lives writing books on 'SUCCESS'. They will tell you how to be a millionaire, how to be the most powerful man or woman in the world, how to climb to the top of any tree, however prickly. Well, if they know so much, why don't they do it themselves? Surely *their* highest ambition can't be merely to go on writing books about Success?

It is the same with books about MAGNETISM. Often, I have seen advertisements in magazines headed. . . .

YOU CAN BE MAGNETIC TOO!

Underneath this cheering news is the portrait of a young
man who looks as if he were accusing you of, at the least,
arson, and he is pointing his finger at you, and little arrows
of magnetism are popping out of his finger. One learns, on
perusing the letterpress, that for a guinea *you* can look like
that and have arrows popping out of you too.

'It's a *gift*,' said Mrs. M. 'A positive gift.'

I looked at her dreamily. She went on talking. I did not
listen. I was too intent on my own thoughts. . . .

Charm! There was another thing you could buy in a
book. I remembered a quantity of advertisements of books
on Charm. One, in particular, showed a photograph of
the authoress, oozing charm to such an extent that she
looked a little breathless, as though she had laced her stays
very tight just before the photographer was going to
take her and was muttering to him (with distracting
charm), 'if you don't press that bulb soon I shall explode'.
Why, if these ladies know so much about charm, don't
they flaunt themselves in front of the nearest palace, so
that when the king . . . whoever he may be . . . drives
out he will stop his coach and take them in? Why don't
they go and purse their lips in the Casino at Monte Carlo,
so that countless millionaires in flannel suits, and young
men in dinner jackets, and honest concierges, will kneel
before them, and offer them their ALL, whether the 'all' is
to be interpreted in terms of money or of muscle?

It is difficult for a simple person, like myself, to understand. If I knew all that about charm I should do something really drastic about it. Quite often. And end up in
a nursing home, at the end of the season.

'I give you up,' said Mrs. M., at last. 'I try to put you

on to a good thing and all you do is stare at me as though I were a fraudulent solicitor.'

'I'm awfully sorry, Mrs. M. But as I told you before, I don't understand these things.'

§ III

And there, I thought, the matter was ended. True, during the next few weeks one heard various rumours about the Montevideo Tin Mines, whose directors seemed determined that Allways must share in their prosperity. A young man with an American accent had arrived in a very highly powered car at Miss Bott's cottage, and had endeavoured to sell her some shares. After an hour's ardent salesmanship she had responded by thanking him very much and showing him the latest letter from her bank-manager, which had considerably cooled his ardour. The Professor, also, was reputed to have had a call. But he had merely taken the prospectus, sniffed, dug up a geological map of Montevideo, studied it, turned to the young man and said that if his directors really wanted to find tin, they would be better employed in visiting the Allways dump on the other side of the hill, where they would find a number of empty cans whose contents now reposed inside him. And no, it was really no trouble at all to show him out.

Therefore, surely the matter was ended?

§ IV

A month later.

I was in the garden again. Writing more things in a note-book. Turning up my diary, I find I was writing:

It's all very well, but the schyzostylus, alias the Kaffir Lily, is a washout. All the garden writers tell you it is a blaze of colour in November, but it just isn't. It is a series of dreary stalks with one rather diffident blossom on top. I have spent nearly ten pounds on Kaffir Lilies and I consider it an insult.

This was a very muddled observation, but when I wrote it, I had not intended it for publication. Just as I had written the word 'insult', I looked up. And the pen dropped from my hand.

Miss Hazlitt was standing before me. She must have glided into the garden like a ghost. She looked pale and distraught and ill. In her hand she held out a newspaper.

I sprang to my feet.

'What is the matter?'

She stared at me. She shook her head. She looked bewildered, and very tired. She still held out the newspaper.

I made her sit down. Even now she did not speak. She only pointed to the paper. I looked at it and read:

CITY SWINDLE

MONTEVIDEO TIN COLLAPSE

THOUSANDS RUINED

I stared at her.

'You don't mean to say . . .'

She nodded.

'You?' I could not take it in. 'You?' And then. 'How much?'

'Everything.'

'Everything!' I shut my eyes for a minute. I tried to think. It was impossible.

I said . . . 'I think you'd better have a very strong cup of tea. Quickly.'

She had begun to cry, very softly . . . those searing tears which are trebly bitter because they come from brave eyes . . . like a man's tears. Not that she looked other than helplessly, tragically feminine at that moment. But she didn't want me to see that she was crying. She had turned her face, and was staring at the hedge, biting her lip.

'I'll go and get the tea.'

I went into the kitchen. My man was out, but the kettle boiled merrily on the stove. I got the tea-pot and two cups, and opened the cupboard for the tea. There floated up to me the sweet and soothing smell of household things . . . the smell of raisins, and coffee, and sugar and rice. There seemed an awful lot of every sort of food. There were nine bottles of capers, for example. Ought there to have been nine bottles of capers, I thought, distractedly. I wondered if mine was an extravagant household. Well, what if it is, I should say, in the ordinary course of things, but somehow it seemed wrong, to-day. To have so much when others had so little.

What would she do? Damn — I'd forgotten to warm the tea-pot first. I took it out to the sink. What would she do? She wouldn't accept charity. That was absolutely certain. Now I can take it back and put the tea in. No, she obviously wouldn't accept charity. Perhaps we might do something she wouldn't know about . . . through a lawyer. A little legacy, perhaps. But she'd probably suspect. Oh Lord . . . what a mess it all was.

I poured the boiling water on to the tea. It hissed. The fragrant steam poured out. I put on the lid. Here was the milk. Where was the sugar? Back to the cupboard. Why do cooks hide things so? Does it give them a grim pleasure to know that nobody else can possibly find anything? Then I remembered that Miss Hazlitt did not take sugar. Neither did I. So I carried the tea out to the garden.

She was better now. She looked at me and forced herself to smile.

'Oh, it is *good* of you to think of this!' And she took the tea as though it were some very precious nectar that I had obtained at great risk.

'Now tell me all about it.'

She told me. It was a plain little tale, pitifully plain. You have read a hundred such tales in the daily papers. He had been so kind . . . no, it was nothing to do with Mrs. M. . . . and had arranged everything so easily . . . yes, the bank had warned her, very strongly, but just when she had been thinking of listening to their warnings, the young man had turned up again.

'Why didn't you come to me?'

'I didn't want to worry you. You were so busy.'

'You make me feel awful, when you say that.'

'What had it to do with you?'

'I might have been able to help.'

'It is a judgment on me,' she said quietly.

·'Please.'

She shook her head. 'Yes. It is a judgment. I was avaricious. I was seeking the things of this world. I have been rightly punished.'

'How can you say such things?'

She covered her eyes with her hand. For a moment there was silence. Then she took her hand from her eyes. She spoke quietly.

'He said ten per cent. That would have meant four pounds a week. Twice what I have now. I could not believe that it was possible, but he swore that it was. And

he was so kind . . . I trusted him. Poor misguided man,
I don't believe there was evil in him . . . I don't believe
he knew.'

I had difficulty in preventing myself from saying a few
very crude things about that young man, but in the
circumstances, I felt it would only make Miss Hazlitt's
lot harder.

'But it wasn't only for myself . . . it wasn't . . . please
believe that?' Her great eyes pleaded with me.

'Have you *ever* done anything for yourself?' I muttered.

She did not seem to hear me. 'I thought I might be
able to do a little bit more for the people in the village.
I haven't been able to do anything yet.'

'You have done far too much already. The point is,
what are you going to do for *yourself?*'

She drew herself up in her chair. She straightened her
shoulders. She looked absurdly brave and absurdly fragile.
In a voice which was firm and clear, she said:

'I shall try for another post.'

'Oh . . .' I began to speak and then stopped.

'Well?'

'I . . . I don't like to think of you doing that.'

'Why not?'

'I . . . I just don't like to think of it.'

How could I tell her the bitter truth — that she was too
old — that nobody would want her, now?

I remembered a letter she had once written me, in which
there was a passage that made my heart ache . . . 'Mrs.
Y. has been so kind about everything, but of course she
says that the children *must* have somebody a little younger,
now that they are growing bigger, and though she has *no*
complaints, she feels that as my neuritis is no better, she
must get somebody who can play with them. The little

boy is *quite* a keen cricketer, and is always asking me to bowl to him. I try, but I can't really do it because of my arm, and that makes him laugh and me too! I expect I must look very funny. But Mrs. Y., naturally, does not like him to treat his cricket just as a joke, because she wants him to grow into a little man. And so, I shall have to go. She has been very good to keep me so long, and has given me such a nice reference, and has said that if she hears of anything she will certainly let me know.'

I remembered that letter now. That had been five years ago. Since then Miss Hazlitt had drifted from post to post, making gallant efforts to play with little boys whose mothers wanted them to grow into little men. She had been almost beaten, when her legacy had arrived, just in time.

And now, to begin all over again! To leave Allways and the cottage, and the garden for which daily she had thanked her God . . . the thought was intolerable.

But already she was accepting it, with a sort of puzzled resignation. I heard some broken phrases which she was muttering . . . 'so thankful . . . these few months . . . have made all the difference . . . should always remember the little garden . . . perhaps I would take some roots of her wild balm . . . would not like to think of it being lost.'

It was then, when she spoke of the wild balm, that I made a vow that whatever happened, Miss Hazlitt must not be allowed to leave Allways. For the balm was one of the earliest memories of my childhood. When I was six, long before either of us had ever heard of Allways, she and I had gone for walks, every morning, in the Devonshire lanes, and this balm had grown at the bottom of a high hedge just as you approach the village of Cockington, from the hill. For all I know it is there to this day, on the right hand side, about ten yards before you turn the corner from where you can see the forge. In the summer its leaves were thickly laid with the dust of the road, and we used to pick it and take it to a clear brook and wash it. Very delightful and exciting it was to see the sparkling water of the brook wash the dust from the pretty leaves, and then to draw out the balm, bright as an emerald, and press a leaf between one's thumb and forefinger, and savour the lemon-sweet fragrance.

This was the plant which she had sought and found, on one of her rare holidays, and had brought to Allways, and set in the shadow of her hedge. Often I had gone round to her cottage, just to smell the balm. It was still too small and delicate to press with the fingers, for the tiny leaves would have been bruised. But if you knelt down, so that your head was close to the earth, there drifted to you the immemorial fragrance of the balm . . . sweeter than the lemon verbena, fresher than the rose geranium. And for me that scent was an incantation that dimmed the years that lay between, a scent that made me a boy again, bending a flushed face over a brook in summer, clutching the leaves of the balm between hands that were as yet innocent of pain.

I went over to Miss Hazlitt.

'If you go on talking such nonsense,' I said, 'I shall put something extremely strong in your tea, and then you will be tight, and a very good thing too.'

She began to protest.

But I was in no mood for protestations. We were all one family at Allways, I said. We were not going to let anything horrible happen to anybody. The rest of the world might be cold and heartless but at Allways, somehow or other, we would see that things were all right.

But how? Even as I talked I asked myself that question, over and over again . . . how were we going to solve Miss Hazlitt's problem without any suspicion of 'charity'?

'It would need a miracle,' I said to myself, 'and the age of miracles is past.'

But the man who says *that*, is always a fool. Especially if he says it at Allways.

CHAPTER IX

TO THE RESCUE

WHY does news travel so quickly in Allways? Why is it that Mrs. Joss, at the village inn, invariably knows that your cat has had kittens almost before the happy event has been entirely admitted by the animal itself? How is it that the road-man, who is working miles away, is completely *au fait* with the ravages made in your kitchen-garden by the pigs that strayed through your hedge? How is it, when you call on La Belle Undine in the afternoon, that her Austin knows that you are going to have fried sole for dinner, or, which is more likely, knows that you are *not* going to have fried sole, because the fish 'hasn't come' . . . a negative habit to which fish is greatly partial in the country?

What is the secret of this strange dissemination of news? One could conjure up an agreeable fantasy of tidings spread by the wind, like seeds, of savoury smells blown from one cottage chimney to another, of words and phrases and sentences scattered like dust through the hedges and over the fields, by the nervous fingers of the wind. For surely, the wind has a hand in it. No human agency could possibly blow the words out of one's mouth so quickly, nor toss them so gaily through the high branches of the elms, over the little hill, through somebody else's back-door.

Anyway, Miss Hazlitt had hardly left me before there was a rat-tat-tat on the door, and a violent barking from Whoops. I realized that work, on a day like this, was out of the question, and so I hurried out of the garden, peered through the darkness of the hall, saw Mrs. M., and admitted her.

Mrs. M. came straight to the point.

'You have heard about Miss Hazlitt?' she rasped, and she slid her mink cape on to the sofa, and took up a dominant position in front of the fire-place.

'Yes. She's just been here. But how did you. . . .?'

'We *all* know.' Mrs. M. sniffed sharply, and rubbed her hands together. '*Everybody* knows.' From Mrs. M.'s intonation one would have thought that the loss of poor Miss Hazlitt's two thousand pounds was front-page news in all the papers. 'Poor misguided woman! If she'd only come to me!'

I blinked at Mrs. M. Had she entirely forgotten that she had spent a good hour trying to persuade *me* to invest all my savings in Montevideo Tin? Could she be so utterly brazen as to suggest that 'she knew all the time'? Apparently she could. For she went on . . . 'these wild cat schemes! Of course the prospectus was attractive . . . I believe I mentioned it to you? Yes, so I did! But I don't think you were quite able to follow it? No! Well, if you had, you'd have seen through it, soon enough. I did. They couldn't catch *me*!'

I gasped at this exhibition of feminine self-deception. However, this was not the time for expostulation. We had to think of Miss Hazlitt. And Mrs. M., with all her faults, *was* thinking of her. For Mrs. M., when it comes to a pinch, is pretty good. She may not have any very soothing words for you if you've gashed your hand, and she may seem quite unnecessarily brutal in the way she daubs the iodine on to a raw wound, but she does the job, quickly and efficiently. Oh yes, there are worse women than Mrs. M. in the world, very much worse!

She was at her best on an occasion like this.

'Obviously,' she said, 'we've got to do something about it.'

'I'm only too ready to help.'

'Private charity is out of the question. She wouldn't take it.'

'It's going to be very difficult to make her take anything at all.' I felt a certain diffidence in telling Mrs. M. about my talk with Miss Hazlitt. But I managed to convey that Miss Hazlitt regarded her disaster as being specially sent to 'test' her, and that, as such, it was really a blessing.

'I know all that,' said Mrs. M., impatiently. 'The poor creature . . . she's the sort that would regard anything as a blessing. If a snake bit her, she'd bless it. All the same, we can't just let her starve. Or go to the workhouse. She'd do either without a murmur, but we *can't*.'

'She thinks of trying for another post.'

'Good God! At her age? It'd be cruelty to animals.'

'So I thought. But what *can* we do?'

Mrs. M. looked at me mysteriously. 'I have an Idea,' she said. 'Will you be free to-morrow afternoon, for tea? Good! Then perhaps you would come along at about four?'

More she refused to say, and all I could extract from her was the fact that the tea-party was to celebrate the first meeting of the Miss Hazlitt Relief Committee, of which Mrs. M. was the chairman. The remaining members consisted in Undine, Miss Bott, the Professor and myself.

§ 11

'I think,' said Mrs. M., 'that we will have our tea *first*, and talk about Miss Hazlitt afterwards.'

We all agreed that this was a very good plan. I suppose,

in theory it was, but actually it tended to rob our conversation of sparkle. All sorts of subjects were broached, but they were hastily abandoned, because they all seemed to lead to Miss Hazlitt. This is always the way when you meet, at meal-times, for business purposes, and decide to defer the business till afterwards. I have occasionally lunched with editors who didn't want to be editors till the arrival of coffee, or with theatrical managers who wished to avoid all 'shop' until the bill was paid. The strain, on both of us, of trying to behave as though we were gentlemen was almost unendurable. But it is a habit which is very prevalent in business circles.

At last, after we had all politely but firmly declined the offer of one of Miss Bott's new kittens, offering various naive excuses, such as 'we didn't think it would agree with the other cat' or 'if you can't be *certain* that it isn't a female' (and nobody could) . . . and after we had all agreed that the Michaelmas daisies were very late this year, and that really, there was nothing quite like them, was there . . . a statement which is palpably untrue, because there are a great many flowers extremely like them . . . there was a long pause.

'More tea?'

'No thank you, really.'

'Professor?'

'No thank you.'

'There is still a scone . . . waiting to be eaten,' said Mrs. M. brightly. 'No? Then Spot shall have a treat!'

She held up the scone, and her elderly fox terrier advanced from under the table, gazed at the scone with acute disgust, shuddered, and staggered back to the shelter of the table. We sympathized with Spot. The scones had been heavy going.

'Well,' said Mrs. M., giving Spot a look which boded ill for him, 'shall we adjourn?'

The word 'adjourn', in this connection, was a little ill-placed, because all we could do was to scrape round in our chairs, and look nervously at the pencils and paper which had been provided for us.

'I think,' said Mrs. M., 'that one subject is uppermost in our minds.'

It was indeed.

'That subject is Miss Hazlitt. I will not waste time on reminding you of the details. I need not even refer to the person who was responsible for all this, though . . .' with a dart at me . . . 'I never trusted him, not for a moment. I will merely put a suggestion before you.'

She paused. She was evidently enjoying this moment.

'My suggestion is this. That, between us, we should purchase Miss Hazlitt's cottage for her, transform it into a general shop, and instal her as the proprietress.'

This was what is known in journalistic circles as a 'bombshell'. It was so unexpected, it opened up so many curious visions, aroused so many problems. It was true that we wanted a shop, for since the death of Mr. Joy, some twelve months back, we had been without a commercial establishment of any sort whatever at Allways. Very tiresome it had been to have to get everything from the town. We were always running out of matches and soap and candles. But the idea of Miss Hazlitt was so revolutionary that all we could do was blink, and murmur polite and meaningless things, like 'wonderful . . . most interesting idea'. But all the time, we were obsessed by the strangeness of it all, and we could not manage to say anything sensible, in spite of Mrs. M., who was saying 'Well?' in an impatient voice, every few seconds.

It was Undine who broke the tension. She suddenly clasped her hands over her knees, with a fierce rattle of bangles, shot her neck into the air, and proclaimed in ecstatic tones:

'I think it's all divine. Lucky Miss Hazlitt! I've always longed to keep a shop!'

This, somehow, struck us as unexpected. We had not visualized Undine in such a role.

'But *longed!*' cried Undine. 'It's been my *one* longing. Jujubes . . . bootlaces . . . and *enormous* dollops of soap . . . exquisite!'

We stared at Undine.

'And the rattle of acid-drops into the scales,' she went on, with rising fervour. 'And those *disgusting* sticks of liquorice . . . too, *too* gruesome! And the heavenly servility of it all . . . one would be a *slave* whenever the door bell rang!' She fluttered her lids, dreamily . . . 'a slave, even if it was a huge ploughboy, wanting . . .'

Mrs. M. was evidently anxious to prevent us from hearing what the huge ploughboy might, or might not, want, in this dream-picture, for she rapped on the table, projected her rabbit's teeth, and said, in staccato tones:

'I am sure that is most interesting, but after all, it is Miss Hazlitt that we are considering. It is her, she . . .' Mrs. M. cleared her throat. These pronouns!

'But you *will* let me serve behind the counter?'

Mrs. M. regarded her impatiently. Undine was doing all her undulations.

'It is a little early,' she said, 'to consider that.'

'Oh, but we've all agreed. Haven't we?' Undine turned to us with a sweeping gesture. 'Let's have a show of hands. For Miss Hazlitt's shop!'

Somewhat feebly, and with considerable embarrassment,

we all raised our hands. It was a strange and rather incongruous little group, with the firelight flickering over us and the shadows gathering fast outside the window.

But that is how the shop at Allways was born.

§ I I I

'And now,' said Mrs. M., 'to details.'

She felt, after Undine's moment, that her authority as chairman was being slightly undermined, and for the next half hour, our noses were kept to the grindstone.

It was astonishing how much information she had already managed to collect. The landlord, it appeared, was quite willing to sell the cottage. No precise sum had been mentioned, but she gathered . . . and there was a long pause after the word 'gathered', a pause which was meant to convey to us that she had been engaged in the highest and most mysterious financial transactions . . . she *gathered* that the sum would be about four hundred pounds.

'This is how I have calculated it,' said Mrs. M. 'House, four hundred pounds. Alterations needed to turn it into a shop, fifty pounds. All we really need is a counter and some show cases and a cash register. That bow-window of hers will do perfectly well for displaying things. The only other large item would be the first stock of groceries, etc. And we certainly shan't need more than fifty pounds worth of those, not till we see how things go. In other words, if we can somehow form a little company, with a capital of five hundred pounds. . . .'

And then the Professor interrupted her.

'Do you think the shop will pay?' he asked quietly.

Mrs. M. looked indignant. 'Well, really, I should hardly be proposing if it I thought it wouldn't.'

'But of *course*,' echoed Undine. 'I shall buy *everything* there. I shall desert Fortnum and Mason's *completely*. They'll die of mortification, but I can't help that.'

The Professor blinked. 'But we weren't exactly proposing to set up a local branch of Fortnum and Mason's. Or were we?'

Undine glared at him.

'I mean,' continued the Professor, 'although I'm sure we very much appreciate Miss Wilkins' kindness, we can't expect Miss Hazlitt to make much out of selling her a few bottles of stuffed olives and an occasional foie gras.'

Undine sat up very straight. 'I really do *not* know what you mean. I detest foie gras. If you *knew* . . . they put the goose in front of the fire until its liver explodes, or something quite fearful. I really *resent* it being suggested that I live exclusively on foie gras. I can *not* imagine where anybody got such a hateful idea. . . .'

How long she might have gone on like this it would be difficult to say, had not Miss Bott interrupted us.

'Personally,' she said, in loud and cheerful tones, 'I'd eat foie gras till *my* liver exploded, if I ever got the chance. But that isn't the point. The point is that Miss Hazlitt's main business will be with the village people. Two half-pennyworth of sweets, a packet of hairpins, a bar of soap, a threepenny bottle of "heart and stomach mixture".'

'It sounds *astonishingly* squalid,' hissed Undine.

Miss Bott's eyes flashed, but she did not take up the challenge, directly. She merely said . . . 'In other words, the majority of Miss Hazlitt's customers will be people like *me*.'

§ I V

I was beginning to feel embarrassed. The atmosphere, which had seemed so clear and bright a moment ago, was now charged with gloom and menace. I was thankful that Mrs. M. decided that this was a moment to call a halt.

She rapped on the table. 'Ladies! Gentlemen! If you would not mind deferring these discussions, perhaps you would care to hear a few *facts*?'

'I am always willing to hear facts,' said the Professor. And he took out his note-book, and jotted down something in it, to Mrs. M.'s evident irritation, for she always felt that he was writing down things about her. However, this was no time for personal animosity.

'I have worked out that Miss Hazlitt cannot afford to make a net profit of less than two pounds ten shillings a week. After all, she'll have to have a boy to help her, and she couldn't get anybody under ten shillings. That would leave her with exactly two pounds a week for herself, which is what she has been accustomed to.'

The Professor made another note. 'And how is she going to make that two pounds ten?'

Mrs. M.'s voice rose sharply, and *she*, in her turn, produced a piece of paper. 'By selling exactly twelve pounds, five shillings worth of goods per week at a profit of twenty per cent, which is the average profit, I am informed, of retail stores, and perhaps the Professor would glance at these figures.' All this was said in one breath, as she thrust the paper under the Professor's nose.

The Professor blinked at it, put it in his pocket, and made another note. Mrs. M. sighed loudly at us, to indicate how hopeless it was to argue with him. Then she resumed:

'But of course there are all sorts of side-lines that might be extremely profitable. Teas, for example. In the summer.'

It was my turn to interrupt.

'But who is going to come to Allways, just to have tea? Even in the summer?'

'People have to have tea somewhere.'

'Yes, but why at Allways?' Perhaps it was my eagerness to try to help Miss Hazlitt that made me see all the drawbacks so clearly. 'After all, there's nothing to bring people here. There's no golf-course. No river. No historic ruins. There's really nothing at all.'

'My nieces often come over,' remarked Mrs. M. in a cold voice. 'At least, they came over three times last year.'

'Yes, but you've only two nieces, and even if they came over six times, and you always took them to tea at Miss Hazlitt's, that would only be twelve teas — or eighteen, counting yourself, and even if she charged one and six (which is quite a lot), she couldn't make much more than ten shillings.'

'It's no use meeting trouble half-way.'

'No. But it's no use counting your nieces before they're hatched.'

This was a most unfortunate remark because Mrs. M.'s nieces were so very definitely and finally hatched. However Mrs. M. ignored it.

'Besides,' she added, 'think of the hikers. All this fresh air craze. Not that *I* believe in it . . . I think women ought to be prevented by *law* from wearing shorts . . . but whatever they wear, I imagine such people still drink tea.'

'I've only seen two hikers in Allways in the last year,' said Miss Bott, 'and they were so tired of hiking that they pinched my bicycle from the toolshed and have never been heard of since.'

Mrs. M. tapped her foot on the floor, and looked up at the ceiling. 'I *had* hoped,' she said, 'for a little encouragement. If everybody is determined to pour cold water on every single word I say. . . .'

'But indeed no,' said Miss Bott, quickly. Undine and I also murmured something conciliatory. And the Professor said, 'I think the idea of teas is excellent.'

'It only needs a little patience,' said Mrs. M.

'We might put in an advertisement,' said the Professor.

And Mrs. M. beamed at me, and said, 'You could write it for us! In your nice, light way.'

§ v

It was then that Miss Bott suggested the library, and that was the first idea that met with universal approval.

'Now we *are* getting some help,' said Mrs. M. delightedly. 'I cannot think why I never thought of it myself.'

'I shall destroy my subscription to the Times Book Club,' ejaculated Undine. 'Not one *word* will I read that doesn't come out of the shop.'

'But we shall have to provide the books,' said Miss Bott. 'And I suppose they'll be mostly be pretty old.'

'I don't care if they're *medieval*. . . .'

'I imagine we can all supply a fair number?' Mrs. M. looked at me again.

'I've got a hundred or two. Pretty new. Review copies, mostly.'

'A hundred or two! At tuppence a week . . . that makes a pound a week from your books alone!'

And so exciting was the atmosphere that nobody questioned the wild optimism of this estimate. For there was indeed a great charm in the thought that the dozens of books which we all had, mouldering in our attics, might be taken out and given a new purpose in life by being included in the village library. These books which had been nothing but an encumbrance in the past would suddenly be endowed with the magical property of earning tuppence a week. True, it might have occurred to the cynic that since nothing would induce *us* to read them, nothing would induce the village people to read them either. But it did not occur to us. We were all too busy thinking how splendid it would be to be able to clear our attics and show our charitable intentions at the same time.

The Professor leant forward, blinked three times very fiercely, and said, 'I've a whole shelf of books I'd be delighted to get rid of.'

'Oh!'

'Splendid!'

'Thank you *so* much.'

The gloom with which the Professor's offer was received was too deep for him to ignore.

'Well . . . don't you want them?'

'Of course . . . but . . .' Mrs. M. paused. She was thinking what we were all thinking, as we remembered the titles of some of the Professor's books which we had respectfully noted on his shelves. Most of these titles were in German, and they were all concerned with terrifying abstractions of Light and Space and Time. And when you opened them, you invariably came upon a page in which some deathless drama of mathematics was being waged . . . something like this:

If we take $a - b = \dfrac{bqz + \sqrt{870 \cdot 000}}{N}$ $(2+2=5)$

to represent speed at which light travels. . . .

And after reading two or three sentences, you put the

book down, and thanked God that your feet were firmly on the ground, and that such things as speed, at Allways, were limited to the flight of the swallows over the duck-pond, or the leisurely tread of cattle through an open gate, or, at the worst, the whirl of bicycle wheels over the dip on the green, when the boys raced on a summer evening, with breathless shouts and a distant tinkle of bells.

How could we explain all this to the Professor? Perhaps we never should have explained it, had not Miss Bott come to our rescue. Thank Heaven, Miss Bott came straight to the point.

'What Mrs. M. means,' she observed loudly and cheerfully, 'is that the village boys aren't exactly going to line up in a queue to get Popoff's Theory of Electrons.'

The Professor blinked.

'Don't think we aren't grateful,' continued Miss Bott. 'But what we want is nice cosy bed-books. And personally I'd rather go to bed with a boa-constrictor than with Professor Einstein.'

'I wasn't asking you to go to bed with Mr. Einstein,' said the Professor amiably.

Mrs. M. drew in her breath under her tongue, as she always does, when the conversation takes a turn of which she disapproves.

'Well, I'm sure it would all be very remote and ethereal if I *did*,' continued Miss Bott, unabashed. 'Parallel lines never meeting, you know, and all that sort of thing. Still, I'd rather not, if you don't awfully mind. And I'm sure the village boys would feel the same. Now if it were Edgar Wallace. . . .'

'But it *is* Edgar Wallace,' said the Professor. 'That was what I was offering *you*. And the only reason I'm willing to get rid of them is because I know them all by heart.'

So that was that.

Up soared our spirits at one moment, down the next. They took a slight header in the latter direction when we began to discuss a tobacco licence.

'She *must* have one,' said Miss Bott.

'After all,' said Undine, 'it's a way of luring people on. They go in for a packet every day, and then, when they're in the shop, the sun comes out and shines on a bottle of tangerine drops and they feel they can't *live* without some.' Pause. Then, faintly . . . 'Don't you think?'

'I see your point,' said Mrs. M. in a voice which assured us that she didn't. 'But I'm quite certain that Miss Hazlitt would never consent to sell tobacco.'

'She's never said anything to *me* about it,' said Miss Bott, waving a 'gasper' with very yellow fingers.

'No, she wouldn't,' said the Professor quietly. 'She doesn't go campaigning about the place. She's not that sort. She doesn't ask the butcher if he's "saved", nor go into the pub and tell them the Devil's waiting for them. Nor does she take my pipe out of my mouth nor your cigarette out of your fingers. But she wouldn't sell tobacco, all the same. Not if you paid her a thousand a year to do it.'

'It's going to cramp her style pretty badly,' said Miss Bott. 'A shop without tobacco . . .'

I agreed with Miss Bott. A shop without tobacco would be like a room without a fire . . . there would be something dead about it.

'Supposing,' said Undine, 'we got some little pamphlets about the evils of smoking too much and put one in each packet of cigarettes?'

It was surely a proof of the distance we had departed from reality that this suggestion was received with complete gravity. For as I look back on it, I can imagine no stranger principles on which any commercial undertaking could have been begun. To warn one's customers, with each packet of cigarettes, of the dire effects which would result from smoking them, to tell them that they were straining their hearts, impairing their digestions, lowering their morale, and generally hurrying themselves at full tilt towards the nearest lunatic asylum . . . this would be, indeed, an odd way in which to build up a flourishing retail tobacco business.

Mrs. M. thought so too. 'I do not think that would be *quite* . . .'

We all agreed that it would not be *quite* . . . Quite what, we did not specify. Quite honest, I suppose we meant. And when Undine suggested that the pamphlets could be put under the counter, out of sight, Mrs. M. shook her head, and said that would be definitely dishonest.

The Professor came to the rescue.

'There is a form of cigarette, made of herbs.'

'Oh God!' said Miss Bott.

After we had all elevated our eyebrows at Miss Bott, the Professor continued:

'It's supposed to be very good for asthma.'

'But who's got asthma in Allways?' demanded the unquenchable Miss Bott.

'Really,' said Mrs. M., sternly, to Miss Bott, 'do let us *try* to look on the bright side of things, sometimes.'

'Well if you think it's looking on the bright side of things to imagine that the whole of Allways is suddenly going to develop asthma, I give it up.'

It was a little difficult to calm the atmosphere again. I give myself the credit for doing that. For, in the interests of peace, I proclaimed that I had often smoked herb cigarettes, that they were quite delicious, and would probably be a roaring success.

It cost me a good deal to say this. For I viewed the idea of herb cigarettes with the very gravest distaste. They reminded me of horrors like coffee with the caffeine extracted, or of non-alcoholic port, or companionate marriage. All these things aren't really so muddled up as you may think at first. They have a very definite link . . . they are all efforts to obtain pleasure without the penalty of pain. And if life has taught me anything, it has taught me that pleasure has to be paid for in terms of pain, at odds of about three to one. Yes, whether you are drinking a cup of coffee, or a glass of port, or making love on a twilit river. Think that out.

'Anyway,' I said . . . 'You can put me down as a regular customer.'

'In that case, I'll risk a packet,' said Miss Bott.

'I have an idea about them,' said the Professor. 'I think . . .' Then he blinked, and made a note. And we all stared at him and wondered what he had written. Mrs. M. whispered to me . . . 'If he invents a new cigarette, *don't*. It would be bound to explode.'

And so, we decided that we would all smoke herb cigarettes. And by smoking them we should all endow ourselves with such charm and fragrance, and chase the phantom of asthma to such distances, that Miss Hazlitt's heart would be softened, and she would feel that if one form of cigarette would exercise such beneficial results, surely another form of cigarette would not be so evil?

§ VI

And thus we talked. And you might say our words were as smoke, from phantom cigarettes, or as quickly to be dissolved as the tangerine drops which had glimmered in Undine's imagination, or as dusty as the books which we had promised for the library, or as illusory as the clients who were to pour tea in the tea-gardens . . . the clients who were still in limbo, waiting to be served in gardens which only existed in our brains.

You might say this, and much more. You might say that it was all a dream, and that we were only giving Miss Hazlitt dreams to sell.

But you would be wrong. For exactly six weeks later, I put my signature to a document which already bore the signatures of Mrs. M., Undine, the Professor, and Miss Bott. Don't ask me what the document was. All I know is that the cottage now belonged to Miss Hazlitt, and that there passed constantly up the lane a succession of grocers' vans and provision carts, on their way to the Stores. The Stores of Allways.

For, as we have said before, Allways is a place where miracles are a daily occurrence. So is every other place, if people only knew it. But you know, and I know, that they don't. Which is one of the reasons why you are reading this book.

CHAPTER X

BABES IN THE WOOD

Miss Hazlitt was installed in her shop on a rainy day in November, a day so rainy that all our water-butts were overflowing, and our thatches dark and soaked, while the little stream by the public-house was so high and fierce that we feared that the road would soon be flooded.

For in those distant days it *did* rain. It rained real water, and lots of it. After two years of drought it seems difficult to believe, but such, you will recall, was the case.

And this rain caused such complications in my private life that for the moment we will leave Miss Hazlitt to settle into her shop, promising to pay her a visit at the earliest opportunity.

§ II

The complications occurred in my wood. This wood, some people coldly assured me, existed only in my own imagination. To them, it was only the field over the garden hedge, with a few trees in it. And true, three years ago, it *had* been just a field. But now, it had far more trees in it than people seemed to realize. If they could have seen my bills from the nurserymen they would have been bound to admit that it *must* be a wood. Nobody could possibly spend so much on trees and flowering shrubs and fail to have a wood. Besides, if you stood in the middle of the field in summer, under the weeping ash, and if you half closed your eyes and faced due south, and looked at the little group of silver poplars with the tiny clusters of mock-orange at their feet, and beyond that to the small but sturdy cluster of silver birch, you felt that you were quite definitely in a wood, provided, of course, that you had had enough to drink.

But to make a wood it is necessary to do a great many more things than put trees into a field. As each year goes by, bringing with it some fresh menace to my newly planted trees — a menace of drought, or of wind, or of blight — I wonder, more earnestly, how any wood ever manages to grow at all, without human assistance! My trees have to be staked, and pedicured and dieted and Lord knows what else. How do ordinary trees manage when there is nobody to do any of these things for them? Nobody to cut away the grass round their trunks? Nobody to check the hungry ivy, nor support them against the south-westers, nor give them a drink when they need it? This is one of the profound mysteries of nature to all amateur gardeners.

The trouble that was now brewing in the wood was directly connected with the rain that was soaking Miss Hazlitt's roof, and filling our water-butts. And it was my father who first sounded the note of alarm.

When I showed him the list of trees I had ordered — which included excitements like tulip-trees, mulberries, maiden-hair-trees, standard wistarias, rare buddleias and all sorts of things which, in my imagination, had already formed themselves into a tropical forest, laden with fruit and blossom, with large rude birds bouncing about on the branches, all he did was to screw his eye-glass into his eye, tap the paper before him and say, 'What are you doing about drainage; it's swampy in parts. I noticed sedge grass too. What kind of grass is that? It's triangular without joints, marsh stuff.'

Now to me, in those dark ages, a drain meant merely a rather disagreeable thing a long way under the earth, which one left to the tender mercies of the local Borough Council. Sometimes the drains 'went wrong', in which case, one went away as far as possible, and stayed with relations until they had gone right again. The only place where drains were at all in evidence was the Riviera, and then the only thing to do was to swim round to the bay next door, or to put on one's clothes and go off to the Casino in a huff.

So I said to my father, somewhat indignantly, 'There aren't any drains in my field. Why should there be? There isn't a house anywhere near. There are only a few very modest cows on the hill above.'

'I'm not talking about sewerage. I'm talking about land drains.'

'Oh!'

From the tone of my voice my father realized that I had not the least idea what he meant. So he proceeded to tell me about land drains, and said that if we did not put them in, half of the trees would be waterlogged. I still had not the least idea what he meant.

So I paid no attention to him. And when he had gone I took the piece of paper on which he had drawn a drainage plan of my field, and I drew large cats poking their heads out of one end of each drain, and small cats poking their tails out of the other end. I gained much satisfaction from doing so, and forgot about the urgencies of life for at least half an hour.

But all through November it continued to rain. Day after day it rained. The roads were full of puddles perpetually puckered with rain-drops, and the little stream at the bottom of the field swelled to a whirring yellow

The
Pond

torrent. I used to go out, swathed to the eyes in a mackin-tosh, and stand under the great elm to watch it. When you have not got a proper stream on your land — only a petulant dribble — it is very exciting when the great rains come and turn your stream into the real thing. You think of the lakes you could make, and the fish you could catch, and all sorts of idiotic pleasures like that. You also think of the islands you could make. You could put the cat on an island and say to it, 'See! You are on an island.'

'The hell I am,' the cat would reply as it jumped back on to the bank. At least, if it were like my cat, it would.

But rain, if it pours incessantly for a fortnight, begins to get on one's nerves. One hurries to the greenhouse, and breathes a sigh of relief to be in the shelter, among the quiet green plants. The chrysanthemums regard one gravely, with great tawny faces. The early white cyclamen arch their thin necks, nestling among their foliage like swans in summer reeds. The solitary orchid poses disdain-fully in a corner, with the air of an exquisitely clad manne-quin flaunting her satins before the plain tweeds and serges of the common folk. The bloom is already trembling on the under-leaves of the cinerarias, a bloom that will deepen as the dark days hurry by, till the leaves and flowers revel in an enchanting competition of colour. But meanwhile, the rain is beating a tattoo on the glass, nervously, madden-ingly, and one cannot enjoy these things. . . .

'The water tank is overflowing on to the floor again, I must have a proper pipe put in . . .'

'But if I do have a pipe where is the water to go to?'

'If it goes outside it will flood the violet bed. If I run it past the violet bed it will lie in a pool on the path and rot the frames. I could move the frames, but there is only one other place for them, and that is under the poplars, where they will get no sun. . . .'

'Oh Lord . . . will it *never* stop raining?'

And one goes indoors, disconsolate, leaves the umbrella to make a puddle on the red brick, and sits in front of the fire, moping, while the rain comes down the chimney and spits spitefully on the great logs.

§ I I I

By the time the new year was in, the trees were standing in water. I used to go out with a spade, day after day, and cut little channels through the grass, from the stem of some particular tree to the hedge. For a while the water would drain away, and I breathed a sigh of satisfaction as the ground round the stems became clear and firm. But one could not do this with the whole wood. The water-channels became horribly complicated, and got all mixed up, and sometimes, when one had dug a channel, one met another channel, and all the water from the whole wood charged down it, so that the last state of the tree was worse than the first.

Mrs. M., of course, knew all about this. At the most unfortunate moments, her head would pop out over the hedge, and she would stare with ill-concealed glee at my pitiful little efforts at drainage.

'Well — how are the water-works progressing? Ha! ha! He! He!'

'Very well thank you, Mrs. M.'

'Looks like a map of the rivers of England, doesn't it?'

'Yes, very,' I said, between clenched teeth, longing to take a spadeful of yellow water and throw it over the hedge into her face.

'There *was* something in what your old father said, wasn't there?'

To which I paid no attention whatever. And the only consolation about the rain was that it was so heavy that Mrs. M. could not stand in it for very long, looking over my hedge. Which shows that it must have been heavy indeed.

§ I V

At last the rain stopped. The earth turned in space, a bright globe, cleanly washed, and the great winds caressed it, and fanned it dry, and the sun hurried through the vanquished clouds, and gave it blessing.

Reading that sentence again, I realize that it would have been much simpler to say 'spring came'. Simpler, but not really quite so true.

For though spring came to Allways, though little blue pools of scillas gathered miraculously under the stems of other peoples' beeches, and the catkins danced about on other peoples' nut-bushes, spring did not come to my wood. Indeed, from the condition of the majority of the trees, you would say that we were in the middle of a strange and bitter autumn.

The silver birches were the worst sufferers. Their lovely bark, which should have been as smooth as silk — (have you ever stripped off the thin grey outer film of a silver birch to find the pale shining stem beneath?) — their bark was rough and pock-marked. And when you bent a twig, instead of springing back with a happy resilience, it either snapped or split, revealing an unhealthy yellow core.

The tulip tree put out one or two sickly leaves, which mildewed and fell off. The horse-chestnuts flourished, it

140

is true — but then you can't kill a horse-chestnut even if you try — and the willows and the poplars seemed quite pleased with life. But at least half the trees were sickly, and struggling, with tiny, pathetic leaves, mildewed trunks and the general appearance of children from one of the worst areas of the slums.

One day I could bear it no longer. I knew, in my heart of hearts, what was the matter, and I decided that I would face the facts. I walked grimly out into the wood, took hold of a silver birch, gave a great heave and tugged it out of the ground.

There was a sickening squelch. And in the hole where the silver birch had stood, there was a pool of dirty water, rapidly filling.

§ v

Two days later my father was tramping over the ground, making snorting noises, taking hold of the trunks of trees, shaking them, listening to the squelchy sound made by the roots, and then making more snorting noises.

'It's a damned disgrace,' he said. 'You might as well chuck most of 'em on the fire. Why didn't you do as I told you, and put in drains?'

'I didn't understand.'

Another snort. 'The ground's as sour as a lemon. We'll have to get old W. on the job at once.'

Old W. came, and he and my father spent the morning marching round my wood, talking mysteriously of 'levels' and 'drawing power'. I followed in a state of puzzled depression, with wet feet.

'If the water follows the spade, we're all right,' said my father.

This phrase was constantly on his lips. 'If it'll follow the spade.' I had incongruous visions of a rustic musical comedy with all the girls singing:

> Fol-low the spade!
> Come to the open spaces!

However these visions were soon dispelled by the fascinating game that my father and old W. proceeded to play. The main drain was dug right across the wood with a lot of minor drains leading off it. To me the whole wood looked as flat as a fen, but both my father and old W. said No — there was a distinct rise in the centre from which the water would flow, outwards, draining into a pond at each end.

But the really exciting part came when they actually laid the drains in the troughs which had been dug for them. Because, all they did was to get length after length of pipe and lay them together, *without any sort of cement to join them*, and then to shovel the earth on top of the lengths of pipe again.

Please try to follow this. It's important.

'But where does the water *come through?*'

'It sinks through the earth, through the cracks between the pipes.'

'But if it goes through the cracks at the top won't it go straight out again through the cracks at the bottom?'

'No it won't.'

'But it stands to reason . . .'

My father screwed his eyeglass at me. 'I've drained forty-acre fields a good many years before you were thought of.'

'Well then, can't you explain why the water runs through the top cracks and doesn't run through the bottom? It seems so very odd.'

'A lot of things in agriculture are extremely odd,' remarked my father tersely. He then turned with a sigh of relief to old W.

I was so astonished by this latest revelation of the mysterious nature of water that when the drains had all been covered in I almost hoped that they would not 'draw', in order that I could prove my father wrong.

On the night after the drains were finished there was a heavy rainfall. I rushed out in the morning and ran to the mouth of the drain. It was quite dry. Water, water everywhere, but not a sign of water in my drain. I returned to the house in triumph.'

'It *is* running through the cracks at the bottom,' I proclaimed. 'There isn't a drop of water coming out at the end.'

'And there probably won't be,' said my father, calmly, 'for another couple of months.'

'What?'

He said it again.

'But why?' This was really the most baffling thing I had yet heard. Why the water should run through the cracks at the bottom for two months and then suddenly stop doing so, and run through the drain, as per plan — this seemed to me almost beyond a joke.

And yet, that is what happened. We put in the drains in May. No water came out of them, into either pond, till the middle of July. Then, one day there was a thunderstorm. As I walked in the wood, after it was over, to see if any damage had been done, I heard a pleasant tinkle. I looked across the pond, and there, from the main drain (whose mouth was almost concealed by a big clump of wild irises), water was merrily trickling. The drains were working. They have worked perfectly ever since.

That is how the first great Battle of the Wood was waged, and I am happy to say that it ended in my favour. Next winter the trees were no longer water-logged, their trunks were no longer covered with green slime, and the ground about their feet was sweet and clean. But there were other great Battles of the Wood to be waged, even longer and more arduous than this, and we shall be obliged to chronicle them when the time comes.

I cannot end this digression without observing that the older I grow the more firmly am I convinced that the Ways of Water constitute one of the major mysteries of the earth. Why does it linger in certain places, and fly from others? Why does it dive deep down here, and well up there? Why, at one moment, is it clear and sweet, and at another sour and sullen? Has it a strange intelligence of its own, a secret spirit whose commands it is obliged to obey — a spirit who broods moodily in many a dark well, dreams over the great lakes, laughs shrilly in the waterfalls, and weeps with the falling of the rain?

CHAPTER XI

THE STORES

AND now we can go back to Miss Hazlitt's shop. And perhaps we may feel inclined to make a purchase?

This hint is thrown out only with the greatest diffidence. For, in a way, I have an interest in the shop, or rather, in its owner. Which accounts for the dialogues which invariably take place, at week-ends, between me and the guest of the moment. It usually goes like this:

Me: I thought that to-morrow you might like to go and look at the shop.

Guest: Oh, I'd adore to!

Me: You might like to buy something, too.

Guest: Why, have you got shares in it?

Me: No. But it's kept by a very charming old lady and it would help her.

Guest: But of *course*. I'll buy some cigarettes.

Me: Well, that only means a half-penny, on a shilling packet. Couldn't you get some chocolate? She makes more on that.

Guest: I couldn't *possibly*. I'm on a diet.

Me: Well, your mother might like some.

Guest: She's on two diets.

Me: Well, there must be something.

Guest: Yes, of course there must. (Brightly): Could I buy some stamps?

Me: I don't think that would help very much. She doesn't sell them. She sells head and stomach pills, though.

K   145

Guest: *How* revolting.

Me: Hairpins?

Guest: Oh really!

Me: Sorry, I forgot. But there must be *something*.

Guest: Yes. There must.

Me: I *had* hoped you'd spend about a pound.

Guest: A *pound*? Whatever on?

Me: Well, things for your home. Cleaning things. Soap. Vim. Rinso.

Guest (coldly): You talk as if we lived in complete squalor.

Me: I beg your pardon. But your mother *must* run out of soap, sometimes.

Guest (still more coldly): If you think so, it would be only kindness to tell her so.

Me: Oh well — of course — if you don't want to buy anything, it doesn't matter.

Guest: But *what*?

Me (shortly): Matches, for example. You could buy a dozen boxes of matches.

Guest: So I could.

Me: And Pond's cold cream. Don't you use Pond's cold cream?

Guest: No. Why should I?

Me: Isn't one a little *déclassée* if one doesn't? All those earl's daughters — what would *they* do without it?

Guest: I can't think. But I'm not an earl's daughter. So I don't have to be so careful.

Me: Oh hell!

Guest: Perhaps I might buy a pound's worth of matches. And then we could hire a lorry to take them up to London.

§ 11

But these dialogues were still in the airy future on the eve of the shop's opening.

A great many thrills had preceded this opening. One of these was the episode of Miss Hazlitt's well.

Ever since she arrived at the cottage Miss Hazlitt had been drinking the water from the well at the bottom of her garden. It was a very ancient well and it had never dried up. For many generations, presumably, the owners of the cottage had relied upon it for their water supply, and nobody had made any complaints.

But one day, when I was calling on her to help arrange the first groceries along the shelves, and to decide such pleasant details as whether the counter was to face east or west, I felt thirsty, and asked for a glass of water.

When it arrived, it tasted exactly like Vichy. Not at all unpleasant, but salty, and with a faint suggestion of effervescence.

I turned to Miss Hazlitt. 'Have you had this water analysed?'

'No . . . why?'

'It tastes rather extraordinary.'

'It has done me no harm.'

'All the same, we really ought to have it analysed. It might be something marvellous, that we could bottle.'

Visions of an Allways spring floated before me — a spring that would become famous all over Europe. We should have special bottles for it, with labels that told one how soothing it was for the *estomac*, and how it charmed away all the ills of the liver. Very rich old gentlemen with purple noses and bouncing *estomacs* would sip it reverently at the Ritz.

So I sent the water to be analysed.

However, when the report on the water arrived it was, as they say in Government circles, 'damning'. Never had such a water offended the outraged nostrils of the analyst in all his long experience. Never had so many gases congregated together. There was almost everything in that water except alcohol. There was free ammonia, organic ammonia, chlorides, nitrates, and many other dark things. True, lead was 'absent', which was, one supposed, a good thing. But under the heading 'microscopical examination' it said there was 'amorphous organic matter, spores and crustaceae'. Which made one think that one was swallowing a tank of the more prickly varieties of shell fish at the Brighton aquarium.

A very sinister little note accompanied the analysis.

'From our experience,' wrote the chemist, 'we would suggest that this water is subject to some very definite contamination. Is the well in the proximity of the churchyard? If so . . .'

I shuddered. The thought was appalling. So appalling that I did not show the analysis to Miss Hazlitt. Instead, I went round to Mrs. M.

§ I I I

'Yes,' said Mrs. M. 'Of course that *must* be it. And it must be stopped at once.'

She put on her cape, and waved away my offer to help her on with her goloshes. I think she felt that it was not quite 'nice' to be helped on with goloshes. If they did not go on properly, one had to grab her ankle, and that tickled, and led to girlish laughter, which might be misconstrued.

'I always suspected that well,' said Mrs. M., as we walked along. Whenever anything goes wrong it is fairly safe to say that Mrs. M. 'always suspected' it. I often wonder why she keeps so many of these suspicions to herself.

But she did not say this to Miss Hazlitt. She came straight to the point. She began by waving the analysis in her face.

'Nitrates!' she boomed.

Miss Hazlitt smiled radiantly. 'Yes?' she said, as though this were indeed good news.

'Bad — very bad!' Mrs. M. began to shout as though Miss Hazlitt were deaf. 'Chlorine!'

Another radiant smile. And Miss Hazlitt said, 'Isn't it wonderful to think of all those things in my well!'

'It isn't wonderful at all,' said Mrs. M. sharply. 'The only wonderful thing is that it doesn't give you a stomach-ache.'

Miss Hazlitt frowned slightly. The frown deepened as Mrs. M. continued. And her face was very grave when Mrs. M. delivered her final shot. . . .

'You have been drinking water that comes straight from the grave-yard! and they've been burying there since Saxon times.'

It was then that Miss Hazlitt uttered a remark which has become part of Allways history. She looked at Mrs. M. with an expression of pained reproof in her clear grey eyes. Very quietly she said, 'It is hallowed ground'.

Now when you put that remark in cold print, without being able to convey the tone in which it was delivered, nor to capture on paper the queer light which shone in Miss Hazlitt's eyes, it sounds, to say the least of it, priggish. It also sounds slightly insane. But when she said it, it sounded, not only beautiful, but true — as though the

water that had flowed through God's acre must, in some
way, be sweetened and purified — as though the rain had a
different quality, and must be blessed.

Anyway it was a remark which completely baffled both
Mrs. M. and myself. We looked at each other with a
hopeless expression, and after a few aimless remarks, we
took our leave.

'Miss Hazlitt has a most extraordinary gift for ignoring
the disagreeable side of any subject,' said Mrs. M., when
we got outside.

'No subject has a disagreeable side, for her.' I pulled
off a long piece of grass and began to chew it. 'Don't you
see? Everything's right in the world for her. It *must* be.
Just because — because God has ordered it.'

Mrs. M. sniffed. 'Well, whatever God may or may not
have ordered,' she said, 'I think *we* ought to open a subscription for a filter.'

With which I heartily agreed. For the whole subject
was, you must admit, gruesome in the extreme. It was
worthy of Edgar Allan Poe in his most morbid mood —
the lashing rain, the deserted grave-yard, the subtle poison
spreading under the earth, from the dead to the living. I
shuddered and tried to turn my mind to pleasanter things.

But when we had arrived at Miss Bott's cottage, and had
explained to her the purpose of our quest, we found that
she took a far more cheerful and less polite view of the
matter.

'Lord help us!' she cried when she heard the news.
'My old aunt's buried in that graveyard, and if you'd ever
known the old brute you'd wonder that Miss Hazlitt is still
alive.'

Mrs. M. wrinkled her nose. 'We think of purchasing a
filter,' she said, coldly.

'You'd need a damned strong filter for my aunt,' observed Miss Bott. 'You never met her, did you?'

'No, I never did, and if you don't mind, I would prefer not to discuss the subject.'

'Well, I don't see any use being squeamish about it.'

For once in a way, I supported Mrs. M. 'I'm extremely squeamish about it myself,' I said.

Miss Bott shrugged her shoulders. 'All right,' she said. 'But we've all got to die sometime. And go into the earth. And mingle with the soil. Dust to dust, and all that sort of thing.' She turned a shrewd eye on me. 'If you'd had a couple of drinks you'd write one of your purple passages about that, wouldn't you?'

I edged nearer to Mrs. M. 'I don't think so,' I said shortly.

'No? Well, perhaps you wouldn't. Anyway, you can put me down for five bob towards the filter.'

§ I V

And now at last, the stores can open.

I had spent a feverish two hours, the night before the opening, helping Miss Hazlitt to get everything in order. I cannot say that we had been very successful. The accounts, for one thing, were in a terrible muddle. But they could be straightened out later. What really worried me was the chaos among the provisions themselves. Packets of tea jostled lamp-mantles, and bars of chocolate were in dangerous proximity to bottles of eucalyptus oil.

The first thing we did was to put all the patent medicines together, and call them The Drug Department. This was great fun. We made a pyramid of Tooth and Nerve Drops, and arranged a little circle of dandelion pills underneath.

What dandelion pills did to one, I have no idea, but they were always in evidence at village shops, so presumably they must do something fairly drastic.

Then we got busy with the confectionery, and I spent a good half-hour arranging bottles of 'rum fancies', 'tangerine delights', and 'mint humbugs'. It was curiously satisfying to dip a scooper into a big bottle of crisp mixed fruit drops, and pour it into the tray on the scales. Two ounces cost a penny, and you got heaps of fruit drops for a penny. Usually the scales refused to balance, and you had to take out a pear-drop to make it right. And then, in a fit of generosity you put the pear-drop back again, so that the customer (who still existed only in our imagination) got extra value for his money.

It was nearly midnight before I left the shop. Poor Miss Hazlitt looked tired out. But she would soon get used to it, she said, and she was sure that she would be able to manage. And she was so thankful for the way in which her life was being guarded. . . .

I left her, and her quiet blessing rang in my ears as I trudged home. Lord — it was cold. The air had the savour of snow in it. I hoped it would not snow to-morrow.

§ v

It did not snow. Nor did it rain. It was a bright, sunny day. The sort of day that tempts people out to buy.

I had promised to be at the shop for the opening. Actually, I was there about ten minutes before. But I was not the first. Undine was already prowling round behind the counter, in a state of great excitement.

'She has been *so* kind,' whispered Miss Hazlitt. 'A *huge* order.' She was holding in her hand a list of various provisions which Undine had written down, in purple ink. I glanced hastily at the list and saw that it contained a number of items of a comparatively exotic nature, which were not in stock, such as tomato juice cocktails and stuffed olives. I made a mental note to write at once to Fortnum and Masons for these delicacies.

'I *can't* bear the suspense,' gurgled Undine. 'Couldn't we open the door now?'

Miss Hazlitt shook her head. 'Not until nine,' she said. She was unexpectedly firm about this, and she also gently exerted her authority to shoo Undine from behind the counter. I was glad to see this — for Miss Hazlitt was bound to have to deal with difficult customers, sometimes.

We watched from the sitting-room window.

'I should have thought there would have been a *queue*,' said Undine, a little indignantly.

'It's not nine yet.'

'Yes it is.' At precisely that moment the church clock pealed the hour. At the ninth stroke Miss Hazlitt drew the bolts of the front door.

The shop was open!

§ V I

Half an hour later, the shop was still open, but nobody had been in.

'Really,' said Undine, 'it's *quite* monstrous! Do you think they *know*? Or are they all dead? Or is there some *appalling* intrigue?'

'You can't expect very much before ten,' I said. But I too, was very disappointed. Curiosity alone, one would have imagined, would have brought some of the villagers to Miss Hazlitt's shop.

'But crowds of people have been going by, and they haven't even looked in at the window.'

'Oh come . . . not crowds! Only the two boys from the farm, and Miss Grant, and her dog, twice.'

'Anyway I shall go mad if I sit here any longer. I shall go and buy one of those *frightening* sticks of liquorice.'

She got up and was just going into the shop when the door bell pealed violently, and she rushed back again.

'It's started!' She clung to me, trembling with excitement.

We peered through a crack in the door, and we saw . . .

It is odd how certain scenes, of no intrinsic significance, remain silhouetted in one's memory for all time. The scene I saw then had that quality. I remember the shaft of wintry sunlight, falling on the counter, and glinting on Miss Hazlitt's spectacles. I remember each detail of the brightly coloured rows of tins and bottles and cartons, and how the rolls of string, suspended from the ceiling, were still swaying in the cold wind that had blown in as the door opened. Most of all I remember the face of the woman who stood there.

She looked like a gipsy. She was holding a very tiny baby in the hollow of her arm. A shawl was flung round her head. She looked cold, and her hands were red. But all these things were unimportant details. For her face was one of the most beautiful faces I have ever seen.

'Oh . . . *oh* . . .' whispered Undine tensely, '. . . it's Garbo!'

And indeed, at that moment, it was. The same lovely neck, like the stem of a flower, the same violet-lidded eyes, the same queer twist to the lips — slanting them away from perfection to a subtler beauty.

'Ssh!'

What would this exquisite creature say? What would she demand. We had not long to wait.

A very high, shrill voice echoed through the shop.

'Box of head and stomach, please!'

I blinked. I looked again. She was lovelier than ever. A faint smiled hovered around the mysterious mouth, the sort of smile which Garbo always assumes when about to drink some peculiarly significant toast. And all for a 'box of head and stomach'. Pills, I hasten to add. It was mortifying. Such a Being ought not to have a stomach. She ought to have only a head. And a Body. I suppose that means she would have to have a stomach too, but one would forget it, or veil it in some way. And never, never would it demand any vulgar pharmaceutical attentions.

I looked at Undine. Her eyes were closed, and her whole being registered Outrage. The expression on her face was one which I have often seen on the faces of very artistic ladies at provincial concerts, when somebody behind them has rumbled, in the middle of a slow movement, or scraped his chair, or rustled his programme. They are showing the rest of the audience what *they* feel about it, how deeply their fine souls are wounded. 'Here we were, in a lovely trance,' they seem to say, 'a trance for which we have paid five shillings plus tax, and this frightful person behind chooses this moment to rumble!' (Or scrape, or rustle, or whatever it is.) They have to show the world what a lot it means to them.

That was how Undine looked at this moment. But the look quickly faded for at that moment the door-bell rang again. Once more the channels of commerce were in full flood.

§ VII

And so the morning passed. I think that in some ways it was one of the happiest mornings I had ever spent. There was so much *music* in it. The sharp clang of the bell, the momentary roar of the wind as the door opened, the slamming of the door and then, soft voices. After which, there would be the high rattle of sweets in a bottle, followed by a tinkle as they were poured into the scales. Or there would be the sound of rice pouring into the scales with a pleasant hiss. And always the murmur of voices, and to finish it off, the chink of money, like the last few staccato chords at the end of a domestic symphony.

When nobody was in the shop we played Miss Hazlitt's old musical box, which was one of her most treasured possessions. It was made in Paris in 1788 and it had eight tunes. I forgot what they all were, but my favourites were Valse des Fleurs, and Menuet Diable. When it played the Valse des Fleurs one had a sense of a very tiny carnival, played by marionettes, who were throwing silver roses, no larger than confetti, into the echoing airs. Up and up spun the roses, their pale petals glittering, and as the valse came to an end a single note sounded, high and sweet, as though the last silver rose had been flung by the last marionette — flung in challenge to the vast darkness of the Future. For the year you must remember, was 1788, which was a year when the silver on the roses was beginning to tarnish, and the marionettes were beginning to move a little jerkily, pulled by rough fingers over which they had no control.

But the Menuet Diable was really the prettiest of all. If this were devils' music the devil must be a charming person.

For his minuet was like a little stream trickling over a worn rock — the notes plashed and glittered as they were struck from the tarnished old cylinder of the musical box. So faint and aery were they that you would say this was only the echo of music — music in a mirror, heard in dim reflection.

By one o'clock Miss Hazlitt had taken seven shillings and twopence, *excluding* Undine's order, and all the other orders which we could safely count on getting from the members of the Hazlitt Relief Committee. This very satisfactory sum was made up as follows:

		£	s.	d.
1.	One box of Head and Stomach pills, purchased by the fair unknown with the suspicious baby	0	0	3
2.	One ounce brandy balls, one-quarter of tea, one tin of 'super' Newfoundland crab, for Mrs. W.	0	1	2

(*N.B.* — This item on the following day was reduced to sevenpence, because the tin of crab was returned by Mrs. W., more in sorrow than in anger. She said the crab, when opened, 'fizzed'. We all agreed that this was the last thing that a properly brought-up crab should do, and the money was returned. Another tin was sold later on, but was also returned, because of its fizzing tendencies. The remaining four tins were then relegated to the outhouse. If any of my readers have a taste for sparkling crab, it might be possible to obtain some for them.)

3. One Queen of the East Henna shampoo, purchased, surprisingly enough, by old Mr. Post, who is quite bald and has, as far as we are aware, no female relations. When he demanded this item Miss Hazlitt asked gently:

'was he *sure* . . . There was no *mistake*?' He   £   s.   d.
had replied, gruffly, that he knew what he
wanted, and the shampoos were hanging on a
card over her head, which closed the conversation. But who or *what* did Mr. Post shampoo? It was very troubling. However, he
paid, for this item, the sum of . . .   0   0   2

4. One book. This was the first book to be
taken from the library, and was a very exciting
sale. A very small boy, origin unknown,
came in, and asked for a book. Miss Hazlitt,
delighted, glided towards the shelf devoted to
religious works, and was about to hand him a
copy of *Little Meg's Lesson*, or some book with
a similar title. She felt that this was a great
'opportunity'. Personally, I doubt the value
of these books for children, because the little
heroes and heroines always seem to be such
frightful prigs, who are in more danger from
adenoids than from the devil. The little boy
evidently thought so too, for he chose, with
great firmness, a book called *The King's
Mistress*. He then wiped his nose on the back
of his hand, paid his twopence, and departed   0   0   2

5. Another box of Head and Stomach pills,
purchased by the same exquisite creature as
before, after an interval of two hours. This
purchase surprised us exceedingly. There
were twelve pills in each box. Surely she
could not have taken them all? Miss Hazlitt
looked at her gravely. 'You have read the
directions — two after each meal?' The girl
nodded, and gave a Mona Lisa smile. Yes,

The Shop

she had read the directions. 'For babies, I £ s. d.
should think *one* would be sufficient,' said
Miss Hazlitt. 'They aren't for biby,' replied
the girl, rocking her child in her arms. Miss
Hazlitt looked at me, through the door, with
puzzled eyes. I am afraid I could not help.
After all the girl might have quantities of
relations with odd heads and peculiar
stomachs, or both. It was not for us to ask.
We were 'in trade'. And so she was given
another box, which she seized as eagerly as if
it were dope. Lord, I thought, as the bell
clanged her departure, supposing it *is* dope?
Supposing it turns her head and does
something frightful to her stomach, and she
takes off all her clothes and stands on her
head in the middle of the lane? What on
earth would one do? However, these were
morbid speculations, and anyway the till was
richer by the sum of   o o 3
6. Three packets of Virginian cigarettes, purchased by three youths, in rapid succession.
I have omitted to mention that we had
gradually weaned away Miss Hazlitt from her
prejudice against tobacco. We began by
reminding her that Sir James Barrie had made
some highly laudatory remarks about a certain
brand, but that did not have much effect. We
then unearthed a number of prominent divines
who were 'devotees of the fragrant weed', to
use one of those pretty expressions so deplored
by modern writers But that did not have
much effect either. Miss Hazlitt had not

much use for 'prominent divines'. She felt   £ s. d.
that the prominence sometimes obscured the
divinity. In the end we chose the simpler and
far more honest argument that tobacco was
sown over the earth by the winds of God, and
that it would not have been sown if it were
evil. Tea, tobacco, coffee—all these things had
sprung up in this strangely coloured world, we
said, for our sustenance and our pleasure.

And I finished it off by saying 'Anyway, I
like it, and if anybody tries to stop me smoking
I shall take to drink'.

At which Miss Hazlitt had frowned. But
there was a twinkle in her eyes. And she
signed an order for a large quantity of
cigarettes and shag. *Not* made from 'herbs',
but from good, honest Virginian tobacco.

The three youths purchased a packet each,
making . . .   o   3   o

The last purchase was a couple of tins of
asparagus for the vicarage, at one and a
penny each. There seems nothing very epoch-
making to say about this, and so we shall just
put it down as   o   2   2

And that was how the shop began.

Would it pay?

Would the village 'respond'?

Would they come to Miss Hazlitt for their medicines,
their sweets, their toys for special occasions, their groceries
for the daily round?

Time alone could answer these questions. In the
meanwhile, you must agree, it was all great fun.

If it could only last. . . .

CHAPTER XII

THE LOST WINDOWS

WE all agreed that for some months we could not expect to form any definite conclusions about Miss Hazlitt's shop — its success or its failure.

'We must wait till the summer, and the Teas,' said Mrs. M. And we all thought of her nieces, and how they were going to come over to drink tea at the shop. I remember wondering if they were like camels, who could store up vast reserves of tea to last them through the following winter.

'They're bound to *adore* it in time,' said Undine. 'Besides, there are so many side-lines, don't you think? Pottery . . . and things.'

The idea of 'Pottery-and-things' gave me rather a pain. Dreadful little dishes with legends written on their bottoms, like 'There's mair in the kitchen'. All my life I have been pursued by arty little dishes inscribed 'there's mair in the kitchen'. And usually the nourishment placed on these dishes was so repulsive that one hoped that no mair would come out of the kitchen. One had tasted quite enough already thank you.

Anyway, we decided that it was still too early to judge. And even if we had not so decided, the event which now occurred would, I fear, have chased all other thoughts from our minds.

§ I I

It was spring at Allways. And you will forgive me if I suggest that spring at Allways is a little greener, a little more melodious and a little more dramatic than anywhere else.

Dramatic is the only word for the way spring came, that year. For weeks the earth had been icebound, like an empty theatre. Then, suddenly, the lights were turned on, up above. The delicate fingers of the wind switched away the dust sheets of the snow. And the empty arena filled, as though with cloaks and dresses and scarves, in a thousand shades of green. And the orchestra began to tune up. A faint ripple of bird-song in the forest, like the flute that always seems to be having such fun, all on its own, in the orchestra pit. And then more melody, sweet and sudden, from the wood wind, and soon, an exquisite chaos of music . . . a phrase here, and a phrase there, up, down, and sideways . . . the lovely, unorganized music of spring, holding in it the echo of summer dances . . . the rough, fresh music which a man can weave to the patterns of his heart's desire.

Drama, drama everywhere. The spears of the daffodils were thrust through the earth with a single arrogant gesture. Or so it seemed. Like a white scarf thrown over a dancer's shoulders the apple blossom covered the bare boughs. Or so it seemed. You found yourself staring at an empty stage, and suddenly, before your eyes, a transformation scene was taking place.

Or so, as I have said quite often enough, it seemed.

And in the middle of this drama, on a day of whirling winds and flying blossom, Leo appeared. Like a very young clown, or a *poltergeist*, not quite certain of his role, but determined to play his part.

§ III

Leo was Mrs. M.'s nephew.

If there is such a thing as a 'typical schoolboy', Leo was that boy.

'Everybody knows that Napoleon used to stink,' was the first phrase of his which struck me as having any real erudition. But after a little acquaintance with him, I was inclined to discount the historical value of this observation, because I found that Leo, with great amiability, but with equal firmness, invariably asserted that all persons of whom he did not entirely approve were 'stinking'.

'Of course, most of the chaps in my form stink,' he said, mildly, one day.

'Couldn't something be done about it?' I asked earnestly, fearing an epidemic.

'Oh no!' he replied, treading heavily on a clump of white daffodils. 'They're quite decent really. But pretty stinking, too. *You* know.'

I was flattered that he should think I knew. But I didn't. My own boyhood was too far away. The queer usage of words, on the lips of youth, had escaped me. It was enough to know that in Leo's opinion I myself did not 'stink'. Much.

Leo was fair, fifteen, and freckled. His fingers had been stained by an ink that was, apparently, indelible, for it never came off, in spite of Mrs. M.'s constant homilies in favour of pumice-stone.

His main hobby, at the moment, was collecting stamps. It was this hobby which, by devious paths, led to the great adventure of The Lost Windows, and so a word of explanation may be excused.

Leo discovered that I had a fairly extensive correspondence. He had a habit of arriving shortly after breakfast, when the lady from the Post-Office had delivered the mail, and he would fidget about in his chair examining envelopes while I had my coffee.

I remember one morning which was typical.

'I say, that's a shilling New Zealand. New issue. I haven't got that.' He rent the envelope in twain, and stuffed its contents carelessly against the coffee pot.

'Look here, young man. A little more decorum.'

'Why?'

'Somebody's soul may be in that letter.'

An unfortunate remark, for Leo snatched the letter and began to read it. 'I say, this is pretty good, it's from a girl who wants . . .'

I seized the letter. 'Leo, you are very young.'

'Oh sucks!'

'And that's a horrible word.'

'Oh — all right.'

Pause.

Then he said: 'I say, you haven't got any fans in Liberia, have you?'

'Of course, I have quantities of fans in Liberia,' I said, indignantly. 'All Liberia is mad about me.'

'Honestly?'

His eyes were very bright and trusting. 'Honestly?'

'Well . . .' *Had* I any fans in Liberia? I tried to think. A negress had once sent me her photograph, and a fervent appreciation of my pacifist activities, but she had added a PS. requesting a loan of five pounds, which somehow seemed to take the bloom off our little intercourse. And then there were all those societies and Black Brotherhood Associations which one was always being asked to join. But I don't think they had anything to do with Liberia. Better be honest about it. Humbly I said to Leo, 'I'm sorry.

I was mixing up Liberia with somewhere else. I don't think I've got any Liberian fans.'

'Oh Hell.'

'Leo! You can't say "oh Hell" till you go to Oxford.'

'Can't I? I can say a lot worse than that. I can say . . .'

'I'm sure you can. But don't, if you don't mind. I know them all. And they bore me.'

'I say . . . you *are* blasé, aren't you?'

'Incredibly.'

And thus it went on.

All this is leading nowhere, you may think. You would be wrong. For one day, Mrs. M. came to me and said:

'I am really getting quite worried about Leo. He thinks of nothing but stamps.'

'I don't see that that hurts him very much, Mrs. M. Besides, it's teaching him geography.'

'It's teaching him nothing of the sort,' she replied sharply. 'He thinks of it only from the most sordid commercial point of view. Every morning I find sheets spread out on my desk . . .'

'Sheets?'

'Yes, sheets of stamps from various firms. Leo gets twenty-five per cent commission on anything he sells. And to my knowledge, he's sold nearly ten shillings worth in the village, since he arrived.'

'If he's as good as that we'd better give him a job in the shop.'

'*Please!* It looks so strange . . . people will talk. Can't you do anything?'

'For example?'

'Well . . . you know a great deal about the district. Couldn't you take him round and show him a few things? There's Fotheringhay for example. Surely he'd be interested in hearing all about Mary Queen of Scots? I should think that as soon as he saw the royal arms in the pulpit, he would be excited.'

On the other hand, I thought, he might sum up the situation by saying, 'Everybody knows that Mary Queen of Scots used to stink'. However, I did not say that to Mrs. M.

'And Pepys' house. It's only ten miles away. He told me they were doing the diary at school this term. It would make it all so much more real to him.'

I wondered if Pepys' diary was a wise choice for a schoolboy with such a very inquisitive mind as Leo. He might make some very outspoken comments on Pepys' peccadilloes. However, again I held my peace.

'Or if *that* is too much trouble, couldn't you take him to our own church, and tell him a little about it? It mayn't have anything very spectacular about it, but it's full of history. And it's very beautiful.'

'But why don't *you* do it, Mrs. M.?'

'Because,' she said in desperation, 'all he ever talks to me about is stamps, and when am I going to write to my cousin in the Straits Settlements? You see, if I write, she's bound to reply, and then Leo will get the stamp off the envelope. But as she invariably writes the *most* insulting letters, and seems to imagine that she's Queen of England merely because she's married a government official, I *refuse* to start a correspondence just for Leo's sake.'

Mrs. M. looked really harassed. And the idea of anybody having to write to a repellant cousin in the Straits Settlements was so barbaric that I could not allow it. So I promised that I would take Leo round to the church that very evening.

A VILLAGE IN A VALLEY

§IV

And now the curtain goes up on a drama. Slowly, it must be admitted. One of those dramas where you want to cut out the first twenty minutes, because it is all taken up with butlers telephoning and saying, 'I'm very sorry, sir, but her ladyship will not be back till seven'. And young women sitting on sofas, lighting cigarettes and saying, 'Of course, ever since Jim married, I think he's been different somehow, don't you? After all, Ada and he had been so inseparable, and since his mother died, and the house was sold, I often think . . .'

So we'll cut the first half hour, for it was that sort of drama. The church was lovely, the vicar was charming, and supplemented my very sketchy knowledge with a great deal of sound historical detail. But Leo, obviously, was thinking of stamps.

Until, something happened.

It is an important moment in the history of Allways, and I should like you to remember it as I do.

There we were, the three of us, standing in the little church, while the vicar made desultory remarks about this and that. In spite of the wind roaring round it, and in spite of the agitated chirping of birds in the ivy outside the window, the church seemed to be shrouded in silence, so that even against the storm one could hear oneself breathing. Indeed I could hear more than mere breathing. I could hear a wide and hearty yawning from Leo, who was standing just behind me, bored to death.

I turned to Leo and frowned at him. Little did I realize how deeply that frown was going to affect our lives. For it caused him to make a final effort to be polite and to join in the conversation. It caused him, in fact, to ask the question about the glass.

He turned to the vicar, and with a painful politeness, he said, 'Why is there only *one* stained glass window? Why are all the rest plain?'

§ v

The vicar looked at Leo. 'But surely you know why?' he said.

Leo flushed and looked a little sulky. He guessed that he had shown himself ignorant in some awful historical detail. He was about to mutter something when the vicar turned to me. 'Haven't *you* told him?'

It was now my turn to blush. For I had not the faintest idea why all the windows but one were plain. I had merely imagined, vaguely, that there had not been enough money to decorate the others. Besides, whenever I am going over a church with anybody who knows anything about it, I keep grimly silent, for my knowledge of architecture is extremely fluffy.

'They say this dog-tooth ornament is about 1130,' says the guide. One nods with all-embracing amiability, hoping that one is looking at the dog-tooth ornament.

'But of course it isn't,' snaps the guide.

One shakes one's head, a little over-violently, in an endeavour to show how definitely one agrees that the dog-tooth ornament is *not* 1130.

'It must be at least thirty years later,' says the guide. 'Don't you agree?'

You do. Quickly, and sharply. And you leave the dog-tooth ornament with a sigh of relief, only to land in endless

169

complications of 'incipient trefoil arches', 'triforium arches' and the like.

We will go back to our story in half a minute. But first of all let me give one brief tip to all those who, like myself, are occasionally landed in architectural difficulties when exploring old buildings. If the guide asks your opinion about something, look him straight in the eye, and say, in firm tones 'Transitional, of course'. For two reasons. Firstly, because the thing you are looking at nearly always is transitional. Secondly, because transitional means neither one thing nor the other. Neither do you. So there you are.

'Haven't *you* told him?' repeated the vicar.

'I'm ashamed to say I didn't know.'

'What? Not know about the Allways glass?' He looked quite incredulous. Then his face creased into a wrinkled smile. 'Well, well . . . that gives me an opportunity of telling my favourite story.'

And so, he told us. And so, I will tell you. Simply, without any details of scholarship, because I don't know any.

'It was in the time of the Reformation,' he said, 'the time when all the Puritans were tearing the beautiful things out of our old churches, because they thought them a relic of Rome. They thought they savoured of idolatory.'

Leo nodded. He knew *that*, all right. They'd been doing the Reformation in school last year. They'd been doing it so thoroughly that the class had formed itself into rival groups of Roundheads and Cavaliers. Leo, needless to say, had been a Cavalier, and had been the hero of many dialogues such as this:

Leo: You're a Roundhead, so you stink.

Friend: I don't stink nearly as much as you.

Leo: Oh yes you do.

Friend (amiably): No I don't. You're a Cavalier. And everybody knows how much Cavaliers stink.

Leo (amiably): Oh they do, do they? Well, I'll show you, you stinking brute.

'I wouldn't be a Roundhead, not if you gave me a hundred pounds,' said Leo, with much more alacrity than he had previously shown.

'Roundheads . . .' Then he stopped suddenly.

'Yes?' said the vicar.

Leo had been about to say 'Roundheads stink'. But somehow it did not seem right to refer to this unpleasant Roundhead trait in church. So he finished off, a little lamely 'Roundheads are rotten'.

The vicar smiled. 'Well, sometimes,' he said, 'when I see the cruel things they did in our old churches . . . when I see beautifully carved angels with their wings torn off, and mutilated brasses, and old stone images chipped and shattered . . . well, I don't feel too keen on the Roundheads myself. After all, the men who made those things were only praising God, as they saw fit, and there are many ways of praising God. The creation of beautiful things is one way.' And he ran his hand affectionately over the carved end of an old pew, that was shaped like a Tudor rose.

'However,' he continued, 'that's not the point. The point is that once, in Elizabethan times, this church was famous for its lovely old glass. You'll find all sorts of references to it, in contemporary histories and diaries. People who were travelling to Scotland used to turn their horses off the Great North Road specially to see the glass of Allways. It must have been amazingly rich, particularly in a certain shade of blue, which was a local secret. And though there naturally aren't any illustrations of it, one or two phrases about it have crept into local legend. You'll still hear old farmers in the inn talk about a sky being 'blue as Allways glass'. The vicar sighed, and then smiled again. 'At least that's what my father told me. I'm afraid I don't go much to the inn.'

'I'll go to-night,' said Leo, eagerly.

'You will do nothing of the sort,' I observed.

Leo winked at me. Then he said, demurely, to the vicar . . . 'And did the Roundheads smash all the glass?'

'No, it was not smashed. It was . . . taken away.'

'The swine,' said Leo, who was now too worked up to curtail his vocabulary. 'I bet the Roundheads sold it. And got drunk on the money.'

The vicar shook his head. 'No,' he said gravely. 'It was not the Roundheads who took it away. It was the Cavaliers.'

'*What?*'

'They took it away,' said the vicar, 'to save it. Piece by piece, with the greatest reverence. And they hid it, till better days. So that the Roundheads would never be able to destroy it.'

Leo gasped. This *was* a story! 'Hid it? Where?'

'Nobody knows. It cannot have been far from here, for they only had a few hours in which to work. And nobody ever *will* know, because the men who took it were all killed, a few days later, in a skirmish just off the Great North Road.'

Leo's face was brighter than any stained glass saint, with the rapture which this story had filled him.

'You mean to say,' he said breathlessly, 'that all the glass from this church has been lying hidden, somewhere about here, ever since sixteen something?'

The vicar nodded.

'Buried in a field perhaps?' He twirled his cap nervously.

'Or in an old house? In a cellar? Or down a well? Oh *sir!*' He turned from the vicar to me. I caught something of his excitement. Till now it had only been a charming story . . . a legend, with the dust thick about it. But Leo's burning interest infected me. After all, the glass *had* been hidden somewhere. It couldn't have vanished into thin air. For all we knew it was lying under our feet, at this very moment, the blue glass, like a secret pool, waiting for the rocks to be split above it, guarding its strange and lovely colours for some distant sunrise.

'Has nobody ever looked for it?' I asked.

The vicar shook his head. 'Not systematically,' he said. 'Sometimes a farmer ploughs up an old brass plate, or unearths a few carved stones, and then it gets into the local papers, and an archaeologist comes out from Cambridge and does a little spasmodic digging. But we've never found anything of any real interest. I'm afraid we never shall.'

Leo gulped. I realized that he was about to let loose a stream of questions so I said, 'We must be going' and we all shuffled off.

As the vicar was about to latch the door, he turned and stared at the one glass window which remained. The light of the dying sun was shining through it, and across the faces of the saints there danced the reflected shadows of the storm-tossed trees outside, giving to their features a troubled, restless expression, as though there were something which they longed to tell us, but could not, because their lips were imprisoned by the glass.

'And the strange thing about it,' he said, 'the sad thing about it and yet, and yet, in a way, the *happy* thing about it . . . is that when the Roundheads came, they left that solitary window alone. There was only one window . . . the Cavaliers had taken all the rest, so that the wind blew through the empty gaps. But when the Roundheads saw that one window, they left it alone.' He spoke almost to himself. 'I think the sun must have been shining through it, as it is shining now.'

§ VI

Leo and I walked home between hedges that strained and whistled in the rising wind. And Leo did all the talking.

'I'm going to find that glass,' he gulped, holding on to his cap to prevent it being blown away. 'Gee! I bet you anything you like I'm going to find that glass. What'll you bet me? What'll you bet me that I find it? That I find the Allways glass?'

On and on he rambled, with bright eyes and crimson cheeks, splashing heedlessly through the puddles in the road. I forgot what I had bet him. I was a little anxious about this new excitement, and the effects it might have on Mrs. M.'s carefully ordered life.

But I remember, after I had seen him home, and had walked down the lane to my cottage, standing outside the door for a moment, and letting the wind blow on my face. It was a tremendous, galloping wind . . . a wind that would take a valley in its stride and ruffle a forty-acre field with a single puff from its titanic lungs. Shelley must have looked on some such sky as this when he wrote:

Thou on whose stream, 'mid the steep sky's commotion,
Loose clouds like earth's decaying leaves are shed,
Shook from the tangled boughs of Heaven and Ocean . . .

The clouds gathered fast. But there was still a patch of blue over the western hill. A strange patch of blue, almost square, with the clouds streaming past it, like blowing curtains. A patch of blue that made me think of a window, the window of an old church.

§ v i i

The storm broke that night, and though there was little sleep for most of us, I did not care. For there are not many better things in life than to lie in bed, in a sturdily timbered room, under a thatched roof, while one's own garden thirstily drinks the welcome rain, and the wind whistles down the chimney, and under the crack in the door.

It is at moments like this that one is inclined to count over one's blessings.

I lie back in bed. The lightning stabs the earth's breast, with a brilliant blade. I count. One, two, three, four five . . . bang . . . the thunder is just overhead. Never mind if it strikes. It would be a good way to die.

I count my blessings. No frightful diseases. That is obviously a strong point. No lumps, spots, croakings or other beastlinesses. I put out my hand to touch wood.

Still fairly young. Young enough, at any rate, for it to be worth my while to plant trees that won't be particularly impressive for thirty years. It is odd how one gets over the fear of growing old, after the first flush of youth has gone. The only thing I worry about, in this age question, is the fact that one day I shall reach an age when I shan't be able to look thirty years ahead in my garden. That will be rather a bitter day. Because all gardeners want to look thirty years ahead. But perhaps, by that time, I shall be married and have a family, with lots of frightful little boys who want their noses wiped, and trample on the new delphiniums.

More blessings. Money. (Good, that last lightning flash was comparatively mild. And the thunder's moving away, like a lion retreating.) Money . . . not very much, but better than it's ever been before. Probably it will all be taken away from me, or will be worth nothing, just when I have written my last word, and feel the time has come to sit back and watch the flowers unfolding. However, that is a morbid thought. The only fact that matters is that there *is* money in the bank. It has accumulated there, mysteriously, because every day I lock myself up in a room and guide my pen over sheets of paper, and then sell those sheets of paper. That, you will agree, is an exceedingly peculiar way of earning one's living. Making odd scrawls on a sheet of paper . . . rather ugly, hurried scrawls, blotched over, scratched out, very painfully erased and amended . . . and then, exchanging those scrawls for beautiful, tangible things, like tulip bulbs, and shelled walnuts, and bottles of mysterious, dusty and exquisitely fragrant Chablis! Very odd indeed. But then, the minute any man except the farm labourer begins to ponder the sources of his income, he will feel inclined to hang his head in shame, unless he is a charlatan, or a stockbroker.

The storm raged, the lightning grew fainter and fainter, till it was only the flash of a distant blade, drawn by a dark horseman over the hills. The thunder growled ever farther away . . . till its growl was almost a blessing, like the purr of a gigantic velvety cat, prowling the fields and forests. And when I woke up in the morning, the sky was a stainless blue, the blue of a glass window, waiting for a master-craftsman to decorate it with the silver wings of the clouds.

§ VIII

But though the thunderstorm had passed over Allways, the other storm had only just begun.

For a few days after the vicar had told us his story, I did not see Leo. Indeed I forgot all about him. For there comes a time in spring, just about the sixteenth of April, when everything in the garden seems to happen at once. You go out after breakfast and make at least six discoveries . . . the first pear blossom is out, a clump of jonquils has suddenly danced into view, a white tulip is just opening its eyes, the japonica is dressed to kill, all the may is bursting green, and the copper-beech, which you thought was dead, is indignantly denying the fact with a hundred buds. Then, just before luncheon you go out again, and do another tour, and make even more sensational discoveries than before. You go in, feeling slightly dazed, and eat luncheon, and then if the sun is still shining you reconcile yourself to the fact that you will have to spend the whole of the rest of the day going round and round the garden. And however quickly you go round there will always be something new to meet you at the end.

Well, there *was* something new to meet me at the end of one of these tours which I was making. No — not new. A very old friend indeed . . . Mrs. M.

But she did not look at all friendly as she walked down my garden path.

'I thought,' she said acidly, 'that you were supposed to have a *good* influence upon modern youth.'

This astonishing accusation momentarily floored me. 'Well . . .'

'All I can say is, you've had anything but a good influence on Leo.'

'Leo? Why I haven't seen him for three days.'

'No? Well, it didn't take him three days to destroy my asparagus bed.'

'But . . . but what's that got to do with me?'

Mrs. M. was so heated that she ignored my question. 'I don't suppose,' she continued, with a rising intonation, 'that I shall have an ounce of horseradish this year. Not an ounce. The seakale bed is carnage. Absolute *carnage*. Fortunately I stopped him from doing any very serious damage to the raspberry canes, just in time.'

I stared at Mrs. M. Had she gone mad? Or had Leo suddenly run amok?

'I don't understand,' I said coldly. 'He always seemed a very polite little boy, as little boys go.'

'He was, until you put those absurd ideas into his head.'

'What ideas?'

'About the buried glass!'

'Oh!' I blinked. 'Oh!' And then, I am ashamed to say, I began to laugh. Loud and long. Mrs. M. stood beside me, occasionally projecting her rabbit's teeth, and prodding her stick angrily into the ground. It was a long time before I felt able to reply to her with propriety.

So Leo had been digging up Mrs. M.'s asparagus bed in the hope of finding the glass! And running riot among her horseradish! Oh Lord . . . this was a little too good to be true. I didn't know how to conciliate Mrs. M., so I bribed her instead. I said, firstly, that I would go and see Leo myself, and tell him to stop this nonsense. And secondly, I promised her some roots of my iris stylosa, which she had long been coveting.

Even so, as we went out, she made a typically Mrs. M. remark. She passed a massed clump of grape hyacinths, which were just on the point of coming into bloom under

178

the big plum tree. 'Were those good this year?' she asked casually.

If you are not a gardener you will not understand the monstrousness of that remark. *Were* they good! Implying that they were so feeble that Mrs. M. thought they were already over. Implying that Mrs. M.'s *were* over, anyway, and had been flowering weeks before mine.

Implying, almost, what Leo said about Mrs. M. at the end of a heated and quite fruitless interview with him in the tool-shed. For Leo, who was still filled with a fierce determination to dig up the whole of Huntingdonshire for the buried glass, brought the whole argument to a conclusion by observing, with elderly sang-froid:

'She stinks.'

CHAPTER XIII

WOMEN IN SHADOW

THERE came a morning in May when Leo's belongings were packed up, and he returned to school. It seemed that the whole of Allways had contributed something to his 'playbox', for in spite of his language, and his habit of treading, like a young bison, on all our most precious clumps of bulbs, he had greatly endeared himself to us.

How the 'playbox' was ever packed, I cannot imagine, for it contained, in addition to three stamp-albums (loose-leaved variety), a larger quantity of sweetmeats than most of us could consume in a year. There were, for example, twelve pots of vegetable-marrow jam from Mrs. M.

'It stinks, but I shall swop it with a new bug,' said Leo. This mysterious phrase, being interpreted, meant, firstly, that the jam was not to Leo's taste, and secondly that he proposed to effect an exchange with a new boy, either by persuasion or by torture. Knowing Leo, I had not much doubt which course he would pursue.

There were quantities of things from Undine too, including a bottle of brandied cherries, on which Leo hoped to get 'squiffy'. Also an electric light set from the Professor, a home-made cake from Miss Bott, and various oddments from me.

And at the last moment Miss Hazlitt had sent a tin of chocolate-covered puff cracknels — a terrifying form of biscuit, which exploded in all directions when bitten.

'Don't eat them all at once,' I said to Leo, 'or you may explode too.'

WOMEN IN SHADOW

'I shan't eat them at all,' he said, 'I shall swop them'.
Whereupon he put one in his pocket.

'Leo, take that out of your pocket at once. It'll melt.'

'No, it won't.'

'But you *can't* want a chocolate puff cracknel in the train.'

'No, but I might meet somebody who did, see?'

'I don't see, at all.'

'B., you old stinker, this is for swops. You never know
your luck. I might get in with a man who had his pockets
full of triangular Capes. And if I did . . .'

Actually, he got in, not with a man, but with a lady of
uncertain age, who looked very like a triangular Cape
herself. For one wild moment I thought I should get into
the carriage too. It would have been worth a good deal
more than a railway ticket to see Leo offering a damp and
extremely sickly sweetmeat to that ice-bound female.
However, common sense made me refrain from the adventure. It usually does, damn it.

The train vanished on the flat horizon, tossing garlands
of smoke in its wake, white garlands that floated away into
the cloudless wastes above.

I wondered if life would be dull, now that Leo had gone.
But the wonder was short-lived. How could life be dull at
Allways when even the toy station — (which, I should
observe, is a good five miles from the village) — was so
full of excitements? For example, there was a huge crate for
the Professor in the waiting-room, and I wondered if it
was his new refrigerator. He had invented a patent refrigerator, which from his description, would appear to
freeze an elephant in about five minutes. I hoped it would
be better than his last one, which was run by paraffin.
Instead of freezing anything, it had caught fire and nearly
destroyed the cottage.

181

There was also a large crate for Mrs. M., from a well-known nurseryman. I was just able to peep through the cracks, and saw something that looked very like fuchsias, just breaking into bloom. And I remembered a chance remark she had made to me, a week ago, about her fuchsias . . . 'You *must* come and see them soon . . . in a week they'll be a perfect picture . . . but they're not quite ready yet.'

'But how do you get fuchsias in May, Mrs. M.?'

'Ah!' she had gurgled. 'That's my secret.'

Now, it would seem, it was my secret too. I tried to peer a little more closely into the crate, but it was impossible to be certain about its contents. However, I was almost certain that those pink blobs, faintly seen through the tissue paper, were fuchsias.

'Not quite ready, yet!' Really, the duplicity of women baffled me. I felt like ordering a cartload of orchids, and pinning them to the boughs of the damson trees outside my study, and letting loose a few crates of humming birds among them and then asking Mrs. M. to tea. And then, above the din of the humming birds I would yell at her 'Quite tropical, aren't we, Mrs. M.?'

The duplicity of women! We shall have more to say on that subject in a moment. But we shall say it in a different tone. . . .

§ 11

I had indeed been wrong in suspecting that life could possibly be dull at Allways — Leo or no Leo. His departure far from diminishing the interest in the lost glass, seemed actually to intensify it. A fresh zest was imparted to all digging operations. When old Miss Grant sank a new well, the piles of clay which were piled in the adjoining field were examined as eagerly as if a vein of gold had been located beneath her spring cabbages. And when fate ordained that two new graves were dug in the churchyard, the vicar could have been able to obtain the services of the grave-diggers free of charge, so certain was everybody that the glass was about to be found.

Even Miss Bott joined in the hue and cry. When I walked down to the post office one evening, a few days after Leo had begun his activities, I passed her back garden and saw her standing in the middle of a vast assortment of old tin cans. There was Heinz's tomato soup, Campbell's vegetable soup, Libby's asparagus, Heinz's oxtail, and quantities of an obscure Newfoundland firm's 'crab salad', for which she had an unholy passion. One day I hope to be bold enough to tell her that I am quite certain that her prediliction for tinned crab salad is responsible for the spots she invariably gets during the months of July and August, when her consumption of crab-meat is most intense.

'Not a hope,' barked Miss Bott, holding up a very mouldy can of W's baked beans.

It was quite unnecessary for me to ask whether she was referring to the glass. So I said, 'You wouldn't expect to find it in W's Baked Beans?'

'I'd expect to find anything in W's Baked Beans,' she replied, tersely. And then chanted:

> 'What time the evening shadows fall
> When darker forms of doubt appal. . . .'

There seemed every reason for darker forms of doubt to appal, when peering into a mouldy can of W's Baked Beans.

'Do stop that. It's idiotic of you. You can't be looking for the glass.'

'No. I'm not.'

She spoke oddly . . . huskily.

'Then what are you doing?'

'Passing the time, young man.' She threw down a tin on to the heap. It made an ugly clatter. She paused, and then walked stockily towards me. Her face looked strangely drawn, and her eyes were very bright. 'Passing the time.'

I stared at her for a moment, and then looked away. Something rather terrible seemed to be shadowed in her eyes. Something . . . hunted. Or was it . . . hunting? All I know is that I felt restless and uncomfortable. I had been happy a moment before . . . happy in the quietness of an October day. And now I was unhappy.

'I'm growing old.' Her voice had a sudden ghastly cheerfulness. 'That's what it is. The falling leaf . . . change and decay.' And then abruptly. 'Are you doing anything this evening.'

'I'm afraid I've got to go back.'

'London?'

'Honestly.'

She kicked a can in sudden irritation. 'You needn't make such a point of the honesty. I don't want witnesses!'

I looked at her quickly. Why had she said that? It was a horrible thing to say.

For a moment our eyes met. Then she looked away. 'You'd better go on, and post those letters,' she said.

I went on. At the corner, I looked back. She was standing in exactly the same attitude, her hands thrust deep in the pockets of her old tailor-made coat. A mournful whistle drifted down the lane. . . .

'Jerusalem the Golden
With milk and honey blest. . . .'

There she stood, with the late sunlight splintering on the old tin cans.

§ III

I forgot to post the letters. I walked on and on, thinking of the thousands of women like Miss Bott, women who lived alone, on little incomes, 'passing the time'.

I remembered a conversation I once heard, between two light-hearted girls of the village, over the hedge.

'I wonder why she never married?'

'What, old Miss *Bott?*'

'She might have been pretty once.'

'Go on . . . you're kidding!'

'I'm not kidding. I tell you she might have been pretty once.'

I walked on.

By a queer trick of the mind, I suddenly began to think of that strange literary confession which Arnold Bennett made, when he was telling how he had received the inspiration for *The Old Wives' Tale.* He had been travelling in a bus. And suddenly, a fat, oldish woman had entered the bus, and had dropped a parcel, and was nervous, and fussy and a little ridiculous. As he looked at her, something happened and it seemed as though the years were lifted, and he saw her through a mist. She was no longer fat, nor old . . . she was slim, and young. 'You were desirable, once . . . you were utterly desirable!' The mist lifted. The old woman had picked up her parcels, and was very red in the face, and there were tears in her eyes. That was how *The Old Wives' Tale* was born.

I thought of the supreme passage in it, a passage which puts Bennett, for a brief space, among the immortals. It is where Sophia, now old and haggard, who had been so slim and radiant, gazes, after many years, on the dead body of the husband who had so long deserted her. In its soaring simplicity this passage is supreme:

> 'By the corner of her eye, reflected in the mirror of a wardrobe near the bed, she glimpsed a tall, forlorn woman, who had once been young and now was old. He and she had once loved and burned and quarrelled in the glittering and scornful pride of youth. But time had worn them out. "Yet a little while," she thought, "and I shall be lying on a bed like that! And what shall I have lived for? What is the meaning of it?" The riddle of life itself was killing her and she seemed to drown in a sea of inexpressible sorrow.'

Sophia was utterly lonely. Miss Bott was utterly lonely. Utter loneliness must be the ultimate hell, I think. It must be like living in a desert where there is not a single green thing to give you shadow and shelter. To know . . . not merely to fear, but to *know* . . . that never, when the postman comes in the morning, will there be a letter from anybody who needs you, needs you vitally, as flowers thirst for water. To know . . . every time you look in the glass, that it is quite ridiculous to suppose that you can ever command love that has in it any element of the physical — all that's gone, long ago, and you have too much common sense to believe that you can bring back the days of dew and dreams by dropping some patent mixture into your eyes, or the days of April by dyeing your hair. You have too much common sense. That is one of the horrible things about it. It gives you an inferiority complex, makes you suspect that there is something tainted in even the purest friendship, makes you awkward, shrinking, hostile, even to those who might be your friends.

I thanked my stars I was a man. These things don't seem to matter so much for a man. At any rate, men who look to me as if they had escaped from a home for elderly monkeys seem, somehow, to be able to inspire the most ardent feelings in girls who are not only sane but beautiful . . . you see them all over the place, the middle-aged monkey-men and the girls.

§ I V

However, these are morbid speculations. If one were to peer behind every doorway in even so tiny a village as Allways, one would often find too heavy a load of sorrow for any man to bear.

The amazing thing is the lightness, the careless grace with which the sorrow is borne. For most of the women of Allways show a bright face to the world, even when their hearts are heavy. Their lives are like their gardens. Even the poorest of them, who can only afford a handful of bulbs, and cannot possibly pay to have an odd man, even once a week, always manage to have the little strip of garden, in the front of their cottages, bright with flowers all the year round, and as tidy as if it were run by the most efficient gardener. They are like those women living in mean streets whose front windows are draped with the costliest lace curtains they can afford, while the rooms those curtains shadow are almost bare.

It is very easy to sneer at the women who have this passion for 'keeping up appearances'. Very easy indeed. But neither very clever nor very kind.

However, lest you should imagine that Allways is inhabited only by angels, I shall now be forced to tell you about a woman who was very much the reverse.

CHAPTER XIV

TROUBLE DOWNSTAIRS

GRADUALLY, the fever of the search for the glass abated. True, it was always at the back of our minds, and we all had an uncanny feeling — which was afterwards dramatically justified by the events — that we had not heard the last of it. But for the moment, as a topic of conversation it lapsed into the background.

Perhaps it was the heat which made us a little diffident about undertaking any digging which was not strictly necessary. For this was the first year in which the English climate decided to emulate that of the Sahara. It has been doing it now for three years running, and I, in common with most of the inhabitants of Allways, have decided that if it does it again we shall give up trying to grow anything but cactuses. We are tired of seeing our roses turned into pot-pourri, by the sun, as soon as they open, and if the cracks in our herbaceous borders grow any wider we shall fall into them, and be lost.

But in those days, the heat and the drought were novelties. Most of us bore these trials cheerfully, saying 'it's bound to rain soon' or 'don't you think it's really a little cooler this evening, quite a breeze, don't you think?' We said these things, not thinking them at all, to keep up our spirits. But there were some people who did not say them, and those were the domestic servants. I don't blame them. I only chronicle the fact. Mine was the only household, that summer, which was untroubled by any signs of domestic unrest.

Though I had no domestic worries of my own, there came a day when, for reasons which are of no general interest, I had to shut up my cottage for a month. And as I could not bear to be away from the garden for so long a period at this time of the year, I accepted the Professor's kind invitation to go up and stay with him for the last fortnight.

It was here that I made the acquaintance of the Professor's Mrs. Drag. And I think she deserves a permanent niche in the great Gallery of Domestic Tyrants . . . a gallery down which every housewife has to make her tragic progress.

The first thing to realize about Mrs. Drag was that she was not Mrs. Drag. She was Miss Drag. She had adopted the title of 'Mrs.' after the custom of cooks in large households, who seem to imagine that the married state is in some way helpful to the culinary art. I have never been able to understand why this should be, because one would have thought that it would be possible to make a soufflé in a state of complete virginity. But this view, apparently, is not shared in the servants' hall.

The second thing to realize about Mrs. Drag is that she was one of the few women I have ever met who desired to be taken for older than she really was. Mrs. Drag, actually, was thirty. But she had snow-white hair — the sort of hair which, if its owner has five thousand a year, causes her friends to comment upon her resemblance to a French marquise. (Why do all wives of French marquesses have snow-white hair, according to popular legend? Are French marquesses so very trying to live with?)

The third thing to realize about Mrs. Drag is that the reason she wished to be thought older than she really was is because she was the most damnably lazy woman who ever had the effrontery to take good money from a defence-less bachelor. And, speaking as a defenceless bachelor, I can assure you that this means that she must have been pretty bad.

However, it was not till I went to stay with the Professor that the full evil of Mrs. Drag was made manifest.

§ II

It began with some mayonnaise sauce. Or rather, it began without some mayonnaise sauce.

A slight recapitulation is necessary.

Both the Professor and I had been away from Allways for ten days, and we arranged to motor up together.

As he got into the car, the Professor put a large box on to the back seat.

'That is the salmon,' he said. 'And some strawberries.'

I made appropriate sounds of approval.

'The salmon is cooked,' he said. 'I wrote and told Mrs. Drag that I would be bringing it, and she asked that it should be cooked, so that she would be able to manage.'

'Manage what?'

The Professor looked a little embarrassed. 'Oh — manage,' he said. And then added, with a sigh, 'I'm afraid I'm a great trial to her.'

I was about to comment, somewhat hotly, upon this absurd self-accusation, when I reflected that it was hardly my position to do so, as a guest. Besides, although I had long suspected that Mrs. Drag was imposing on the Professor, it was a little difficult to be quite certain about it, because the Professor's habits were not as other men's. If one heard that an ordinary bachelor dined constantly off tinned things — tinned herrings, tinned tongue, tinned vegetable soup, tinned lobster, tinned fruit salad, and all the other dreary make-shifts which are the fate of that large section of the population which has no servants to prepare food for it — one would have come to the conclusion that his housekeeper was extremely lazy. But one could not say this about the Professor, because he had meals at such odd times, and very often he forgot to eat at all. This was not affectation on his part. He really did completely forget that he had not 'put things into a hole in his head', as he described it.

It was the same with the question of cleanliness.

If the rooms of an ordinary bachelor were thick with dust, if the ash-trays had obviously not been washed for weeks, if there were spiders' webs on the beams, and stains on the brass, and so much wood-ash on the open fire that it would not draw properly, one would have said that his housekeeper was a . . . well, that is what *I* should have said. But how could one be quite sure that it was not the Professor's fault?

For all over his cottage were piles of dusty papers with DO NOT TOUCH written on the top sheet, followed by the picture of an animal.

The Professor drew animals all over his notes. Very crudely drawn cats, with huge whiskers, peered out of the corners of abstruse geometrical problems. Snakes protruded forked tongues through a thick undergrowth of arithmetical calculations. And on each piece of paper which bore the words DO NOT TOUCH, there was an animal.

Mrs. M. thought it 'in very poor taste' when she once called on the Professor and saw a huge bundle of papers on the hall table, with the words DO NOT TOUCH written across an elephant's behind.

§ I I I

We arrived at Allways at half-past eleven. As I stood in the hall I heard the Professor asking Mrs. Drag, very politely, if we might have lunch at one.

In reply to this comparatively reasonable request I heard a long and querulous plaint which ended with the sinister words:

'There isn't a *staff* in this house!'

I stood in the hall straining my ears. The Professor spoke again. And once more the long plaint began, in a mumble which I could not quite catch. But the last words came with the utmost clarity . . . 'There isn't a *staff* in this house!'

So that was how the land lay! No staff! That was Mrs. Drag's technique of attack. She was a poor oppressed woman, slaving all the week, getting up her strength to open the Professor's tin of herrings, without a staff to help her. Wretched, battered, tortured creature! No staff!

In the disgraceful absence of a staff, I carried up my suit-case to my room.

I met the Professor in the hall. And it is here that the real leitmotif of Mrs. Drag begins.

§ I V

The Professor looked scared and pale.

'She says that everything has been going black before her,' he said.

I blinked at him. For a moment I had forgotten Mrs. Drag. It had been such fun wandering round my bedroom — peering at the old daguerreotypes on the mantelpiece, the lady with corkscrew curls, the Victorian pater familias standing with a shame-faced expression by the side of fourteen children, as though he were about to say, 'I really wasn't *solely* responsible for all these'. And then there had been a chestnut tree outside my window, a whopper of a chestnut tree, with a vast arm on to which I could have stepped from the window itself, and crawled along it, and laid myself flat over the pools of delphiniums which had gathered in the Professor's herbaceous border. Indeed, I had made a secret plan to do so, early the next morning. It would have been grand to lie on the limb of a chestnut tree, looking down on to pools of delphiniums. One would have been able to narrow one's eyes, and think of the sea, and sniff the morning air, and think of breakfast, and crawl back again, and curse oneself for covering one's trousers with green mould.

So when I heard that strange remark . . . 'She says that everything has been going black before her . . .' I said 'Who says that everything has been going black before what?' And then I realized what he was talking about.

'Oh, Mrs. Drag?'

'Yes.'

'Black? Everything going black?'

'Yes. That's what she said. I expect it's the heat, don't you?'

'She *looks* as strong as a horse.'

'It is very hot though,' sighed the Professor. Then he added, 'She said that everything went black before the odd man too, yesterday'.

'That's nothing new with him,' I observed bitterly. 'Whenever he comes out of the pub, everything goes *quite* black before him.'

The Professor blinked. 'Anyway,' he said, 'let's go in to lunch.'

We went in. Mrs. Drag entered with the salmon. I observed her, covertly. She looked like an advertisement for Bovril, from the health point of view. But morally, she looked like an advertisement for those ladies who have not got an electrical washing machine, or do not use Rinso, or suffer from 'night-starvation'. Scowling, fretful, harassed. You know the sort of thing — it is composed of four pictures. The first shows Ada (who has no washing machine) leaning back exhausted in her chair.

To Ada, enters Minnie. Minnie *has* a washing machine, and in consequence she has also a grin like a Cheshire cat, and appears to be dressed by Molyneux.

The following alluring dialogue then occurs:

Minnie: Why, Ada darling, you look terrible. What is the matter? Why aren't you out and about on this glorious spring morning?

Ada (helplessly): Oh . . . it's this dreadful washing day. I shall never get finished.

Minnie: But darling, look at me! (Ada does so, with conspicuous loathing.) I did *all* our washing before breakfast in twenty minutes. I *adored* it. And I'm just off to lunch at the Ritz.

That is the end of Tableau One. Tableau Two is short and sharp. It shows Minnie breathing heavily into Ada's ear, and whispering, 'What *you* want is a new Super-Vladivostok Washing Machine'.

Personally, I have a shrewd suspicion that Ada wants something very, very different, and wants it very, very badly. But she takes Minnie's advice. And Tableau Three shows us a new Ada, waltzing round the Vladivostok Washing Machine, with a balloon coming out of her mouth on which is written the welcome news, 'I feel a different woman now I've got a Super-Vladivostok Washing Machine. All my woollens are washed like magic, and Jim says he never slept between such snowy sheets'. She says all that to herself, alone in the wash-room, so the Super-Vladivostok evidently encourages conversation as well as cleanliness.

Tableau Four shows the interior of an enormous Rolls-Royce. Ada is in deepest evening dress, smothered in orchids, and Jim, in equally deep evening dress, is leaning over her, apparently biting her on the ear. But he cannot be biting very hard, for out of his mouth a balloon is coming, on which is written, 'Ada, darling, you are like a fairy to-night. What is your secret?'

And Ada, taking a deep breath, and fluttering her lids, softly breathes, 'Nothing but the Super-Vladivostok machine, precious, it washes curtains, silks, laces, undies, and woollens, with equal ease, and no really modern housewife can afford to be without it.'

After which, let us hope, Jim really does bite her on the ear, hard.

§ v

Mrs. Drag's face then, was the face of Ada in Tableau One. And I was very glad when it had vanished from the room.

But as soon as she had gone, the Professor, who had helped me to some salmon, looked round vaguely and said: 'I don't see the mayonnaise sauce.'

I looked around, and did not see it either. 'I expect she's forgotten it. I'll ring.'

I got up to go to the bell.

The Professor spoke with considerable agitation. 'Oh — I don't think I'd ring,' he said.

'Why not?'

'Well . . .' He paused. And then added, in a weak voice, 'I don't mind doing without, if you don't'.

'Is that the reason why I mustn't ring.'

'Well . . . perhaps Mrs. Drag hasn't made any.'

'Why not?'

'She mayn't have had the time. Besides she mayn't have been very well. She said that everything went black . . .'

I was rude enough to interrupt the Professor. 'Now, listen. We've both been away for ten days. Mrs. Drag has had exactly ten days in which to let everything go black before her.' I ran my finger over the dusty table, drew the Professor's attention to the line it left, and observed that she *had* let everything 'go black', quite literally.

'But that's beside the point,' I said. 'Ten days really *is* enough for one woman to make two beds and a little mayonnaise sauce. She could make one bed on Monday, and then lie back and let everything go black before her till the following Thursday. *Then* she could make the other bed . . . after which, I suppose, everything could go black again. Then round about last Monday, she might have begun to think about making the mayonnaise sauce. And after she'd got over breaking an egg or two, and coped with the blackness which *that* effort must have entailed, she might possibly have staggered over with some butter, or milk, or whatever one puts in mayonnaise sauce, mixed it, and then have gone into a long, deep swoon of blackness.'

'There *may* be something organic.'

'You know there's nothing of the sort,' I replied, almost angrily. 'You're just being a damned coward.'

'I'm afraid I am.'

'Very well then. I shall ring the bell.'

And before the Professor could protest, I rang it.

We waited.

We waited a very long time. Not in silence, because there was the sound of muffled bangings and crashings in the kitchen.

Strange thoughts flew through my head. Had the mere sound of the bell made everything go black before Mrs. Drag? And was she trying to grope her way towards us in the dark? The thought was a little alarming — I could almost see her crawling on all fours, emerging through the door like some large hostile animal, and glaring through sightless eyes.

But suddenly she appeared. And she was not in the least crawling. She was standing proudly, almost haughtily, erect.

Politely I said, 'Oh Mrs. Drag, I think you've forgotten the mayonnaise sauce.

She stared at me. 'Pardon?'

The Professor gave her an agonized blink. 'Mr. Nichols rather thought . . .' he said, '. . . there might be some mayonnaise sauce?' And then he blinked very rapidly at the salmon, which seemed to him, at the moment, about the only object in the room which was not likely to answer back.

'I haven't had the time.'

The outrageousness of Mrs. Drag's remark almost took my breath away. It defied argument. There was something almost magnificent about its effrontery. I could only echo feebly, 'Not the time?'

Mrs. Drag stood stock still, with a look on her face which a viper, robbed of its young, could not have bettered. 'I've been doing the strawberries,' she said.

Very innocently the Professor said: 'Oh, you have been cooking them?'

'No, sir.'

This answer seemed to crush the Professor completely. However, the battle was veering to our side. I ignored the Professor's agonized signals to cease fire. 'Then what have you been doing to them?' knowing full well that all she had done was to pull out the stalks.

Mrs. Drag gulped. It was a great moment. I had manœuvred her into a position where she *had* to admit that all she had done, in the past ten days, was to make two beds and take the stalks from one pound of strawberries, and that these activities had been too strenuous to allow of the manufacture of mayonnaise sauce.

'I . . . I . . .'

'Yes Mrs. Drag?'

And then Mrs. Drag swayed. A highly theatrical, calculated sway. A sway that would not have deceived a babe in arms.

'Oh, oh . . .' she cried.

The Professor jumped to his feet. 'What is it . . . what is it?'

'Everything's . . . going . . .' Mrs. Drag shook her head dramatically. And then, without any further ado, she tottered from the room.

'The next word,' I said to the Professor, 'is . . .?'

'Black,' said the Professor. And I am happy to be able to record that he said it extremely curtly, without any trace of sympathy.

§ VI

That round, it must be admitted, ended in favour of Mrs. Drag. When a woman knocks herself out, in any contest with a man, decency decrees that one should count ten before going on with the struggle.

So hot was it . . . so deliciously, brazenly hot, that I would willingly have counted ten times ten, and forgotten all about Mrs. Drag, and allowed the days to drift by in a dreaming procession of blue and gold. And for a time I did, and spent a glorious week, prowling round the Professor's garden, which was one of the queerest gardens I had ever seen.

The first thing that struck me about it was the strange number of butterflies which were always hovering there. If you wandered down his little central path at noon, there were butterflies everywhere. You had a sense of Carnival. It was as though a laughing crowd of mysterious revellers had tiptoed up to the other side of the hedge and were tossing handfuls of confetti, that landed on the flowers and then fluttered away again, blown by a fairy wind — magical confetti that hovered and danced and melted into the blue sky when you tried to catch it — confetti thrown by fingers which were not of this earth, in celebration of a wedding which, this day, next day, some time, never . . . might be danced under the chequered shadows of the trees.

'Are you the king of the Butterflies?'

I asked him the question one day, after tea, when most of the butterflies have usually gone to bed.

'Of course.'

'But seriously . . . why do they always aim for this garden?'

'Because I know the flowers that attract them. Look at the foot of that wall. How many Red Admirals can you see there?'

'One, two, three . . . seven.'

'Do you see what they are perching on?'

I walked closer. The Red Admirals did not stir. They remained poised there, like a toy fleet of aeroplanes in an absurd land of make belief, waiting for some signal which would speed them away to a battle of flowers.

'All I can see is stone-crop.'

'That's all it is . . . common stone-crop. But Red Admirals love it.' He walked up to it, and passed his hand over the Red Admirals, with a queer mesmeric gesture. If any other man had done it, they would have flown away. But still they did not stir.

The Professor straightened himself abruptly, and pointed to a bed of stocks.

'Do you see? There's not a single Red Admiral on those stocks. But there are . . . one, two . . . Oh Lord, there must be nearly twenty Scarlet Ladies.'

He looked beyond me, and his eyes brightened. 'Ah!'

I followed him. 'What is it?'

'Do you see all those orange-tips on the nasturtiums? Ye Gods, isn't that beautiful?'

And indeed it was. For the nasturtiums were Golden Gleam, and no orange is more glowing, more burningly alive, than the orange which this particular butterfly carries so gaily on its wings. There were a dozen orange-tips fluttering over those nasturtiums, and if you narrowed your eyes, and framed a little picture for yourself, you had the impression of a ballet in miniature, a barbaric, flaunting ballet, achieving itself in a tiny patch of country garden. You could almost hear the music, the clash of floral cymbals, the rolls of drums, played on withered leaves by blades of grass.

'And over there,' said the Professor, 'the Peacocks are making the most of the mignonette.'

They were. There were eleven of them.

'Why do they like certain flowers? What's the explanation of it?'

The Professor blinked. 'You are always asking for explanations,' he said, almost impatiently. 'You shouldn't. That's *my* job. Your job is to accept, to assimilate, to drench yourself in colour, and then . . . to fill your pen. Don't ask me to explain things. Not to-day.'

We walked down the path together. The air was dizzy with painted wings.

§ VII

Meanwhile, everything was still 'going black' before Mrs. Drag. Only at the most convenient moments, of course. When there was an extra bed to be made, or a special sort of salad to prepare, or a room to be cleared out. Only at moments like these did the skies suddenly darken before Mrs. Drag. At least, that was what I suspected. And soon I was proved to be right.

This is what happened.

Mrs. Drag had a violent objection to going out into the garden for anything. That was the odd man's job. If the Professor humbly asked for leeks for lunch, to go with the mutton chops, Mrs. Drag said she would 'see if Morris could get her some'. It was unthinkable that she should walk down the little brick path to the patch where the leeks grew and pull up some for herself. It was the same if we wanted a salad.

'Oh no, sir!' said Mrs. Drag firmly. 'You never asked me for any this morning. I might have been able to get some, though it's very difficult, in the country.'

Everything, according to Mrs. Drag, was very difficult in the country. Eggs were extremely difficult, for example. There was some conspiracy to prevent Mrs. Drag from getting eggs. Butter was most difficult, too. The difficulty of apples, also, was grave, although we were surrounded by orchards. But salads presented the most hideous difficulty of all. From the way she talked you would think that a lettuce was a rare form of edelweiss, which grew on a distant crag, and could only be obtained by skilled mountaineers, covered with spikes, at full-moon.

'There is a box of cress in the greenhouse,' suggested the Professor, greatly daring.

'Oh!' Mrs. Drag gave him a look which could not possibly be described as clean. There was a pause. Then she said, 'Morris has gone. I really don't know where he keeps the key of the greenhouse'.

I saw that this was a crisis. So I said, 'Morris hasn't gone yet, Mrs. Drag. You'll find him in the greenhouse now'. And I took the Professor firmly by the arm and observed with vibrating clarity, 'Won't it be lovely to have heaps of delicious cress to-night?' And mumbled him off into the garden.

'You oughtn't to have done that,' said the Professor in a scared voice. 'She hates going out in the garden for anything. Especially in the summer. She's afraid of sunstroke.'

'What, at six o'clock in the evening?'

'That's what she says.' The Professor blinked, took out a piece of paper, made a rapid calculation on it, and then abruptly turned away, walking absent-mindedly straight through a clump of phlox.

§ V I I I

I stayed where I was, bent down, and pretended to examine some Shirley poppies. But actually I was examining Mrs. Drag, whose movements were clearly visible through the door.

Mrs. Drag was well aware that she had an audience. For an expression of tragic fatigue was quickly printed on to her face. She came out of the door for a moment, shaded her eyes with her hand, stared at the setting sun, shuddered and retreated, as though she had been suddenly confronted by a blast furnace. Then there was a pause, in which I observed that the kitchen curtains were slightly parted, proving that she was glaring out to make sure that I was still there.

Then she came to the doorway again, wearing black glasses. These were flashed in my direction, to prove that her condition was indeed dire. And finally she took a huge picture hat from a hook, lifted it with a supreme effort to her head, adjusted it, and sat down.

I still examined the Shirley poppies. I learnt more about poppies in that breathless five minutes than anybody has ever learnt since the Reverend W. Wilks first raised them, with such loving care, at Shirley. And it was through a haze of Shirley poppies that at last I saw Mrs. Drag, fully accoutred against the menace of the setting sun, stalk darkly down the garden path towards the greenhouse. The light flashed dramatically on her black glasses. The cool breeze flirted with the brim of her hat. But Mrs. Drag did not swoon or falter. She walked straight on to the greenhouse.

And we had cress salad for dinner. Rather earthy cress salad, which made grinding noises when you bit it. For Mrs. Drag had been far too fatigued to wash it. As you may remember, there was no 'staff' in this house.

§ IX

The end of the Drag drama is approaching.

It happened that the Professor received a telegram, summoning him to London, and as it was really so hot that one could not sit still, I arranged to drive him up in an open car, and bring him back again in the cool of the evening.

'We shan't be home till late, Mrs. Drag,' said the Professor.

She heaved a deep sigh. One felt that she was a poor prisoner on the rack, being given a moment's respite.

But when we arrived in London, the Professor found that he would have to stay the night. And London was so insufferable that I decided to flee back to Allways without delay. I bought a cold lobster, and a carton of mayonnaise sauce (so that Mrs. Drag would have no trouble), pressed the accelerator and sped back over the Great North Road.

All went well till I reached the end of the lane. And there, just opposite the little toy garage, a tyre burst. It burst very loudly and emphatically. I made the appropriate remarks, drove the car with a great deal of bumping into the yard, delivered it to a very moist and panting young man, retrieved the lobster and the mayonnaise sauce (which smelt strongly of petrol), walked up the lane to the Professor's, and was about to lift the latch of the garden gate. . . .

When I paused. Electrified, I paused, staring in front of me, clutching a clammy luke-warm lobster, that was pushing its protesting claws through the frayed newspaper. For, from the Professor's lattice-gate, you had a clear view of the kitchen and the little terrace in front of it. And there, outside the kitchen door, sitting, without a hat, in the blazing sunshine, and revelling in it, was Mrs. Drag, reading the newspaper!

I stayed stock still, feasting my eyes upon this blessed vision. I noted every detail. Within three feet of Mrs. Drag was a pool of deep shade, cast by the arm of the chestnut tree. She could have moved into it merely by shifting the angle of her chair. Hanging on the open door leading into the kitchen, I observed Mrs. Drag's hat — that same hat which so often she had painfully lifted to her head, as though it were a protective helmet, when she had been compelled by her cruel masters to battle with the dangers of the sun. And on the kitchen table, despised and neglected, lay the black goggles which she had affected as the final proof of the tortures she was enduring.

No shade — no hat — no goggles — the whole of Mrs. Drag's duplicity was revealed at one fell swoop.

I closed the gate with a loud click.

Mrs. Drag started, stared, became rigid.

I walked slowly up the path.

Mrs. Drag began to rise in her chair.

I beamed upon Mrs. Drag. Call me merciless, caddish, anything you like . . . you would have beamed too if you had suffered under her dominion.

'Sunbathing, Mrs. Drag?'

Those were the only words that were spoken. For the excitement of the moment was so intense that it would not have been surprising if everything had instantly gone pitch black before both of us. And I did not wish to be discovered by the odd man, lying over the prostrate body of Mrs. Drag, with a lobster round my neck.

§ x

On the following day, when the Professor returned, Mrs. Drag gave notice.

She was not accustomed, she said, to being ordered about by gentlemen (if they *were* gentlemen) who were merely visitors.

She wished to remind the Professor that there was no staff in this house.

She could not be here there and everywhere, she said, and it was not as if the Professor lived in the town, where you only had to ring up for things on the telephone.

Besides, she added, in *this* house, there was no staff.

She said that the country was very much dirtier than the town, and the Professor would be surprised if he knew, but of course he didn't, because he never paid attention to these things.

Moreover, she averred, this house contained no staff.

And so it went on, in a long monologue, and for all I know, it might still be going on, had not Mrs. Drag suddenly remembered that she was standing in the blazing sunshine without a hat on, and that she had a reputation for delicacy. So she clapped her hands to her eyes, and walked heavily away, supporting herself by theatrical clutches at the furniture.

A little while later, Mrs. Drag departed, and from that day to this, complete and final blackness enveloped her. And peace reigned at the Professor's in the shape of a young man of startling efficiency, called Blake. At least, that is what he *said* his name was.

However, that is another story, which must wait for the time being.

CHAPTER XV

CONVERSATION

It was September before I returned to my own cottage, and
September is such a rapturous month in the country that
for a week I shut the garden gate and indulged in an orgy
of prowling.

A great deal of prowling went on round the clumps of
autumn crocuses, which had been planted in drifts, in the
wood. These were really almost too good to be true. If
you prowled over to the stream, and then turned your head,
they looked like pools of coloured water, with the slowly
paling leaves above them. If you prowled back to the
cottage and went up to the bedroom window and stared
out, through the acacias, they looked like a sort of celestial
laundry, laid out to dry.

Do you prowl about your garden like this? Have you
a lot of 'favourite views'? Do you spend your time going to
an archway and gazing over a certain clump, or stopping
half way down a path, and turning your head to the right?

Glaring through gaps, pushing your head over hedges? I suppose it is a form of incipient madness, but it is a very agreeable form. I am quite sure that in many parts of my garden the earth is worn bare, like an old carpet, because here, in April, was the best place to see the daffodils, or here, in June, the syringa smelled the sweetest, or here, in September, the autumn crocuses shone most brightly.

At the risk of offending all those persons who think that no man ought ever to have a lump in his throat which is not caused by his Adam's apple, I do not mind admitting that autumn crocuses give me a lump in the throat. They are like the last fling of youth — they seem to herald the spring, when the chestnuts are yellowing. By rights, you feel, they should be flowering in a brightly enamelled world where white lambs prance on fields of emerald green. But they come to a world of rain-streaked skies and sudden frosts, and often their petals are marred by the drifting leaves.

§ 11

For a whole week I continued to prowl. Only two months now to November, and in November all the new trees would be coming for the wood. One must be ready! So I would go out to the bare field, and prowl for hours round the bamboo sticks which had been stuck in the ground, to indicate where the new trees were to be, and examine the labels tied to the sticks in order to be sure that everything was in order. Sometimes, when I felt very rich, I would say to myself, wildly, 'I am going to fill that gap over there with guelder roses — hell, it's worth it — ' and then I would rush to the study, and write out twelve labels, each one marked 'one guelder rose'. Then another rush to the tool-shed, for twelve more bamboo-sticks, and a canter through the field to the gap in question. Then — ah then! — the fun began! For you had to take a few steps back, and decide where the first guelder rose was to go. And then you stuck the first stick in. If the earth was very hard you had to force it in, and anybody looking over the hedge would think that you had a very odd way of employing your leisure — pushing sticks into your stomach with an agonized expression. Then you stepped back again, and little by little, you grouped the other bamboo sticks round the first stick.

And by the time you had finished, so far were you away from the world and its troubles, and so vivid had your imagination become, that it seemed as though the bare sticks had sprouted and were growing green branches, that blew in the wind, laden with the heavy clusters of the guelder roses, the snows of summer.

Yes, I was very far away from the world and its troubles, during that one week. But they were soon to come on me again.

For one day, there was a meeting of the Miss Hazlitt Shop Committee. I had to go. The accounts were gravely disturbing. She was not even paying her way.

'And what is more,' said Mrs. M. gravely, 'I don't like the look of her.'

'How do you mean?'

'It's my belief she's ill.'

'Has she complained of any pain?'

'Does Miss Hazlitt ever complain of *anything*?'

I cursed myself for having been so negligent, and undertook the task of submitting a report, and trying to straighten things out.

§ III

I have always envied the people who can let things slide. It must make life so very simple. There are quantities of people in this world who always kick off their boots in the middle of the floor, who always crumple up a newspaper and then leave it in the garden, who lose things and expect others to find them. These are the people who, when they have any money of their own, spend it, and then, when they haven't, spend yours. They are the people who know that 'somebody' will always clean up the mess, when it gets bad enough, because there are a sufficient number of 'somebodies' in the world who hate mess, and chaos, and bankruptcy, to such an extent, that they will sacrifice themselves in order to avoid it.

I am one of those 'somebodies'. It isn't anything to be proud of. It is merely a matter of temperament. And it was because of this that the little committee suggested that I would be the right person to put Miss Hazlitt's affairs in order.

But how? What was one to do? It was not as if one were dealing with an ordinary person. Far from it. One was dealing with such an extraordinary person that I cannot explain to you the difficulties of the situation until I have reported one of the strangest conversations I have ever had in my life.

I had asked her to come and see me in the evening, as soon as the shop was closed, 'to discuss a business matter'. And this is what happened.

§ IV

It was a day of storm and shadow.

In the morning, I had spent an anxious time in the wood. I saw, over in the corner, a silver poplar straining against the wind, holding desperately to the earth by its frail roots, waving its thin arms in panic. I ran over to it, pressed my shoulder against the young stem, and was filled with fear at the force of the wind — it was like pushing against a blustering giant. Hardly had I staked the silver poplar than I saw a young cherry in dire straits — leaning over, almost giving up the fight, the shrill, malicious wind tearing the pale leaves from its delicate crest. I succoured the cherry, but even as I did so, I saw other little trees, groaning firs, and rocking willows, all staggering under the bitter onslaughts of the wind. It was too much. It was like watching people drown. For all these trees were newly planted, and the tendrils of the young roots were being torn from their frail hold. But I could do nothing. And so I went inside. The wind slammed the door after me, as though it were telling me to mind my own business.

And even indoors, it was triumphant. Shrill, shrill through the keyholes and the door cracks, wailing its evil tidings. It tried to put out the fire in the hall, and scornfully puffed its smoke in my face. It tore at the curtains in my bedroom . . . it made of the whole earth a lamentation, there was no shelter anywhere.

And then, at evening, it died down very suddenly. There was a hush over the world and the tired branches ceased to tremble. The sun came out and the air was pierced with bird-song. And there was the sound of steps coming slowly down the path.

I looked up from my desk and saw Miss Hazlitt.

§ v

This chapter is called 'Conversation'. I had almost forgotten it. It does not matter. But there must be no lingering, though she had stopped under a white jasmine, and was reaching up to it, running her fingers over the flowers.

Yet, I would like you to see that picture, for in it, white was laid against white, by chance, and danced in a delicate rhythm against the dying wind. There was the white of her hair, and the starry white of the petals at her feet. And in the sky, there drifted a cloud as white as wool, like a swan on a twilit river. And everywhere there seemed to be the white stars of the jasmine . . . for they were all around her, and they bent towards her, while she ran her fingers over them.

Conversation!

I had asked her over 'to discuss a business matter'. But as soon as she arrived, it seemed impossible. For *she* had come to talk about . . . well, I suppose one may call it 'the things of the spirit'. She had not seen me for some weeks, and she did not wish to talk about business, for she was hungry for my salvation. No, that sounds all wrong. I despair of putting Miss Hazlitt on paper. I seem to suggest that she was lazy, shirking things, living in a dream. It wasn't like that. It was rather that these things simply did not exist for her.

I looked at her standing there. Time enough to talk about pounds, shillings and pence when we had talked of other things. I said to her:

'You don't look as if you belonged to this world.'

She let free a spray of jasmine which she had been holding down. It danced back to its green home, and swayed above us.

Very gravely she said:

'If you are born again, you don't belong to this world.'

'Born again!'

It is odd how the traditional teaching of an Englishman

makes him feel that there is something 'not quite nice' about religious conversation. We are perfectly prepared to discuss, in the frankest terms, the problems of sex, we don't mind revealing the extent of our incomes, nor the state of our digestions, but when somebody like Miss Hazlitt quite calmly and quietly refers to God or the Bible or Jesus Christ, we have a curious nervous reaction about it. It is almost as if something naked were being exposed to us, which we found a little shocking.

Why? It is very silly, when you come to think of it. One doesn't get this feeling when people are talking about other religions. I have heard Buddhists speak with the same calm exaltation of their God, and all I felt was an intense interest, faintly tinged with envy . . . the envy which any man must have who is still not *certain*, who can believe, but only up to a point.

This was the burden of our conversation in the garden. I had discussed it with her before. It always seemed impossible to make her see what I meant.

'Faith is a *gift*,' I said. 'We've talked this out before, but I *cannot* see any merit in faith. It is like having an ear for music, or a gift for engineering. What if a man's mind *forbids* him to believe? A man may be short-sighted, as far as his eyes are concerned, why can't he be short-sighted as far as his brain is concerned too?'

'Oh please, please don't reason about these things. You *mustn't* reason!' Her voice was trembling with anxiety. And then she said something which to me was extremely wise and illuminating.

She said: 'Spiritual things are spiritually discerned.'

I could write a book about that sentence. But we will leave it for a moment, like a flower that one lays in the shadow of a hedge, to pick up later.

'Yes,' she said, 'faith *is* a gift. It is the gift of God. We have only to take it. But before we can do that, there is a first step to be taken, the step of repentance.'

'But supposing I don't feel repentant?'

A shadow passed her face.

'We are born in sin,' she said.

'But why, why?' I could not help it if I were being cruel. This doctrine seemed to me so cruel itself. I said:

'You say that a little baby, a few hours old, is sinful. But that seems to me terrible. What has it *done?* It didn't ask to be born. It came into the world because it couldn't help itself. It doesn't know anything . . . it couldn't sin if it tried. What has it *done*, except breathe a little, and cry a little, and go to sleep? How can you say that is sin?'

'It is not what I say but what God says.'

You see. Once again I was knocking my head against that stone rock of old Bible teaching on which she stood so firmly, high above the waves of worldly dissension.

'But supposing this little child that we're talking about was brought up by atheists? Supposing it had never had an opportunity to hear even the name of Christ? Would it still be doomed? You wouldn't punish a child because it couldn't read, if nobody had taught it the alphabet, would you? Why then should you punish a child who didn't believe if it had never been given anything to believe in?'

'God's ways are always right. He will not judge the heathen as he judges us.'

'And how will he judge us?'

'We shall perish if we do not believe in Him.'

If anybody else had said that to me I should have been violently irritated. But one could not be irritated with Miss Hazlitt.

CONVERSATION

All the same, the conversation did not seem to be getting anywhere. And so I began to excuse myself. . . .

'But please . . . please don't go.'

'I've an article to write. And the proofs of a song to correct.'

'Your work can wait.'

That *did* irritate me. 'Yes. Yes, it can wait. If I like to break my contract . . . and put all sorts of people to a great deal of inconvenience. And lose a lot of money.'

'There are more important things.'

I looked at her. She stood there, supremely detached . . . she seemed almost luminous in the evening sunlight. 'It must be grand to feel like that,' I thought. 'Perhaps there *are* more important things.'

§ VI

Martha and Mary!

The eternal argument!

It was almost inevitable, after my reference to my work, that we should have to thrash it out . . . for Miss Hazlitt said, 'Not all the works in the world will save you, if you do not believe'.

'Let's sit down and get this straight.'

'Oh, I want to, so much!'

We sat down under an old pear tree whose branches were heavy with fruit.

'Supposing,' I said, 'there was a Martha who was, essentially, a good woman . . . a woman who was kind and truthful and loyal. And supposing that she just *couldn't* believe, however much she tried? She might think Christ a wonderful man, and she might try to follow his example, but she couldn't believe that he was the son of

215

God? Her mind just couldn't swallow it. *Couldn't* - remember — though she tried and tried. What then? Wouldn't the fact that she had led a life that was pure and unselfish, and had made many sacrifices for others, wouldn't that make her, at least, worthy of some consideration?'

Miss Hazlitt looked at me with clear, stern eyes. . . . 'In God's sight, her life would be of no avail.'

'Then . . . then . . .' I hesitated to say it, but I could not help myself. 'I think that is a cruel philosophy.'

She shook her head. 'You don't understand,' she said.

I didn't. How could I? For my feet were on the earth, on the green grass, and from over the hedge the sounds of the village drifted in a pastoral medley. My eyes revelled in the brightly painted flowers in the border beside us, a border which looked as though some modern artist had squeezed out all his tubes at once, and dotted the canvas with the most glowing colours he could find. I was part of all these things, they were my life. She loved them too, but it was as though she saw them through a veil . . . no, that is not right, for no woman knew more about country things than she did. It would be truer to say that for her they were all bathed in a light that was not of this world.

She *was* not of this world. For to my argument of cruelty she responded with the story of the Passover. How strange did that queer and brooding Oriental fantasy sound in a cottage garden! 'From out of their houses came the children of Israel, and anointed the lintels of their doors with blood. And as a result of that act, their eldest sons were saved from death.'

I closed my eyes. I saw the squalid houses, with the blood smeared over the lintels, and the sun pouring down, and the flies buzzing. Through a crack in the door I saw the wizened face of an old Jew . . . and the waxen face

of his son . . . saved by the blood. My mind revolted.
I opened my eyes. Thank God, the roses were still there,
tinted more variously than all the colours of Jacob's coat. I
heard Miss Hazlitt saying . . .

'It is the same with us. We are saved by the blood of
Christ. It is the blood of Christ who speaks.'

§ VII

I tried another argument.

The argument of the cat and the mouse.

'How do you reconcile *that* with the conception of a
merciful God . . .' I asked her. 'What sort of light does
it shed on the idea that not a sparrow falls to the ground
without His knowledge?'

She shook her head. 'You forget that it was Satan who
brought sin into the world.'

And now, I nearly *did* laugh. Because the very word
'Satan' makes me feel a little irreverent. It somehow
suggests a poor old actor in red tights in a Christmas
pantomime, popping out of a trapdoor, rather breathlessly, and cowering back into the wings before an ultra-
blonde Fairy Queen.

But to Miss Hazlitt Satan was a real person. As real as
the black bats that scar the star-laden skies in June. For,
you see, she was not looking at life as I looked at it. She
was looking at it in a mirror — the mirror of the Bible.
Into those clear pages she gazed, and they were as crystal
to her, and it was in their shining depths that she saw
reflected the green things of this world, and the clouds and
the waters, and men 'like trees walking . . .'

The texts of the Bible, to her, were as fresh as the white
daisies at her feet. That was why she had no difficulty in

answering the argument about the cat and the mouse. She had a text ready for me:

'It will not always be like that,' she said. 'When Christ comes "the wolf shall dwell with the lamb". We know that from Isaiah, don't we? When Christ comes, there will be no sin.'

§ V I I I

We rose to our feet and walked on.

And then again, something happened which would have made me laugh if anybody else but Miss Hazlitt had been at my side. For she put her foot on a stone, and tripped, and nearly fell. She could not have hurt herself, because we were walking over the soft grass. But somehow, this silly little incident, which would normally have made me laugh . . . (for as Henri Bergson has shown us, the man tripping on the banana skin is the essence of all laughter, which has in it an element of cruelty) . . . this silly little incident passed off with complete gravity. And with no thought of the strangeness of it all, I accepted Miss Hazlitt's quiet observation, as she straightened herself:

'Whom the Lord loveth, He chasteneth.'

This is not easy writing. I pray that it may make easier reading.

For I want you to understand Miss Hazlitt. She was as a lamp in the little village of Allways, a lamp set in a lonely window, and though we often did not realize it, nor admit it, the light from that lamp often lit up our quiet lanes on nights when the skies were sullen black, when we had lost our way.

Yet, we questioned that light. At least, I did. One can't stifle one's reasoning brain, one can't drift round a lamp, like a bemused moth.

'Whom the Lord loveth, He chasteneth,' I echoed. There was an austere beauty in the words.

'But why?'

'Because it helps us to know Him.'

'But why should pain help us to know God?'

Once again, I felt, she was the governess and I was the little boy. And once again I tried to accept the wisdom that came from her. In the old days it had been 'William the Conqueror, 1066'. Or, 'Canada exports so many millions of bushels of wheat a year'. Or 'Cornwall is a county in England. The capital of Cornwall is Bodmin. And Bodmin is on the river Camel'. 'Bodmin on the Camel,' I used to whisper to myself. And I always thought of a fat old merchant, called Bodmin, in a turban, making a jerky progress over the river, on the back of a camel.

But always I trusted her, and tried to understand. And even now, I tried to understand when she spoke of suffering and evil — the two bugbears of the rationalist who tries to see the face of God through the thick curtains of his mental night.

'God is not the source of Evil,' she said. 'God *allows* evil. You should read the book of Job. And you should realize what it means when Satan says "Let me but touch his body, and he will curse you". Yes . . . you should read the book of Job.'

Read the book of Job!

And the roses were dancing in the wind. . . .

CHAPTER XVI

MARTHA, MARY, AND OTHERS

THE evening deepened. Our conversation continued. It led nowhere. It petered out, like a stream that loses itself in parched earth. I am sorry to have to report so undramatic a denouement . . . it would have been better, for the purposes of this book, to tell of a vision at twilight, a spiritual renaissance under the darkening skies, with the last sunlight washing the grey stones of the church on the hill. Better for you, and better, certainly, for me. But it did not happen, and so, it cannot be recorded.

Instead, at long last, we got down to business. The business of the shop. We walked back to it together, while I braced myself up to the ordeal of asking to see her accounts.

I do not think I ever got over the thrill of entering Miss Hazlitt's shop. It is probably absurd to feel so excited about such a simple thing, but if you could see it all as I saw it, perhaps you would be excited too.

You see the shop at the end of the road as soon as you come out of the gate that leads from my kitchen garden. There it is, about a hundred yards down on the left, with its neat thatch, its heavy canopy of white roses and its sign, painted in green, 'Teas provided'.

As soon as you have closed the door of the kitchen garden, you have to call wildly to Whoops, the dog, who always assumes, when you leave the garden by this door, that you are going for a walk, and has already dashed about half a mile down the road, far beyond Miss Hazlitt's shop, and is standing in the middle of the road, his body facing to the hills and the open country, his head turned back, towards you. For, you see, he really knows that probably you are not going a walk at all. You are only going to that damned shop. That is why he feels it is so important to lure you *beyond* the shop, by a sort of canine suggestion. Once you have got beyond it, he feels, you are safe.

But you do not get beyond it. You pause in the door. You call to that black blob in the distance. Slowly, with a tremendous sense of the dramatic, the tail descends. If dogs could shrug their shoulders and say 'The hell of it', Whoops would do so, then. But whatever he may say to himself, the tail descends. He turns. And slowly, like an undertaker following a hearse, he comes back.

'Whoops. Come *on!*'

You are chafing with impatience. But he does not hurry. Not he! One black paw forward, then another, in measured tread, with a terrible sense of martyrdom radiating from him. 'Lord,' you think, 'if anybody sees him coming to me like this they will think I am a dog-beater. It is too bad of Whoops to do these things in public. I shall have to take him out for at least an hour before bedtime.'

And then at last, he is here. You open the door. 'Go *on!*' He stands, looking at you like some very maltreated orphan in a particularly violent storm. You jerk your head towards the shop. Slowly, disgustedly he stalks in. Usually, he stops with his hindquarters in the doorway, so that the last part of him has to be pushed through.

The opening of the door is heralded, as you may remember, by a bell. I am always glad when the bell has ceased to echo because, somehow, it tinkles so loudly that it seems to suggest you have come to buy much more than you really intended. It has something barbaric about it and you feel that after it there should be heard a voice, booming 'Peacocks for the sultan'. Or words to that effect. As though a negro slave had struck his cymbals together as his royal master entered the market.

Boom! 'Bring out your spices!' That is what ought to happen. What does happen is. . . .

'Boom!' 'Halfpenny worth of mint 'umbugs,' in a thin piping voice.

And that, as I studied Miss Hazlitt's accounts, was what had been happening a great deal too often.

§ 11

These accounts were extremely difficult to follow. Not because they were inaccurate, nor untidy — on the contrary, they were scrupulously accurate, and each item was entered in a copper-plate handwriting. No . . . the difficulty came from balancing the ordinary account with a special account which was labelled 'Credits'. This was an extra book which Miss Hazlitt kept to enter those items for which people had not paid, and obviously never would pay. A large proportion of these were medicines, although there was a considerable amount of groceries as well.

I took the first account of the book.

'But this is nearly eight months old,' I said. 'Whose is it? J.R.? Who is J.R.?'

'I'm afraid it's old Mrs. Robson.'

'But she's dead . . . she died last month.'

'I know. I wish I could have done more to help her.'

'Well, you've provided the family with nearly seventeen pounds worth of free medicines and free food.'

Miss Hazlitt looked very guilty. She twisted her hands nervously together.

'Mr. Robson said he would pay as soon as he could. But they've had a great deal of illness in the family.'

It was on the tip of my tongue to tell her that as long as old Robson had fourpence in his pocket, it would go to the local pub. Miss Hazlitt had not the faintest hope of getting her seventeen pounds. And that was only one item.

'What's this?' I asked, pointing to a long list of items, mostly for a penny . . . this sort of thing. . . .

1 bar milk chocolate
1 ounce orange drops
1 ounce sherbert
2 halfpenny Butter Scotch
1 stick Edinburgh Rock
1 ounce 'hundreds and thousands'
1 ounce Oriental Delights

She looked guilty again. 'It was for the little Smith girl. She never had any pennies. Her mother's paralysed.'

'But my dear, this is a *shop*. It's not a charitable institution.' It was horrible to have to say that, but what else could one do.

'I know.'

'I'm afraid you'll have to stop these credit accounts.'

'I'm afraid I shall.'

'Now let's see. What has been the average takings for the last quarter.'

Miss Hazlitt's face brightened. 'Six pounds a week!'

'Six?'

I was standing with my back to her. It was lucky that she could not see my face at that moment.

'Yes. Isn't it wonderful?'

I did a lightning calculation in my head. Six pounds a week. Taking the average profit at twenty per cent — (an exceedingly optimistic estimate) — that meant that Miss

Hazlitt was making a profit of just over a pound a week. And that was for the summer season! The summer season, when, according to Mrs. M., the tea-gardens would be a riot of gaiety, and the demands for lemonade would be almost excessive, and the sale of acid-drops would be phenomenal!

I stood there, in the quiet little shop, which had that heavenly smell of bootlaces, liquorice, milk chocolate, and tea, which all village shops eventually acquire. I turned and looked at Miss Hazlitt. She stood there by the window, smiling at me with eyes so radiantly trusting and happy, in spite of the wrinkles of pain beneath them, that I couldn't say what I wanted to.

'Six pounds a week,' I muttered.

'Six pounds a week.'

I looked at her again. She was still smiling. This was an impossible situation. Miss Hazlitt just wasn't of this earth. She was not. If she *had* been, her attitude of utterly unruffled composure would have been wildly irritating. That's what I want you to understand.

In the constant dramatic clashes which occur, throughout our lives, between the Marthas and the Marys, I am nearly always on the side of the Marthas. I am nearly always on the side of the women who can't go to church because they have to wash up, the women who haven't read the Bible because they've been sitting up all night with a child who's got a nasty cough, the women who can't send flowers to the Easter festival because they're too tired to go into the garden to pick them. In all the stainless beauty of Christ's teaching, the Martha-Mary episode is the one story which, to me, doesn't ring true. I do see Martha's point, so bitterly clearly. And the children of the Marthas I've known have been better than the children of the Marys, they've been sturdier, more honest, with greater humour and kindliness, and their hands have been clean and strong, the sort of hands you like to grip, in friendship.

But now . . . what was I to do? For Miss Hazlitt could not conceivably be cast for the role of Martha. Oh — if you could only have seen her face, just then, you would not have felt any possible irritation against her, merely because she was not paying attention to such things as accounts and grocery bills. For the light of God was upon it . . . a sweet light that filtered through the old windows, and lit up her pale skin till it looked like a parchment on which some message would soon be written.

'Six pounds a week,' I said again.

She nodded, and sat down. 'Isn't it wonderful?'

§III

I got her out of the room. As I helped her over the little threshold I gripped her arm. And I remember that it had the fragile feeling of the old jasmine branch which I had trained round my window the day before . . . a withered branch . . . a branch that you would say was dead. Yet, inside that branch there drifted, every spring, the ghosts of a thousand starry blossoms, and in its secret channels there was buried a scent of almost intolerable sweetness, waiting to be born as soon as the sun should give its blessing. I thought of that branch as I felt Miss Hazlitt's arm.

I sat her down by the fireplace. She smiled and closed her eyes. I went back to the shop and stood behind the counter.

Bootlaces, liquorice, milk chocolate, tea. I sniffed the curious air of the shop. It was strangely invigorating. It brought me back to earth. Bootlaces. A halfpenny profit on them. How could we sell more bootlaces to Allways? Liquorice! But that wasn't any good in the summer . . . that was only demanded in winter, when the leaves were off the trees and a chill wind drove down the tiny street, and sent children coughing to their beds. Milk chocolate . . . well, that was better. People would always eat milk chocolate, though I observed with trepidation that some rather gruesome stains had appeared on Miss Hazlitt's packets, indicating that she had omitted to put them in a cool place.

I wondered if we could brighten up the library a little — send circulars round the village — pledge ourselves to get at least three books a week. Surely, that ought to give us a few extra shillings? We might enlarge the window, and hang an extra sign outside, to attract casual passers-by. We might put in a little advertisement, in the local paper, about the teas. We might even have a few celebrities down for the week-ends. I could ask Ivor Novello to serve behind the counter for an hour. People would probably pay at least a guinea for half a pound of lump sugar if Ivor served it to them. And they would take the sugar away to a dark place and suck a lump, with awful sighing noises, when they were feeling particularly repressed. Gladys Cooper might be lured up to sell shampoo powders one afternoon. People would be so dazed by her beauty that we should probably be able to pick their pockets while she was wrapping up the shampoo powder. We might even get some politicians . . . Mr. Winston Churchill might induce people to buy Indian tea. But on the other hand, he might not.

I sighed. It was getting late. And these dreams, while they were amusing enough at first, began to wear a little thin. For after all, they were dreams and we were up against realities.

You may think that this was all much ado about nothing. 'Why didn't you make her a little allowance and have done with it?' You may say. For two reasons. Firstly, there seemed no way of doing it without her finding out. And secondly, even if there had been a way, it would have been so utterly alien to Miss Hazlitt's character, that the very thought of it was enough to make one dismiss the idea.

§ I V

And now what?

It was a question which I asked myself, time and again, in the days that followed.

They were painful days. For the discussion of her affairs led inevitably to the discussion of other people's affairs. And by many little reticences, shame-faced admissions, blushes, and gaucheries, I learned that the inhabitants of Allways had already done all they possibly could for the shop. And it was little short of a miracle that they had done so much.

When you have only a very few pounds a week, and you know that no power on earth will make you any more, you can't gaily throw fivepound-notes about the place as if they were confetti. (That remark is probably the most crashing platitude that has yet startled the world but a lot of comfortable people are apt to forget the truth it contains.)

In those few days that followed I learned more about the economy of Allways than I had ever learned before.

Instead of 'economy' I should have written economies.

'Will you come in for coffee?' It was a stock phrase at Allways. I had usually interpreted it to mean that people would be bored by having one to dinner. It didn't mean that. It meant that there had been no such thing as 'dinner' — there had only been a little tinned soup, and some cold meat, while the 'maid', who always looked so smart when she opened the door on special occasions, had gone home, to 'do' for her mother.

'What will you have to drink?' The phrase often came glibly from Mrs. M.'s lips, on the evenings when I dropped in to see her. 'Whisky and soda? Beer? Liqueur?' And there they all were — the bottle of whisky, the bottles of beer, the decanter of brandy and the bottle of Cointreau. Without thinking, I had helped myself to a whisky and soda. But if I had noticed, I would have seen that it was the same bottle as before, and that not a drop had been touched since my last visit.

The same story is written in every line of the dresses of the ladies of Allways. They look smart enough, and their wearers are, very evidently, 'ladies', but what stories those dresses could tell, if they could speak! For this one, that looks so pretty in spring, is only last spring's model, with new cuffs and a bright new collar. And this, which makes its 'first' appearance at church, in the autumn, has really been to church many times before, only it had a different fur, and it was longer. And the flimsy summer things, which you see at garden fêtes, the pinks and the blues, with the wide hats, were greens and yellows before they went to the dyers, before the new bows were pinned on, and the hats were grimy and old, which are now so sparkling and attractive.

And in the houses, it was the same. When the stair-carpet had frayed at the edges of the steps, you did not buy a new carpet. You slid the whole carpet down a few inches, so that the frayed part no longer showed. And when the bedroom carpet had faded you did not buy a new one, you 'turned' it, so that it stared up at you with a surprised but unfaded expression, with all its roses upside down. And you did not give the cat the fish that had been left over. *That* was made into fish pie for yourself, while the cat had a pennyworth of special 'cat's fish', which is a strange bony monster, not recorded in the average book of natural history. And when so many plates of the dinner service had been broken that you had not enough to go round, you did not buy a new dinner service. You had the broken plates 'riveted', and on the rare occasions when you had a dinner party the maid was told to be very careful to give *you* the riveted plate, which sometimes resulted in strange confusions, in plates being snatched from under the nose of the guest and hastily transferred to the hostess.

All these little things became clear to me, and I realized, in the matter of Miss Hazlitt's shop, that Allways could not do more than it had done. The women of Allways were putting up a magnificent fight against genteel poverty, against falling dividends and rising prices. I could not express my respect for them without lapsing into the worst sort of sentimentality, so I will not try. All the same, the Miss Hazlitt problem was still unsolved.

And now — what?

CHAPTER XVII

SMOKE BEFORE FIRE

THE problems of life, at Allways, never seem quite so harsh or so crude as in the world outside. A dilemma presents itself, worries us for a little while, and then it seems to drift away, like the smoke of an autumn fire in the kitchen garden, when all the weeds, the docks and dandelions and dead roots are smouldering in a black, savoury mass. The fire goes on, but for days, sometimes for weeks, it is forgotten. And then, a chance wind will set it glowing again, and over the clumps of battered cabbages and ragged broccoli the acrid smoke will blow, in drifts of blue and grey.

So it was with Miss Hazlitt's problem. It was there. It would have to be faced, one day. But meanwhile, all I could do was to work quietly in the background, trying to find a way out. It would have been a restless task had I not realized that she, more than any woman I have ever met, was happy, with a happiness that could not be pierced by any slings and arrows of outrageous fortune.

It is strange that the simile of the fire in the kitchen garden should have flashed across the page, for these were the days of log-gathering, the days when, after tea, in the sallow twilights, when the wind had a savour of frost and the spindle-bushes glowed like warming torches, you set out, over the fields, in search of the treasure of the trees. You breathed deeply, and hummed a tune under your breath . . . a good tune, it must be, a wide and lofty tune, like the main theme of the Dvorak New World Symphony

. . . for this was exciting business you were on. You were out to draw fire from the cold earth. That was what it really amounted to. Yes . . . as you bent down, and heaved a branch from the grass, and clasped it to you, and smelt the damp lichen that clung to it, already it seemed that it was warming you, already you saw it glowing on your hearth, in the wild dark winds that were cantering down from the north.

§ I I

During the first few days your task was easy. There was a rich haul under the lonely elm that stands in the centre of the field at the end of the wood, and all along the banks of the stream there were stray fragments of willow (an extravagant wood), of oak and of coarse-grained ash. Sometimes, as a special tit-bit, you were rewarded by a branch of crab-apple, which had been beaten down by the storms of summer, and dried by the winds . . . an enticing branch that snapped easily when you trod on it, and emitted fragrant essences when you consigned it to the flames.

But after you had scoured the neighbouring fields and lanes you had to go further afield. That made it a strenuous job. Of course, you could have taken the car, but that you felt, would be 'cheating'. It would have been akin to using blotting-paper when you were doing a water-colour in the nursery. No nice child uses blotting-paper when it is painting a pink cow and the pink is trying to run down in driblets under the cow's stomach. That is 'cheating'. Anybody can paint if he uses blotting-paper. But it is not ethical to do so. Nor is it ethical to use a car when collecting logs. You must use only your two legs and your two arms. The fire, I swear, will burn more brightly if you abide by these unwritten rules.

And if you are a real countryman, you soon become cunning in the ways of logs. You know that there is a coppice on the hill where the wind is cruel, and where the elms are old and brittle, and you will set out after a night of storm and gather many branches. You will know that there was an ash that was struck by lightning, down by the pond near the farm, and you will hover about it, like an amiable vulture, till the last armful has been taken.

You will learn, too, the logs that deceive by their beauty, but give no heat, and the logs that look so dull in the field but glow so magnificently in the fire. In the first class is the silver birch. Many is the bright bundle of silver birch that I have carried home, and many the basket of pale-barked wood that I have proudly arranged by the fire. And many the time that I have sadly shovelled away a bucketful of half-digested ashes, asking myself when I will realize that the silver birch refuses to be burned? Its sap is cold and virginal, it will not yield to the hot caresses of the flames. It shrivels and turns grey . . . there is no passion in it.

But the apple wood! Ah . . . there is a wood of intoxicating fragrance. If you can find a derelict orchard, and rid yourself of the haunting melancholy that must come to any man who sees these boughs bereft and broken, that were once so brilliantly laden, then there is a treat in store for you, if you have a fireplace, and box of matches, and a few evenings to spare, when the darkening airs are damp and chill.

All right. Tell me that these are tiresome rhapsodies. That it would be much easier to order a sack of coal, and to leave it at that. Tell me that the energy expended in making my little log-pile could have been more profitably employed in writing articles on 'Should short women marry tall men?' I am sure that it would have been much more profitable. But if I had not been allowed to go log-gathering something would have died within me, and the brightest and most expensive fire of the latest and most hygienic asbestos would have given me no warmth.

For this was nature's way of 'making' money.

'This is *free*,' I said to myself, as I staggered back, over the fields, with my arms full of logs.

'Free! A fire for nothing! Warmth out of the earth!' I said it again as, with a sigh of relief, I let the logs fall in a heap on the pile. My arms were aching and my chin was covered with green moss and several peculiarly sinister woodlice had to be shaken from my trousers, but these were only minor details. The main thing was that I had been getting something for nothing.

§ III

However, once again, we are being lured away down unprofitable paths, and unless this book is to be like a pile of silver birch, all smoke and no fire, we must fan the embers of our story. Fortunately, it is not difficult to do so, for suddenly, in October, Leo descended on us once more. And life always became a little more intense when Leo was about.

He had undergone an operation for appendicitis at school, which accounted for his presence among us during term-time.

'How did he get appendicitis, Mrs. M.?'

'It was a *direct* result of the O.T.C.,' she said harshly.

'The O.T.C.?' This was indeed news. O.T.C.'s had

never been quite my favourite institutions, and if they gave boys appendicitis, here was a grand argument against them. Though the connection seemed a little remote. 'There was some sort of field-day,' she said. 'All the boys had rations of very hard pork-pies. And the minute they had finished their pork-pies they were given the order to advance, which meant that they had to hurl themselves on to the ground on their stomachs, over and over again. Complete madness.'

'But I thought you insisted on Leo joining the O.T.C., Mrs. M.?'

'So I did. I think he should learn to defend his country. But I do *not* think that *any* sort of useful pupose is served by cramming little boys with pork-pies and then making them hurl themselves about on their stomachs.'

'C'est la guerre.'

Mrs. M. snorted. 'Anyway,' she said, 'it has all been most annoying. And Leo is *no* help in the house, poor darling. He's never been so *willing* before . . . in fact there's quite a change in him . . . but then, you see, he's not allowed to lift anything at all heavy. And he really is obeying doctor's orders, for once in a way.'

I had my own theory as to why Leo was so anxious to obey doctor's orders. For when he came round to see me, and walked in the garden with me, the following dialogue took place:

'Do you know what would happen if I lifted that stone, B.?'

'I haven't the least idea.'

'My guts would come out,' observed Leo, with relish.

'Then please don't try.'

'They would,' he said earnestly. 'Honestly, they would. What d'you bet me?'

'I'm not going to bet on such a loathesome thing.'

'Oh, be a sport. I don't suppose they'd *all* come out.'

'The smallest quantity would be more than enough, Leo.'

Leo sighed. 'I wish you'd be a sport,' he said.

However, though I would not lend myself to this somewhat gruesome experiment, Leo found plenty of other ways in which to occupy himself. For Miss Hazlitt had given him a little plot of earth, for his very own, which he decided to turn into a garden. And though he was not supposed to subject himself to any sort of strain (as he regretfully reminded Mrs. M. whenever there were any sort of jobs to do) — he expended a very great deal of energy in digging this plot, lining it, planting it with bulbs, pulling the bulbs up again, and generally making an incredible mess of himself and his surroundings.

The strange thing about it was that from Leo's schoolboy garden I learned quite a lot of gardening tips which I had either forgotten, or never known. It was from Leo, for example, that I learned about baking the earth of the seed-boxes before you sow the seeds in them, in order to destroy the sperm of any weeds that may be dormant in it. How this elementary gardening tip had hitherto escaped my knowledge, I cannot imagine.

Leo discovered it by accident. One day we were standing in the greenhouse together, looking at a row of seed-boxes, which had been sown in September with a quantity of strange seeds which had arrived from New Zealand. I suppose I ought to have waited till the spring, but I have never been good at waiting, when it is a question of sowing seeds. I always want to sow everything a month earlier than the directions on the packet, in the pathetic hope that the seeds will come up earlier, and will not have to hurry themselves.

The seeds which I had sown in these boxes were of a most exciting shape and colour. Some had been like tiny squashed black pancakes, resembling the headgear of the modern lady of fashion. Others had been triangular, with small moustaches sprouting out of them. Some had been so small that they were as dust . . . it was impossible to believe that from this brown powder there would ever be a blowing or a growing . . . impossible to believe that here there was any perfume in waiting, nor any unborn tendrils.

Had any of them come up? The earth was covered with a medley of green. 'I wish I knew which were weeds and which weren't,' I sighed.

'Why didn't you put weed-killer on the earth before you sowed the seeds?'

'Because its got arsenic in it,' I said, in superior tones. 'And you read so many murder cases that you ought to know that arsenic stays in the ground for at least three years.'

'Well — why didn't you boil it?'

'Don't be silly.'

'Well, *bake* it, then?'

I looked at Leo. I suddenly realized he was talking sense. I also realized that this was something that every gardener ought to know.

Leo built a little brick shelter, to hold a sheet of old iron, on which we heaped a pile of fine-sifted earth. Then we lit a fire underneath, and baked the earth — the pleasantest form of cookery you can imagine, for the earth gave off a delicious scent. And when it was thoroughly baked, we took it straight into the greenhouse so that the wind, which is always alive with seeds, even though we may not see them, could sow no alien growths.

And now, thanks to Leo, the seed-boxes in the greenhouse remain bare and virgin until the seeds which one

The Inn

has actually sown push their heads through the earth. And I suppose that I ought to be thankful that this is so. And I ought to advise everybody to do the same. But really, I am not sure if I shall. For there was something very exciting about those little intruders. Were they really flowers, or were they 'gate-crashers'? Had they the social standing of a penny packet or were they wanderers, seeking shelter for the night? Were they cultured, or were they only 'weeds'? It is, one supposes, a sign of grave moral turpitude to confess that one didn't much care. For they were often beautiful, even if they were uninvited.

With the least encouragement I could develop the last few sentences into several chapters. I will refrain from doing so, and will merely content myself with hoping that you agree with me about the weeds, and also about the 'gate-crashers'. For unlike certain hosts, my idea of a really good party would be one in which nobody came who had been invited and everybody came who hadn't.

All the same, I continue to bake the earth for my seed-boxes. A little drearily, perhaps. But each year, I make the fire a little less hot.

§ I V

And now, at last, we can get going again. For it would take too long to recount Leo's various experiments in his garden. It would also be throwing an unjust emphasis on these proceedings. For all of them, to Leo, were mere pastimes.

It was the glass, the buried glass, which really excited him. He had never forgotten the story which the vicar told us on that spring evening, as we stood in the church, with the wind whistling through the tower. The glass formed a sort of leitmotif to his entire life. Time and again it would tinkle through his conversation, giving it unexpected flashes of poetry. For instance, one day he knocked over a vase of everlasting flowers, which were growing a little dusty.

'What are these Woolworth-looking things?'

'Everlasting flowers. The French call them immortelles.'

'Immortals? But they're faded and dry. Look at these red ones. They're only a dirty pink now.'

'I know.'

His eyes glistened. 'I bet, when we find the glass, it won't have faded. There'll be pieces like red flowers which have just been cut. Don't you think so?'

I looked at Leo and smiled. 'Like red flowers which have just been cut.' Why was that phrase so vivid? Because, I suppose, it came from the lips of a schoolboy to whom red was really red, and not merely a convenient piece of literary colour to be splashed over a grey page. I thought of Browning's line:

'When reds were reds and blues were blues. . . .'

He must have been thinking of a church window, when he wrote that line.

However, I had long given up any hope of finding the glass. It seemed one of those dreams which just don't come true. Besides, at the moment there were too many other things to think about.

§ v

Miss Hazlitt had been ill again. What was the matter, I did not know, for in spite of all our entreaties, she refused to see a doctor. But there came a day when she confessed that until she was better, the shop would be 'a little too much for her' if she had to be on her feet all day. And she asked Leo, very gently, if he would like to come and serve behind the counter, from five to seven.

Leo leapt at the opportunity. He came tearing to me. 'B.! B.! I've got a job. I'm going to serve in the shop till old Miss Whatnot's better.' Then he asked, with the callousness of youth, 'I don't suppose she'll be all right for at least a week, will she?'

'I don't know, Leo.'

'Of course, I'm awfully sorry,' he said, in slightly subdued tones. 'But still . . .'

'Do you think you can manage it?'

'Rather! If that Jackson boy comes in I'll give him hell.'

'You *must* be polite to people.'

'I'll be polite to him, all right. I'll pour brandy-balls down his throat till he chokes.'

'I think I'd better come too, at first, to lend you a hand.'

'All right. And then when I get sick of it I can go and dig my garden.'

And thus it was arranged. In some ways I welcomed the opportunity. For it meant that I would be able to get some first-hand knowledge of the shop, its customers and its takings. It was high time that Miss Hazlitt's affairs were put in order.

For the first three days nothing very much happened. Leo and I took it in turns to serve behind the counter. Very few people came in. Leo soon got bored with waiting and departed to his garden, where he was digging a pond.

'If I go much deeper, I shall bust my guts,' he would say, amiably, from time to time. However, I had come to the conclusion that Leo's . . . well, those parts of Leo . . . must be 'unbustable'. For he had already reached a depth of about six feet and showed no signs of flagging.

While Leo was digging I spent the time in examining wholesale catalogues, checking stock, and adding up accounts.

It was on the third day that it happened. It was just getting dark.

But as this is the one great event in the later history of Allways, I think it deserves a chapter to itself.

CHAPTER XVIII

ROMANCE

'Oh! B.! B.! Quick! Come here!'

There was a note of uncommon urgency in Leo's voice. Had he hurt himself? Had the notorious inside portions of him at last emerged, as he had so often threatened? I threw down the catalogue which I was reading, and ran into the garden. It was already almost dark.

'Leo! Leo! Where are you?'

'Here!'

I looked across the garden and saw him kneeling by a huge pile of earth. Fearing the worst, I ran across the border, trampling on a clump of chrysanthemums in my agitation.

'B.! I've found it!'

'Found it?' I was still panting, and was a little annoyed. Leo seemed perfectly all right. No gruesome physical disorders seemed to be affecting him. But he looked very strange, in the half light.

'Found it?'

He was holding out his hand. It was shaking with excitement.

And in his hand he held a piece of blue glass.

In a sort of dream I heard him saying, 'There's lots more, down here. A whole box-full, B. And another box, underneath. And it's all colours of the rainbow, B., and there's a lot of lead round it. Oh B. . . . I *nearly* bust my guts when I found it'.

Silence. There didn't seem to be anything one could say.

'B.! What's the matter? It *is* the glass isn't it?'

'It looks like it, Leo.'

'Why do you look so funny then? You're not angry, are you?'

'No. Of course I'm not angry, Leo.'

I stared at the glass. It was curiously shaped, like a fan. Round one corner there was a piece of old lead. Attached to it was a brilliant fragment of yellow glass. It glittered in the dusk, like the tip of an angel's wing.

The two pieces fell apart.

'Leo, old man,' I said, 'do you mind saying absolutely nothing at all, just for a minute?'

He gulped and nodded. His eyes were very bright.

§11

I held up the glass. The blue in my right hand, the golden in my left. The two pieces glittered against the grey sky of twilight. The blue was almost transparent. Dimly through it you could see the shadow of the cherry tree. You could not see through the yellow. But even in the dusk it had a strange radiance about it, as though it were burning, sending out a flame of gladness at its deliverance.

If a man had been able to speak, at a moment like that, this was what he would have said:

'Here you have endured, through the centuries. Here you have lain in the dark earth, you who were fashioned that the sunlight might pour through you and give you life, you who were made, by humble hands, for aery places, and set on high, that you might praise God by your silent, lofty beauty. Long ago, you praised Him. The sun shone through you, and you sweetened it with your reds and your blues, and poured it, like wine, over the starched linen of many a devout cavalier, till he, looking down at his hands, through half-closed eyes, might think that they had been stained with the blessed blood of Christ. Over the pews of the church you cast a largesse of green and red, till they were as gay as cherry trees, and with your dancing humours you lured away the eyes of little boys, who sat there, so patiently, in the England of the seventeenth century. . . .

'And then, one day, there were rough voices about you, and the sound of hurried hoofs, and a rending and a splintering, and the very soul was torn from you. And the windows which you had so gaily and gallantly irradiated were turned, in a single hour, to empty sockets. Blind, mournful, ghastly sockets staring out into an alien world. And the rain swept in through the windows, and ran in little trickles down the nave, while the Cavaliers retreated, and the Roundheads marched on. The Roundheads marched on, sternly, haughtily, and perhaps, in their cavalcade, as they passed a ruined church, they jerked their heads towards it, in approval, and thrust out a gauntletted hand to show how grandly they were serving God's purpose, by tearing out the bright eyes of the buildings which had risen, like young acolytes, before him. But somewhere, in a curving lane, muddy, panting, with the thorns of the may tree tearing their cold hands the Cavaliers were hiding . . . *with the glass!* Yes . . . they carried you in bags, and sacks, and boxes, and they cursed you when the horse stumbled, and you sent out a warning tinkle. But how could you help it? You knew no better,

You were made to praise God. And in that silvery echo, through the lanes, when you were marred and scattered and bleeding, with no light to give you life, no unity, your pattern shattered, your purpose mocked, you yet could praise God, in a faint voice, like the voice of distant bells, with a tinkle, as your pieces struck together.'

§III

'And now, the Resurrection. And the Life. A grubby little boy has found you. A little boy in strange clothes, who speaks a curious language which you do not understand. And kneeling beside him, a tired man, who is dressed as strangely, but does not speak at all. And holds you out before him, looking through you with eyes that seem to hurt him, for he is blinking so strangely. Yet, I hope, you do not mind being held by him, for he tries, however humbly, to understand. See! He is holding you up to the sky, that the light may pour through you again. It is only twilight, but then, you have known many twilights, have you not? Soft twilights, when England was very young, and there was a haze over the green fields of Piccadilly, and the waters round our shores were as translucent as the eyes of the young rovers who were setting out to build a new world. Soft, gentle twilights, with a sheen about them, for the nightingale who was trembling outside your paling shadows, on the brink of song, was a nightingale who could trace back his ancestry to the very bird who sang to Shakespeare, when he was writing a little play called *Romeo and Juliet*. . . .'

My hand tightened over the glass. It was a moment when I could have wished that I might cut myself, in sacrifice. I remembered the supreme couplet of Shelley.

Life, like a dome of many-coloured glass,
Stains the white radiance of eternity.

I also remembered that there was a boy of fourteen beside me, staring at me with wide-open eyes.

I laid the glass down reverently on the earth.

'Leo,' I said, 'stop all this sentimental nonsense. And give me your spade.'

CHAPTER XIX

TREASURE TROVE

'Of course,' said Mrs. M., 'it belongs to the Crown.'

It was three days later, and the great Allways Glass Sensation was at its height.

We were resting in the barn, Mrs. M., Leo, the vicar, Undine and myself. The glass was spread out on the ground before us, lying on four white sheets. In spite of our unwearied endeavours, we had only managed to re-assemble about half of it, for the pieces were small and the design was intricate. But already we could tell that the subject was the sacrifice of Isaac by Abraham, for in the centre we had pieced together a hand, powerfully modelled, clutching a dagger which plunged towards a white breast. The top right corner was almost complete, and showed the angel of God, in a whirl of glittering rose and purple. The face of Abraham, too, was finished . . . it stared at us, from the white sheets, grim and terrible, and as the sunlight filtered through the high windows it seemed that spasms of righteous indignation shot over his face.

The execution of the design was superb. Of that there could be no question. It was no paltry treasure that we had discovered, no minor piece of antiquarian interest. It was a magnificent window, worthy to rank with the most enchanted visions of those great but unknown men who made the English churches.

'Of course,' repeated Mrs. M., 'it belongs to the Crown, and . . .'

247

'Oh . . . oh!' interrupted Undine. 'I believe I've found a teeny-weeny bit of my cloud. Leo! Look!'

Leo snatched her piece, somewhat ungraciously. He felt that his position of authority had been grossly under-rated. After all *he* had found the glass.

He licked the glass. 'That isn't a cloud,' he snorted. Then his eyes brightened. 'But I say, I believe . . . yes, it *is* a bit of old what's-his-name's whiskers!'

And though Mrs. M. sssh'd him, and the vicar tried to look shocked, and Undine pouted, we could not really be angry with him. For this was the most delicious jigsaw puzzle that any of us had ever played, or were ever likely to play. I do not know who enjoyed it most. Leo was certainly the shrillest in his expression of pleasure.

'I say, what's this bit that looks like a carrot?' he would say, holding up a narrow piece of ruby glass.

And the vicar would cry 'Oooh, that is part of the dagger!'

And Mrs. M. would cry, 'No . . . *no* it's part of the angel's dress!'

And Undine would heave an ecstatic sigh and say, 'I can't fit a *single* thing to my lovely piece of blue, but I don't *care*. . . .'

And I would take the glass to the water-butt and wash it. That was really the most delightful job of all. One took a piece of muddy, dusty glass, that looked as if it could never have any colour, dipped it in the cool brown water, and rubbed it gently. And then, under the water, you suddenly saw it begin to glow . . . blue or red or green, and when you took it out, and held it to the sunlight, it sparkled like a jewel fresh from the polishers.

§ 11

'Of course,' said Mrs. M., for the second time, 'it belongs to the Crown. That little man from the *Evening Mail* said it did. And after all, the *Evening Mail*. . . .'

I promise to give you the answer to Mrs. M.'s reiterated interjection in a moment. But her mention of the *Evening Mail* makes me feel that some little explanation is due to the reader, in order to counteract the wild rumours which raged in the press, during the Allways Glass Sensation.

How the papers ever got to hear of it, no man will ever know. Leo said it was Mrs. M., Mrs. M. said it was Undine, and Undine said it was me.

It was certainly not me, nor was it Leo, for our first action, after we had carefully collected as much of the glass as we could, was to carry it reverently to Miss Hazlitt's old barn, stack it in a corner, lock the door, and go off to tell the vicar. We decided that Miss Hazlitt should not be told about it yet, for the doctor had warned us that any undue excitement would be bad for her.

I shall never forget the vicar's behaviour when we broke the news to him, in his little study. It was one of those occasions where emotions are so intense that they get mixed. His joy was so utterly unbounded that his face puckered up as though he were going to cry. He was like a little boy . . . he could say nothing but 'oh . . . oh . . .' in a trembling voice, and his lips formed prayers of thanksgiving. Then he seized a torch, and darted through the hall, scaring the cat, and leaving the front door open. We followed breathlessly.

The next thing I remember is the light of the torch on our strange little trio. I expect we looked ridiculous. One often does, on one's knees. For when he had seen the glass, and handled it with loving care, the vicar fell on his knees. And somehow, we felt that it was the right thing to do. Even Leo felt that.

The vicar's voice came softly through the shadows 'O God, we thank Thee for this great blessing, and we humbly ask that we may be made worthy of it, and guided rightly, now and always. . . .'

We whispered Amen.

And then, there was the meeting with Undine, in the hall of the vicarage. Before I could stop him, Leo had blurted out the whole story. That meant, of course, that Mrs. M. would have to be told. And the Professor. And Miss Bott. And everybody. It was a pity, but it was, of course, inevitable. You can't stop news travelling in a village. All we hoped was that we should be allowed to deal with this little matter in our own way, without any interference from the world at large.

Alas for our hopes! Within-twenty four hours, London had heard of the great Allways Sensation. And before we had made any plans at all, a reporter was knocking on my door.

§ I I I

God forbid that I should ever speak unkindly of reporters. I have myself knocked at too many unfriendly doors, waited in too many draughty corridors and endeavoured to infuse life into too many mummified celebrities to regard the newspaper reporter as other than a hero. But this reporter really was the limit.

He arrived in a foul little sports car, painted mauve, with an open exhaust . . . the sort of car that you see

TREASURE TROVE

buzzing down the Great West Road at ninety, with a highly suspicious siren making up her lips at all the drivers she passes.

He had prawn's eyes, plus-fours, and a grating voice, and he said so many hearty things within the first five minutes that I felt I should explode. He even said, when learning that my dog was a happy blend between a poodle and a chow:

'Pretty wizard mixture, what?'

The interview took place in the Garden room.

'Now, about this story. Let's get the facts.'

I told him as much as I felt was good for him. When I had finished, he stared at me.

'Well, d'you mean to say you brought me up from London for *that*?'

I refrained from reminding him that I had taken no part in bringing him from London.

He threw his cigarette out of the window: '*That's* no story,' he said. 'No story at all. This has got to be worked up. Now . . .' He took out a note-book, and an indelible pencil, which he licked, so that it left a purple streak on his tongue. 'About this village of yours. Got an oldest inhabitant?'

I shook my head.

'Village idiot?'

I shook my head. 'Not in residence,' I observed, with heavy sarcasm.

'Say, what sort of a village is this, then?'

'It is Allways. And we are quite sane, and astonishingly young.'

He looked at me impatiently. 'I'm afraid you don't see what I'm getting at. I'm trying to write a story out of nothing . . . .'

'Nothing?'

'Well, what *is* there? How would *you* write this story?'

'I shouldn't. It's my village, you see.'

'Yes . . . but supposing it were your *job*, and you *had* to?'

For a moment, I felt sorry for him. After all, it was his job. People who slam their doors in the faces of reporters might sometimes remember that. 'Damned impertinent nosey brutes,' they mutter, 'prying into our private affairs.' Perhaps. But they forget that they themselves are only too eager to read about *other* people's private affairs. And by patronizing the newspapers which publish these things, they are responsible for the existence of the reporter class. So they ought not to complain when the wheel of fate spins the pointer of publicity in their direction. I apologize for that ghastly metaphor, but it expresses what I mean.

But how could one tell this little monster how to write the story? One would have to begin by telling him to read a little history. After that, to study a little architecture. After that, to read the essays of Ruskin, and then to forget them, and to follow that up with a course of Charles Lamb. In other words, to change his mind. And even after he had changed his mind, one would have to ask him to change his trousers. One couldn't write decent prose in plus-fours like his.

However, as I did not feel energetic enough to ask him to change his trousers, I said:

'If you would sit down for ten minutes, and have a glass of sherry, I'll write the story for you. I know exactly what you want.'

'That's damned good of you.'

He took some sherry, and we both sat down . . . he on the floor, I at my desk. I began to scribble something which I hoped was fairly interesting, reasonably accurate, and not too intolerably vulgar.

After I had written a few sentences, he said: 'Of course, I haven't really got the rustic touch.'

'No?'

I wrote on.

'I mean, not like you. I mean, you can turn it out by the yard, can't you?'

I paused. 'Turn out what?'

'All this rustic stuff. My God . . . that's an easy way of earning a living!'

I resumed my writing, murmuring politely, 'Then why don't you do it too?'

'Oh well, I haven't got the rustic touch. Not like you.'

I felt that if he went on telling me that I had the rustic touch I should be changed into an old-world pergola, completely surrounded by Dorothy Perkins, so I asked him if he would mind holding his peace for a few moments, until I had finished the story.

In a few minutes I handed it to him. He read it. Turning slightly pink, he gulped, and said. . . .

'I'm terribly sorry. But this isn't any good.'

'Oh? What's wrong with it?'

'Well — I mean — for one thing, there isn't a single laugh in it.'

'There wasn't meant to be.'

'No. But — I mean — there ought to be, don't you think? Quite a lot of quiet fun, what? I mean, one might get quite a big laugh out of that old vicar of yours.'

'One might,' I said shortly. 'Though who would laugh at what, and when, is not quite clear to me.'

'And then,' he added, 'I don't think you've quite got the sob-stuff, have you?'

'I'm sorry.'

'And obviously, on the whole,' he continued, warming to his task, 'I think it's sob-stuff, don't you?'

'Frightfully.'

'It's got all the elements, hasn't it?'

'Every one.'

'Religion, I mean. That's always good for a couple of pars. Might work a moral into it. And then . . . .'

'If you don't mind,' I said, 'I have to take the dog for a walk.'

'Oh!' he paused abruptly. 'You're . . . you're not offended?'

'Not at all. I shall look forward to reading your story with the greatest interest.'

And at last he went.

I read his story. If you don't mind, I will not print it here. There are some things one prefers to forget.

After that, the newspapers swarmed on us. I was cowardly, and wouldn't see them, but everybody else did. Undine was photographed in countless positions, each more angular than the last, because, you see, she had an idea that she herself was a figure in a stained-glass window, and stuck out her elbows and jutted out her chin, to give the right effect. The *Sketch* and the *Tatler* had a terrible time toning down Undine's elbows.

Mrs. M. refused to be photographed, but delivered herself of a great many oracular utterances, which sounded strange when translated into journalese. Mrs. M. usually began her interviews by saying, 'I always suspected . . .,' which appealed to one paper so much that they headed the article 'The Woman Who Knew'.

But on the whole, the papers were fairly kind, and some of them told us a lot of things we did not know. The only thing they did not tell us was to whom the glass really belonged. At any moment, we felt, some government official would descend on us and take it all away. In the meantime, we sat in the barn, having the time of our lives.

§ I V

'Of course,' said Mrs. M., for the third time, 'it belongs to the Crown.'

'Oh sucks!' said Leo.

'Leo!'

'Sorry. But what's the king want with the glass?'

'It belongs to the Crown. Even a schoolboy should know *that!*' Mrs. M. cast a Macaulay eye at Leo, and shot out her rabbit's teeth at him, in a menacing grimace.

I found myself wondering if Mrs. M. would have been quite so keen on the Royal Prerogative if the glass had been found in her own garden. Under her rhubarb bed for instance. I wondered. . . .

But she interrupted me. 'We shall have to observe the proper procedure,' she said. 'Everything in order. It *must* be presented to the Crown.'

My mind set off again, willy-nilly. Me, Mrs. M., Leo, Miss Hazlitt at Buckingham Palace. Carrying sacks of glass over our shoulders. What should we do? Who would say what, and why? And how should we be dressed? Leo obviously, would wear his Etons, and look very pink and debonair in them. I could drag out my old morning coat, which was getting too tight under the arms, and Miss Hazlitt would wear her black silk. But Mrs. M.? How would she rise to the occasion? It was all too puzzling.

§ v

On the following evening we decided that the only thing to do was to ask the Professor about it. Of course, we knew that eventually . . . at any moment, indeed . . . officialdom would step in, and we should be forced to do everything 'through the proper channels'. But we all felt that it was very dull to do things through proper channels. After all, it was Allways glass. It was our little adventure. We wanted to keep it to ourselves as long as we could. So we went to the Professor for advice, as he was the only person in the village with any reputation for sagacity.

Sitting there in the deep arm-chair, with the old books around him, and the reading light shining on the dusty old test-tubes, he looked more like a medieval wizard than he had ever looked before. Even Mrs. M. seemed a little awed, as though he were an oracle that we had come to consult.

'Here is what Blackstone says about it,' said the Professor.

'Who is Blackstone, anyway?' asked Leo, somewhat sharply. He was still convinced that the glass ought to be his.

The Professor blinked at him. 'Blackstone was the author of certain commentaries on the laws of England, which have had a considerable influence on legal procedure.'

'I suppose he's about a hundred years old,' observed Leo with a sniff.

'If he were alive to-day,' said the Professor, 'he would be exactly two hundred and thirty-four.' Which quelled Leo.

The Professor read:

'Treasure Trove, called in Latin, *thesaurus inventus*, is any money or coin, gold, silver, plate or bullion, that is found hidden *in* the earth, or other private place, the owner thereof being unknown. In which case the treasure belongs to the King. But if he that hid it be known, or afterwards found out, the owner and not the King, is entitled to it. Also if it be found in the sea . . .'

'Well, it certainly wasn't found in the sea,' interrupted Mrs. M., 'so *that* doesn't apply.'

'And it doesn't say anything about glass,' said Leo.

'It's almost *too* much, isn't it?' crooned Undine, who had hitherto been silent. *'Bullion!* Delicious, bulging word . . . it makes me think of that *supreme* Jewess, what is her name, you know, one always sees her at first nights, what *is* her name?'

Then she trailed off rather raggedly, because the Professor was blinking at her as if she were some strange animal who had strayed in by mistake. And when the Professor does that, one can't be facetious for very long.

'In 1886,' he said, 'Judge Baylis wrote as follows in the *Journal of the Archaeological Institute* . . .'

He licked his thumb, and opened the pages of another large volume. Leo heaved a very theatrical sigh as he did so. But I must admit that for once I did not sympathize with Leo. We seemed to be on the track of something exciting.

'Firstly,' said the Professor, 'the treasure must be found hidden in the earth or in the walls, beams, chimneys or other secret places above the earth, but affixed to the soil.'

'Well,' said Mrs. M., 'we've had that out before.'

'Secondly,' said the Professor.

But what his 'secondly' would have been, no one will ever know. For at that moment, there was a tap on the door, and we all started. The door opened. And there, very pale, with her cloak thrown over her head, stood Miss Hazlitt.

We all rose to our feet. Somehow, in the rush and tumble, we had forgotten all about Miss Hazlitt. She had been told of the glass at last, and she had been allowed out of bed to see it. For a whole hour she had wandered round the barn, holding up pieces to the light, looking through them with a quiet smile. She had even delivered herself of a little homily to Leo on the subject of Abraham and Isaac. But we had not really consulted her about the ownership of the glass, although it had been found in her garden.

I think we all felt a little guilty about it, as she suddenly appeared. It was as though we were conspirators who had been disturbed.

'Am I disturbing you?'

'But of course not.' The Professor stepped forward. 'Please sit down.'

Mrs. M. hurried over with a footstool. 'Are you sure you ought to have got up?'

'I am quite well, thank you.'

Undine put a cushion behind her back. Miss Hazlitt smiled happily.

'Please . . . please. I did not wish to cause all this trouble.'

There was a moment's pause.

I remember thinking, just then, how extraordinary it was that this little woman, this plain, bespectacled old maid, should be receiving attentions from us all which could not have been more spontaneous if she had been Royalty. It was not a question of ordinary politeness, nor even common kindness. We should all, I hope, have been nice to any old lady who had been unwell — we should all have given up our chairs and done all we could to make her feel at ease. But here, it was Miss Hazlitt to whom we looked to put *us* at ease. It was Miss Hazlitt, whom we had rescued from bankruptcy, Miss Hazlitt, who was at the beck and call of every village boy for a pennyworth of acid-drops, Miss Hazlitt who had nothing, and was nobody, who quietly but emphatically held the position of 'chief lady' in the room. And if you had ever been in the same room as Mrs. M., you would know that this was, in itself, an extraordinary feat.

Moreover, she held this position solely by right of what she *was*. Like Royalty. Not by what she did or said, for that was little. But by what she *was*.

She merely sat in her chair, and smiled. That moment of silence seemed to last a very long time. It was broken by Leo.

'I say, Miss Hazlitt, about this glass . . .'

That was the signal for everybody to talk at once. Through the babel I heard. . . .

Professor: *Thesaurus inventus* is any money or coin, gold, silver, plate or bullion. . . .

Undine: Personally I think it's all *too* marvellous . . . I shall *die* if they find any bullion . . .

Vicar: I feel certain that Miss Hazlitt will agree that the glass must be restored to . . .

Leo: Stop nudging me, B. I found the beastly glass. I found it. B., you're hurting. . . .

Out of all this, in clarion tones, came the voice of Mrs. M.

'It belongs to the Crown,' said Mrs. M.

'It belongs to God,' said Miss Hazlitt.

And that, as they say, was that.

§ VI

Of course, as I look back on the whole thing, I realize that Miss Hazlitt's decision was the only right and proper one. Legally, morally, and above all, aesthetically. And if Mrs. M. had not been so insistent in her championship of 'the Crown', and if Leo had not been so shrill in his own demands, we should have paid more attention to the quiet asides of the vicar, who, throughout the whole drama, had reminded us that the glass was the glass of Allways church, and as such, it should be restored to its proper place. But the vicar was not only a man of God, and not only a gentleman, but he was suffering from his annual visitation of asthma. And the combination of these three things was enough to rob his voice of the authority which it would normally have had.

'It belongs to God.'

There was nothing much to be said after that. Nobody disputed it. The matter was settled. The Queen had spoken. At the right time, and in the right way, we felt, the glass would be restored to the window, and the light would dance through it once more, the same light that had once danced through it in the years when England had been very small, and very earnest and very young.

And so, after a little more conversation, to bed. Mrs. M. went out into the hall for her goloshes. 'No Leo . . . that's the wrong foot,' we heard, in a stage whisper. 'No, it's all rumpled up over the heel. There, that's better. Now, where is your scarf?'

Undine followed, and reappeared, a moment later, with her immense Antique Lanterne, which she turned on for our benefit. It cast a garish search-light round the little room, for although its casing was ye oldest in the worlde, and though it had a large cast-iron spider on the handle, it was fitted with a highly efficient battery.

'Can I light you home?'

Miss Hazlitt rose, and thanked her. They went out together.

The Professor and I remained.

'Women are beyond me,' he said, and sighed.

CHAPTER XX

A GREEN HILL FAR AWAY

FOR most of that winter, and some of the spring, I had to be away from Allways. For nearly three months I was obliged to look at the world from the fortieth floor of an hotel in New York.

There are worse places than that from which to regard the world, I suppose, but I can't say that I liked it. I used to peer over the window-ledge and see the stream of human ants below. And although it was all very grand and impressive, and aroused the loftiest thoughts of Man's Conquest of Nature, I preferred my bedroom window at Allways, which is so close to the ground that you can easily jump from it, without hurting yourself.

It must be a sign of galloping middle-age to carry your home in your heart, like this. To scribble in your diary these two memoranda side by side:

Thursday. January 10th. Dine with J at Ambassador's 8 o'clock not dressed, go Harlem afterwards.
Write B. to plant twelve hollies in gap between pond and road.

It is terrible to be thinking of a cottage when you are in a palatial hotel. To gaze at a radiantly beautiful fountain, all lit up in shades of puce and purple, and decorated with exquisite chastity by bunches of Moorish bananas, and to think 'what a waste . . . if I had a quarter of that water in the sunk garden I could grow water-lilies which would make Mrs. M'.s hair turn white overnight'. Even more terrible, when sitting in a Harlem dance palace, watching a thousand oozing couples swaying together, to be reminded by the star saxophone-player of the cow in the farm that always wakes you up in the small hours.

Such reactions, one supposed, are the signs of a narrow, provincial, and utterly unfashionable mind. In the faint hope that some of my readers may be equally weak and despicable, I will make the ultimate confession, which is that I actually carried photographs of Allways about with me, in a leather photograph case. That, we will admit, is definitely not chic. It is positively suburban.

I didn't care. I used to prop the pictures up on the window-ledge, and stare at them. The cottage looked very strange against the background of sky-scrapers. A little blurred building, with dim trees and shrubs around it. And behind, the wild towers of the great city of To-day, the white, slashing lines of the sky-scrapers, the million windows, glaring at each other with arrogant distaste.

§ 11

But even if I had not had the photographs to remind me of Allways, the mail would have done so. I was kept in constant touch with everything. The new planting of trees for the wood had been carried out successfully, in spite of an error in delivery, by which they had arrived two days too soon, and had been forced to lie in the field, covered with sacking, while holes had feverishly been dug for them in the frost-bound earth. Undine was getting up a concert. The shop was progressing wonderfully, and Miss Hazlitt was very happy.

The mail arrived in two batches a week. One day, as I inquired at the titanic rabbit-hutch in the hall, where the letters were kept, I found a very large batch waiting for me. Nearly all of them were from Allways. I sped up in the lift, jangling my door-key impatiently, promising myself a happy hour.

But the hour was very far from happy. The first letter I opened was from the Professor. This is what I read:

I am very sorry to have to tell you [he wrote] that our good friend Miss Hazlitt has been very seriously ill. I know what a shock this will be to you, but I felt it better to warn you because there is a faint danger . . . so faint that I feel sure we need not take it seriously . . . that matters may have got beyond our control by the time you return.'

I stopped reading the letter. 'Beyond control' . . . what did that mean? I dreaded to read on. It was only with a great effort that I could continue.

God forbid that I should criticize her, especially now, but if only she had behaved normally, and reported herself to the doctor when she first felt the pain, she might not be where she is now. But as you are aware, she never complains, she is always resigned, everything is God's will, everything for the best. And so . . .

I'm sorry. I am telling you all this very badly. Here are the facts. Miss Hazlitt was taken to Peterborough hospital for a very serious operation, a week ago. The shop is shut up. Lord knows when it will open again. We have got a woman in, to look after things and to feed the kittens.

I went to see her yesterday. She gave me the most extraordinary lesson in heroism that I have ever known.

In the past I have sometimes had harsh things to say about religion, and I still feel that the Church has often used its influence in the service of obscurantists throughout the ages. But when one sees examples of Christ's teaching like Miss Hazlitt, one hesitates to criticize a philosophy which can have such magnificent results on individuals.

I was the first visitor she was allowed to see. 'But what is she suffering from?' you are asking. I've written this letter over and over again to try to break it gently. But I can't. And you'd better know. It is a malignant growth. In the breast. I wish to God I could tell you this, instead of writing it.

They had performed the first operation a few days before, but another is due as soon as she is strong enough to stand it.

I shall never forget the extraordinary happiness — yes, happiness — of her smile as I stood by her bed. She had a little bunch of crocuses by the side of her bed, which Mrs. M. had picked for her. 'My own crocuses, my very own!' she said. You remember how her voice seemed to sing when she was describing even the simplest pleasures? Well — it had that same singing quality now, though of course it was very weak.

She could only say a very little but her whole talk was a song of praise. It was the crocuses that seemed to please her most. She was afraid that Mrs. M. must have been put to a great deal of trouble — it was so kind of her — everybody was so kind — and now that the flowers were here, in this little glass by her bed, she could enjoy them almost as much as if she were sitting at the window of her sitting-room, watching them dance in the cold wind, against the dark earth.

Enjoy . . . that was the word she used the most. And even when she spoke of the coming operation she said, 'Isn't it wonderful? You see — they would not operate again if there were not hope.'

I think there is hope. H—— is a brilliant surgeon. I had a word with him after I had left her and he said, 'Miracles do happen, sometimes. And Miss Hazlitt believes in miracles!' It was rather a cryptic remark, but he is not the sort of man who tells one lies just for the sake of saving one a *mauvais quart d'heure.* At least, he wouldn't do that to *me.* We had a rather acid correspondence about glandular therapy in the *Lancet* last year . . .

And then, to my astonishment, the letter suddenly stopped, and for nearly half a page the paper was covered with extraordinary symbols . . . partly algebraical, partly geometrical, and partly animal. For the mention of the *Lancet* had apparently started the Professor off on an entirely new train of thought. And, as usual when he was working out a problem, he drew animals. There was a large snake hissing at a giraffe, and a whale spouting, and six cats rushing across a roof after another snake. And then, as though nothing had happened, the letter resumed:

I fear that all this will make bitter reading for you, and as I said before, I would have given a lot to be spared the task of writing it. We drew lots as to who should tell you — Miss Bott, Mrs. M., Undine, the vicar and I. The lot fell to me.

Mrs. M. is very worried about the shop. Not for any personal reason . . . she has been grand all the way through, but because she realizes that if Miss Hazlitt comes back. . . .

And then, once more the letter stopped. This time, for good and all. A maze of figures finished it, and underneath, a big circle with a sparrow sitting on it.

I stared at the circle and the sparrow. I suddenly realized that the telephone had been ringing for five minutes. I got up and took off the receiver. I went to the window and looked out. It was just growing dark. The million arrogant eyes of the sky-scrapers stared at me with that remorseless cruelty which only New York knows.

I went back to the telephone. I called up a shipping agency. Within a week, I was sailing home.

§ I I I

Although April was well advanced when I left New York, there was little sign of spring in America. The trees in Central Park were bare as ever, and though the florists in Park Avenue were full of blossoms from the south, the flowers looked pale and frightened, like poor little rich girls who didn't know what it was all about.

But in England, spring was holding high revel. Never had the grass been greener, nor the cliffs whiter, nor the birds more absurdly sweet. Even the station seemed to echo to the sound of thrushes and blackbirds. I remembered that lovely phrase which somebody once coined for Elizabethan England, when the air rang with rhyme and poets strode down every alley. 'A nest of song-birds.' That was how England seemed, that day.

But it was because of the garden that my home-coming was made so exciting. For all the joys that a garden can give you, the chief joy is the excitement which it adds to the wanderer's return. As soon as you land in England you start staring about you to see what is 'out', and as the train bears you to London you keep wiping away the moisture on the window-pane to look at the little suburban gardens which flash by, for they will give you advance tidings of what awaits you at home.

There are, of course, more important things which you ought to be doing. You ought to be making your head ache over the evening newspapers and congratulating yourself that you are at last 'up-to-date', instead of being several hours behind. You ought to be absorbing the latest details of a trunk-murder case — for after all, it is terrible not to know that the police have discovered a blood-stained handkerchief in Manchester to which 'they attach the utmost importance'. *You* ought to attach the utmost importance to it, too, but somehow, you don't. Why? Because you are not a good citizen? No. Because you happen to be a good gardener. And as such you realize that all this 'news' is just silliness, just tap-room gossip for tired minds, just a sort of mental *apéritif* for people who have no flowers to tend, poor devils. For people who are shut in four walls, with no escape, whose only blossoms are the faded blossoms on the wall-papers, which never change, but grow more pallid and more monstrous and more mocking with the passing of the years.

It must be sad to come home, if you have no garden waiting for you. For then, you have no alternative but to read the silly news-sheets instead of spending your time in the best of all ways, in looking out of the window. But we, who are gardeners together, need not occupy ourselves so drearily.

Look! Over there, a bright splash of pink against a line of washing, is a double pink cherry. That means that the little avenue you planted two years ago, will now be a blaze of colour. And the daffodils are not over yet — it

must have been a very late year. That means that if you
rush up to the country at once you will catch them in their
last beauty, for you live much farther north and there
will be a good week of daffodils ahead of you.

And of course, you *do* rush up to the country at once.
You have to exercise a great deal of self-control to prevent
yourself from running down the path. The dialogue that
takes place with the gardener is staccato and artificial. You
can't pay attention to what he is saying. There are too
many things to be seen.

'Were the crocuses good?'

'Fine, sir. We had lots of people stopping and looking
over the hedge. But the mice are still bad. A regular
torment, the mice are.'

'What about the new trees?'

'They look pretty well, sir.'

'Had much rain?'

'Not enough.'

'Has the wind been bad? I say . . . this tree wants
staking. And we must keep this grass down. And . . . my
word, that cherry avenue's a success!'

'Thought you'd like it, sir.'

You drift away by yourself. You don't want anybody
near you, not for this first hour. You want to gloat, or
growl (as the case may be), in private. You don't even
want a pencil and paper, not at first, to make notes on.
Time enough for that to-morrow. You just want your little
hour.

But it was only an hour that I could afford, on that home-
coming. For Miss Hazlitt was calling me. And even though
I hurried through the garden, and brushed down the little
avenues of the wood, I felt guilty, as though I might arrive
too late.

CHAPTER XXI

THE LAST MIRACLE

SHE was in the garden, under the apple tree. And as soon as I saw her my heart sank. For it seemed that it was a ghost that was lying there, in the wheel chair, a ghost that might drift away into the branches above.

And it was with a ghost's voice that she welcomed me, and excused herself for getting up, for she was 'a little weak'. But she said that she was very contented, and that the little village girl who was looking after the shop, and helping her, was being so kind and efficient.

'And the garden!' For a moment the old ring of delight came back to her voice, that strange, singing quality which was the happiest sound I have ever heard in a human voice.

'Have you ever *seen* so many flowers?' she went on. 'Look! *They are all doing their best for me, in case I may never see them again.*'

'Please . . . please don't say that.'

She put her hand on my arm. It was as light as one of the leaves that fluttered overhead. 'But there is nothing to be sad about!' Her face was radiant. 'Where I am going, there will be flowers too . . . far lovelier than these.'

§ I I

It was then that the miracle happened.

The breeze freshened. And the flowers and the branches swayed in it, dancing, pirouetting, twisting and turning so eagerly, as though they were trying to show her that they

were brighter than any of those ghostly flowers which were
waiting for her, in the dim fields of the spirit. Yes, it was
as though there were a wild whispering from branch to
swaying branch, through the green channels where the
sap runs, and the gold is minted for the blossoms. 'More
speed . . . more speed!' they seemed to sigh, in the
restless wind, and with each breath of the wind one had a
strange sense that the hidden gold was drifting down, down
to the green blossom, till soon, it would hang heavy on the
branches, and all the trees would rejoice in its riches and its
glory.

And among the irises, too, there was a stirring, as though
the butterfly flowers that slept there were restless to spread
their purple wings. 'Somebody is waiting for us . . .
somebody is waiting!' And the winged petals, so delicately
folded, throbbed in the sunlight, that filtered through their
green casings, and the purples deepened, and their myriad
eyes of tawny gold were opened wider, wider.

I looked at Miss Hazlitt. She was lying back with half
closed eyes. I wondered what she was seeing. The white
snows of the cherry blossom in her garden? Or the deeper,
purer snows of the trees of Paradise, whose branches are
the clouds and whose roots are laid in the stainless fields
of the sky?

'I am very happy,' she whispered. 'I am very thankful.'

Even as she said it, her face contorted with a spasm of
pain. The thin hand gripped my arm with a feverish
force which I should not have thought possible. I knew
something of the agony she was enduring, for the doctor
had told me, before I had gone out to see her, that it was
almost incredible that she should be able to endure these
attacks without morphia.

'I can't understand it,' he had said. 'Any other woman

would be screaming half the time.' Then he had looked at me with a certain amount of suspicion in his honest eyes. 'Do you think she has any drugs of her own . . . that she takes without my knowledge?'

'Yes,' I said, 'she has.' I was very tired, and I felt the doctor was rather stupid.

'Ah!' He rubbed his hands together. 'I thought so. Her condition, altogether . . . her pulse too . . . but most of all, her extraordinary calm . . . now, d'you know what drug it is?'

'Yes. It's very simple, really.'

'Well. . . ?'

'She believes in God.'

I was sorry when I had said it. I had not meant to be rude to the doctor. He was an honest man, doing his best. But a little knowledge of the power of mind over matter would not have hurt him.

It was a pity he could not have seen Miss Hazlitt at that moment. For he would have realized that no human drug could possibly have fought for her as her faith was fighting, no earthly anodyne could possibly have brought relief so quickly, nor smoothed the furrows from her features, nor enabled her to say once more, in a voice that did not tremble: 'I am so thankful.'

The wind freshened again. It blew, sweet and cool, on to her forehead, which was damp with the agony through which she had passed.

She smiled. She said:

'Yes . . . the flowers are doing their best to hurry.'

She lifted herself in her chair. She stretched her arm out. '*And look — they are staying up for me . . . too!*'

Staying up?

Then I understood what she meant.

§ I I I

And now I felt that a cloak of magic was drawn over the little garden, that she and I were sitting in enchanted chairs, under trees laden with silver from the land of Faery. That was my Pagan reaction to her Christian conviction.

Somewhere, I felt, a wand was being waved . . . a wand that could wantonly dominate the forces of nature, swelling the pear blossom at its will, checking the daffodils, hastening the sap here, staying its departure there.

For as I looked out, through the dying light, I saw many things that made me rub my eyes . . . there was a lingering among the flowers, a tardiness, as though they were loath to leave. 'If she must go, then we would be here, to say good-bye.' It was a bitter thought, and I put it from me. Yet, it was strange how the winter honeysuckle still breathed its sweetness, over there, by the water-butt. In ordinary years, it had long ago dropped its last flower, and given itself up to greenery. And here we were, and it was nearly May. . . .

Nearly May! Yet the winter jasmine was still spangled with flowers. They shone there, in the twilight, like late lamps burning in a secret wood. The daffodils still danced as though they could never weary, forgetting that for a whole month they had turned the fields to a dancing floor, and swirled and laughed and tossed their heads in the wind's music. As for the primroses, they bubbled on and on, yes, they bubbled and they foamed over the banks, and sparkled, cold and sweet . . . they poured in endless profusion over the ditches, jostling the periwinkles, joining hands round the jonquils, and bearing

s   273

their brave and delicate torches into the deepest darkness of the shrubbery.

'Nonsense!'

'Tiresome sentimentality!'

I *know* that all this is nonsense, and that it may be tiresome sentimentality. But I also know that it is true.

For there are some miracles in which a man must believe, or perish. And one of those miracles is the kinship between mankind and the green things of the earth.

There is a lovely phrase, which country people use, about a man having 'green fingers'. If you have green fingers, the flowers know it, and they let you do with them as you will, and they gain something of your spirit, and flourish, and you gain something of theirs too, and are at peace. I believe that I have green fingers myself . . . in spite of all my failures and stupidities. I believe, when I touch a plant or a tree, that there occurs some contact more subtle and intimate than the mere laying of human hands on vegetable substance, I believe that my blood and the blood of the tree are mingled . . . green to red, and red to green, as the blood of a man who has died is mingled with the earth.

Dust to dust, ashes to ashes.

That is the litany of death, the dirge that blows always through the damp church aisles.

Green to red, red to green.

That is the litany of life, the chant that blows through the forest, when a man is on his feet, under the sunlight, with the wind in his eyes.

And so, I swear, there was this queer magic brooding about Miss Hazlitt's garden in those late April days when life seemed to be deserting her. For the flowers loved her,

and were trying to help her. I make no more apologies.
I just leave it at that.

For flowers know if you love them.

§ I V

The flowers *were* doing their best for Miss Hazlitt. She
never saw them again.

That night she took a turn for the worse. I don't like to
think of the agony she must have suffered, for, towards the
end, she herself asked for morphia — she who had always
refused it. The doctor told me, afterwards, that she
whispered that she would have 'just a little, because otherwise I might cry, and I would not like to . . .' She could
not finish the sentence for some little time, then at last, she
beckoned to him. The drug was just beginning to work.
'I did not finish my sentence,' she said. 'I meant to say,
"I would not like to go home, crying".'

Those were the last words she ever spoke.

She died at dawn. For most of the night her good
friends at Allways had waited. One by one I persuaded
them to go away. There was nothing they could do.

It was just growing light when the doctor came down and
told me. As soon as I heard his slow step on the stairs I
knew that it was all over. I told him I would go up later.
He nodded.

I went out into the garden.

The cool air was shrill with the first clamour of birds.
Shrill . . . shrill . . . they stabbed my aching head. God,
why can't you tell those damned birds to stop? Why must
they go on, with this mockery of song, when she lies dead
in that little room?

Shriller, shriller. Would those birds never stop? I

lifted my head to the skies. They were cold and curdled. They were like a blank stage over which the bird chorus was calling . . . a deserted, rehearsal stage, with only a few cold clouds, like properties which had been left over-night.

'This is ghastly,' I thought. 'It's unworthy of *her*, to go on like this. What would she want me to do? Pray for her, I suppose. But I can't. Not yet. Later on, perhaps, but not now.'

I looked round the garden. What could I do? What would she like me to do. And then, suddenly, I knew.

I have gathered many bunches of flowers, spent many happy hours of life, searching for brighter yellows and more brilliant blues. But no bunch which I have ever gathered in the past or shall ever gather in the days to come, can be as sweet or as fragrant as that which, an hour later, I laid by her side.

CHAPTER XXII

LIGHTS OUT

AND so the lights fade over Allways. And from the pages of this book. If any glow has illuminated them, we must blow it out, and sit back, and watch the ashes of these dreams, as they turn from red to grey, from grey to black.

And so, one day, I suppose, the lights will fade, in bitter reality, from Allways. It will go downhill; it has no purpose in life; it is just a little piece of England where a few people lived, and were happy. There is no reason for such places, nowadays. If there were a golf-course . . . but the fields are not fitted for that. If there were a river . . . but there is only one tiny stream, which is extremely temperamental. If there were coal . . . but there is only homely clay. If there were iron . . . but there is none. The only iron is in the hoofs of the horses, as they plod, plod through the dust of summer and the puddles of winter.

No, I fear that Allways, and the scattered villages which resemble it, will go down. Maybe it will live for fifty years more, maybe a century. What does it matter? The new world is killing it, slowly but surely.

Take one little example, the village shop. It is still there, though Miss Hazlitt has gone.

But people have no use, nowadays, for a little village shop, with a tinkling bell, and it irritates them to find that the single lattice window is so thickly overgrown with yellow roses that they have to look twice at the shelves, which are bathed in a green gloom, splashed with gold, so that all the bars of soap, the bottles of sweets, and tins of polish seem as if they were sprouting . . . as if they were magic products from a little shop in the woods. They do not like to have to peer about like this. They like great stores, blazing with electricity, and filled with a million things which they do not really want.

You and I know, of course, that if these people were sensible they would realize that they could get all that they could ever need in the village shop, in a quarter of the time and at half the expense. Instead of fighting their way to an elevator they would only have to put out their hand from one shelf to another. Instead of walking down miles of corridors, they would only have to peer down to look under the counter. And instead of being called 'Moddom', by a girl who does not care whether they fall dead before her, they would be called by their own names, and they would hear all the local gossip.

If something new arrives at our shop it is a real event. Not an event like a new cold cream in a London emporium, where they arrange ten thousand pots of the cream in a miniature reproduction of the Taj Mahal, and play a coloured fountain in the middle, and get quantities of bulging actresses, powdered like clowns, to sell it. Nothing quite so ineffably dreary as that. No . . . if a new cold cream arrives at the village shop, the total instalment is probably four pots, which are proudly arranged on the counter, with a little card written in ink, telling the village maidens what marvellous things it will do to them. For some days these four pots are regarded with wonder by all of us. And then, one morning, there are only three, and before lunch we all know that Mrs. M. has purchased a pot. And for weeks ahead we have the excitement of looking at Mrs. M.'s face, politely but earnestly, to see if the cream is really going to work.

This seems to me, I confess, more fun than anything which the great stores can provide. Most people will not agree with me. They cannot believe that a thing can be good unless they see ten thousand of it, in a blare of coloured lights. That is one of the many reasons why Allways is doomed.

§ 11

I will not trace the probable course of the decease of Allways. It would hurt too much. The shop, I suppose, will be the first to go. Then the post office. The new generation will not have the patience, when they want to telephone, to walk into a charming kitchen, and if the post-mistress (who has the exquisite gentility of a long line of country ladies), should inquire after their health, they would regard her as a bore. They do not like the purchase of stamps to be a little social event . . . (the stamps are handed to you with a smile, and a kind word, as though they were some secret passport to happiness . . .) no, they will want to buy their stamps from a machine. They will want to do everything by machinery. For all I know, they will want to make love by machinery.

I don't like to think of it. Better to be vague about it. To admit it with a shrug of the shoulders. Just to say — 'Time will pass'.

Time will pass. And the great trees that shadow the village green will grow weary, and fall, and the saplings will take their place, and spread their arms wider and wider, exalting in the sun that blesses them, and the rain that purifies them. And they too will grow weary, and droop at last, and die.

And there will be alien trees at Allways.

§ I I I

But one day I shall come back. It would be worth
centuries of torment, of celestial boredom, of ethereal
anonymity, to come back to Allways again, for a little
while. To come back, and see what has happened to it,
when one is a ghost.

It will be dark, I suppose. It is always dark for a ghost.
And there will be no calendar to tell me what year it is,
only the calendar of nature, which will be written in the
coloured leaves of the trees, the widening curves of the
river, and the slowly wheeling dial of the night sky, whose
every second is commemorated by a silver star.

And I would pray that I might approach Allways from
the wood where the bluebells grew, the wood whose
November shadows once sparkled with the fire of the wild
spindle, whose April twilights were mysterious with the
moth-winged bloom of the wild white cherry.

That is where my ghost will start, for its last journey. It
will stand there, in the shadows.

And it will be waiting, listening . . . listening for a
companion, for it would not make this journey alone.

There he is!

Again, there in the far distance, a faint bark! Very
faint indeed, as though it came from over the hills of the
moon. But once more, much nearer to the earth — oh,
the Fates have been kind indeed . . . I try to call, to
whistle, to tell my dog that I am here. But there is only a
faint rustle in the leaves, however desperately I shout.

Will he find me? A ghost has no scent . . . will he find
me? Oh please . . . please. I start to meet him. And even
as I glide forward, there is a rustle in the bracken, the

rabbits flee affrighted from the phantom who pursues them, and there, through the clearing he flies towards me, and we are together again, as we used to be, when the world was very young, and we were its masters.

And so we set out together. For many moons, I expect, the rabbits will whisper, with horror, of the phantom dog who suddenly and silently bore down on them with icy breath, the dog whose bark was like a distant trumpet, whose bite was so fierce and yet could do them no harm.

§ I V

In the livening breeze, and under the eternal stars, my ghost will set off, down the hill, will revive its tenuous veins with the vigour of the wind, and raise its heavy-lidded eyes to the moon. Thus, silently, my limbs will jerk themselves down the hill, while I whisper desperately:

'See! The stars are just coming out! They were mine once, they are mine still!'

On, on, jerk the creaking limbs, in the appalling silence. 'See! I can still feel the wind! Cold, so cold . . . through my bones . . . it was not so cold, once . . . when my bones were covered. No, it was not so cold, it was warm and fragrant and desirable . . . oh! it was utterly desirable on a night in June, when I had blood, and hands that could take branches, and break them, and fingers that could seize flowers, and pick them, and press them to my face. But now I have no blood, no hands, no face. What have I? What am I? Oh God . . . tell me what I have, what I am, that I may know!

§ v

Allways!

We are in it now. Past the forge. It is still there . . .
though there are some strange buildings which I dare not
look at. Past a big clump of trees by the village green. . .

But what are these other trees? This immense avenue
stretching before me, cavernous and infinite in the aqueous
light of the moon? These were never here . . . I do not
know them. They are all alien to me . . . this is not Allways! My dog and I stand at the entrance to the avenue,
two black dejected shadows, like beggars at the door of
a great mansion, at night.

And then, the clouds drift away from the moon. And
through the Gothic tracery of branches I see, once more the
little hill where the bluebells grew, and the valley that is
shaped like a heart, and the familiar S of the winding
stream. It is still Allways. And these trees, that I planted,
these trees, that were only as high as my shoulder, on the
last year I saw them, are welcoming me home.

Thank you, trees. When I was alive I used to say 'things
do grow, if you will only be patient'. But in those days I
was not patient. I never saw the trees I planted. Not with
my living eyes. But I am seeing them now, with the eyes
of a ghost. They were worth waiting for.

We start down the great avenue, my dog and I. But
now our footsteps are slow and halting, and our eyes
downcast. For we are nearing home. And we do not know
what sort of home it will be. We do not know if there will
be anyone there to welcome us. We are afraid.

On and on . . . slower and slower. Here is the bend
in the road. We shall be able to see it, when we turn the

corner. But we are not sure whether we want to turn the corner. We pause in the chequered shadows.

I look down. 'Well,' I whisper. 'What about it? Shall we go back?'

He tries to wag his tail. He is shivering a little.

'It used to be home,' I plead.

He wags his tail, very feebly.

'We have come a long way and it was cold, among the stars . . . there might be a fire, if "they" are kind . . . it would be a treat . . . we should remember it, for many years, for centuries perhaps, even for eternity.'

And so, we turn the corner.

§ VI

Above us, a wild rushing in the trees, for the wind has risen.

Before us. . . .

A shape.

Just a shape. For what else can I call this ruin of the thing I had loved? It stands there forsaken, deserted . . . its roof has long fallen in, there are thick strands of ivy coming from *inside* the windows.

I step closer. I am shaking with impotent anger. 'How dare they . . . how *dare* they?' And my whole being is wreaked with an agony of longing, to have power once more, and strength, and the authority of this world. To have power, if only for a few hours! That must be the longing of all ghosts who revisit their old homes, who see the havoc that is wreaked by the fools who come after them, who wail disconsolately through ravaged gardens and weep in despair over the woods that their descendants are destroying. For a few hours only, to come back, to issue orders, to set men to work, to enforce obedience, to start the business of salvage, to bring beauty once more into the desert that the others have made, in the wake of one's death.

'How dare they. . . .'

But ghosts have not much strength. When I first cried out, there was a cold breath, and an owl had fluttered, startled, from the ruined walls. But now, my force has gone, and the owl is back again, and is perched, in arrogant possession, on the wreck of a window-ledge. The window-ledge of my old bedroom.

I stare at the owl. I do not attempt to cry out any more. I have been hurt too much. And with the perversity of those who are in an extremity of pain, I press closer, to more pain. . . .

And I drift through the doorway.

I have come home.

The moonlight shines through the roof. But the centre beam is still standing. Grand old beam . . . it's still there. But the ivy is choking it, dragging it down. Feebly I lift out my hands, but they are as star-dust, they have no power. They fall to my sides.

I see in front of me a square ruin, thick with weeds and brambles. It is the Garden Room. My head bowed, for I cannot bear much more, I drift through it. There is still a gap where the window was. Here I am. The garden is before me. I dare not look.

I had better go back.

I whistle to my dog. He looks up at me.

I turn. But I do not seem to be able to move.

I *must* move. I dare not look at the garden. It couldn't be borne . . . even a ghost, with ice in its veins, couldn't

stand this last humiliation. I must never see the garden
again. It has gone, and I must go back through that
ruined door, and up the lane, and over the hill and into
eternity. Never must I look back.

But I can't move. Something is happening to me. A
stirring in the blood . . . almost, a feeling of warmth. As
though someone had laid his hands on my shoulders, and
were turning me, against my will, were whispering 'Be of
good cheer!'

It is happening. Call it what you will . . . call it a
reincarnation, a fluke of astral fluid, or an odd psychic
phenomenon . . . it does not matter. All I know is that
the old magic is working, once again. The old call is
being obeyed, the call that was always too strong to resist.

The call of the garden.

'I remember . . . I remember.'

I remember, on bitter nights in January, how I would
arrive at the cottage, long after Allways had gone to bed.
And in spite of the wild winds and the driving sleet and
the animal hunger in me that craved for a warm drink,
I would fling wide the French windows, and grip a torch,
and make my way to the little patch of snowdrops under the
damson tree, and feel amply rewarded if I found one pale
blossom staring at me, startled, in the light of the torch,
with the frost sparkling like diamonds on it. It never
mattered, in the old days, what the hour was, nor the month
. . . the darkest hour of the blackest week of the year
could not hold me back, could not keep me indoors, when
I arrived. Somewhere, on some branch, there would be
a bud to be welcomed. Somewhere, in the kindly shelter
of a sturdy shrub, there would be the lifted tip of an
emerald spear, thrust aloft through the dark earth by
an impatient herald of spring.

That is *me*. It is the strongest part of me, that will endure through death and through the cloudy wastes that we call Afterwards, and will shine through the uttermost mists. That is my strength, that cannot be denied . . . the strength that must break down all doors that bar me from the garden.

And that is what is happening now, in this little scene from the Future, that I am foretelling.

I turn, once again. I go forward. I pause . . . look up. The garden is before me.

Something happens.

§ V I I

And once again, over this little patch of earth which I have so dearly loved, there will be a sighing and stirring, and the scents will drift back over the centuries, for my delight. The white roses will flutter, like ghosts, from the heart of Time, and light upon their aery branches. Once again the lilies will ring their bells and the lavender will spear the night-air with sweetness. Once again I shall walk down the path . . . 'you are mine, still mine, always mine . . .' And Antinous will be there, on the little lawn, smiling in the moonlight.

For the beauty of the garden has not died. It *could* not die. No garden can ever utterly die. Even if it only flowers, a dim memory, in the heart of a ghost.

And so this book ends on a platitude. Better that it should end so, than on an epigram. For a platitude has a glow of truth in it, that burns on through the centuries. An epigram is a firework that sparks for a moment, but is revealed as an empty case in the morning.

Beauty lives. That is the one platitude that I know. It is

not guesswork. It is knowledge. And it is knowledge which bears infinite comfort.

Whatever we may find behind the dark curtain, when it falls with our falling lids, when there is silence and the bird-song is stilled, whatever we may find when we step on to the stage where all must play their part . . . we shall find flowers.

INDEX

THIS INDEX OF PLANT NAMES was prepared by Roy C. Dicks. Scientific names have been corrected and updated where necessary.

INDEX